Workshop on Multimodal, Multilingual Natural Language Generation and Multilingual WebNLG Challenge (MM-NLG 2023)

AA001532

Prague, Czech Republic
12 September 2023

ISBN: 978-1-7138-9033-1

Printed from e-media with permission by:

Curran Associates, Inc.
57 Morehouse Lane
Red Hook, NY 12571

Some format issues inherent in the e-media version may also appear in this print version.

Copyright© (2023) by the Association for Computational Linguistics
All rights reserved.

Printed with permission by Curran Associates, Inc. (2024)

For permission requests, please contact the Association for Computational Linguistics at the address below.

Association for Computational Linguistics
209 N. Eighth Street
Stroudsburg, Pennsylvania 18360

Phone: 1-570-476-8006
Fax: 1-570-476-0860

acl@aclweb.org

Additional copies of this publication are available from:

Curran Associates, Inc.
57 Morehouse Lane
Red Hook, NY 12571 USA
Phone: 845-758-0400
Fax: 845-758-2633
Email: curran@proceedings.com
Web: www.proceedings.com

TABLE OF CONTENTS

Confidently Wrong: Exploring the Calibration and Expression of (Un)Certainty of Large Language Models in a Multilingual Setting

Lea Krause Wondimagegnhue Tsegaye Tufa
Selene Báez Santamaría Angel Daza Urja Khurana Piek Vossen
Vrije Universiteit Amsterdam
{l.krause, w.t.tufa, s.baezsantamaria, j.a.dazaarevalo, u.khurana, p.t.j.m.vossen}@vu.nl

Abstract

While the fluency and coherence of Large Language Models (LLMs) in text generation have seen significant improvements, their competency in generating appropriate expressions of uncertainty remains limited. Using a multilingual closed-book QA task and GPT-3.5, we explore how well LLMs are calibrated and express certainty across a diverse set of languages, including low-resource settings. Our results reveal strong performance in high-resource languages but a marked decline in performance in lower-resource languages. Across all, we observe an exaggerated expression of confidence in the model, which does not align with the correctness or likelihood of its responses. Our findings highlight the need for further research into accurate calibration of LLMs especially in a multilingual setting.

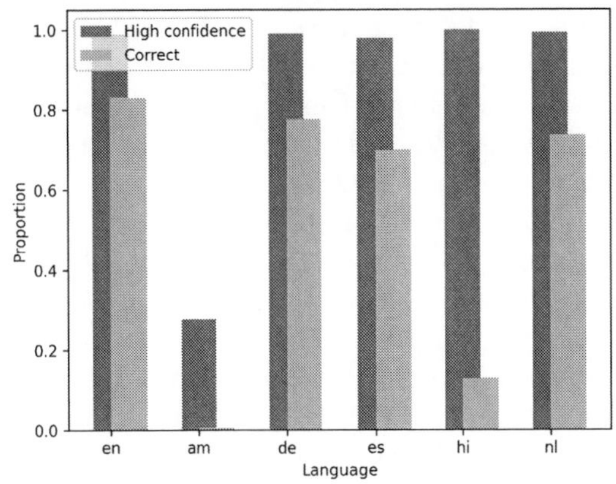

Figure 1: Proportion of *High Confidence* (HI) answers and *Correct* answers for each language. For Amharic, all non-HI answers (72.3%) were unintelligible (NI).

1 Introduction

Accurate estimation of one's own certainty and the confidence in provided information is pivotal not only for humans but also for machine learning models, particularly those intended for broad use. When someone asks a person a factual question, they search in their memory for the answer and produce it when they find it. If they are not able to find it, they reply *I don't know*. It is also the case that the more hesitant they feel about knowing a fact, the more they fill their answers with hedges such as *I guess* or *uhm* to express they are not certain (Smith and Clark, 1993). Ideally, a capable LLM should be able to express its uncertainty about the facts for which it has weaker evidence when generating an answer. A significant body of research has examined the phenomenon of overconfidence in humans, shedding light on their tendency to overestimate their knowledge and capabilities (Lichtenstein and Fischhoff, 1977; Brenner et al., 1996). In parallel, a substantial amount of work has been dedicated to the calibration of models in machine learning, typically with a focus on English-language data (Guo et al., 2017; Si et al., 2022; Chen et al., 2023).

However, if multilingual support is stated when releasing an LLM, claims about model performance based solely on English datasets are not enough, and the capacity to show accurate performance across multiple languages is essential. As such, we investigate the *calibration*, *performance*, and *verbal expression of certainty* in an LLM (GPT-3.5) in a closed-book QA setting across six languages: Amharic, Dutch, English, German, Hindi, and Spanish, for which we release our dataset and annotations[1]. Our methodology for this investigation is based on a similar exploration conducted by Mielke et al. (2022), albeit their research was solely based on English-language performance.

Our findings reveal that while the performance of the model on high-resource languages is commendable, a significant drop in performance is observed in lower-resource languages. Interestingly, our results further demonstrate an excessively confident model, with confidence levels appearing to be unrelated to the correctness and, in most cases,

[1] https://github.com/lkra/multilingual_confidence_calibration

Proceedings of the Workshop on Multimodal, Multilingual Natural Language Generation and Multilingual WebNLG Challenge (MM-NLG 2023), pages 1–9
September 12, 2023 ©2023 Association for Computational Linguistics

to the likelihood of its responses. Highlighting the need for continued research and improvement of calibration of language models, particularly in a multilingual setting.

2 Related Work

Calibration and expression of confidence In NLP, sequence generation poses a special challenge for understanding and estimating uncertainty. Malinin and Gales (2022) developed an ensemble-based probabilistic framework, while Kuhn et al. (2023) proposed the concept of semantic entropy as a measure of uncertainty in LLMs. Additionally, Si et al. (2022) introduced MacroCE, a novel calibration metric for LLMs.

Efforts to improve LLM reliability have been introduced by studies such as Si et al. (2023), which devised prompting strategies for GPT-3, and Kadavath et al. (2022), who explored LLM self-evaluation. Finally, the interpretation and generation of uncertainty in LLMs have been examined by Zhou et al. (2023) and Mielke et al. (2022), who looked at the impact of naturalistic expressions and linguistic calibration respectively. Their findings provide valuable insights for our exploration of multilingual LLMs.

Closed-book QA Question-answering (QA) traditionally relies on information retrieval and a model that generates answers from the retrieved text. Roberts et al. (2020) first proposed a *closed-book* QA approach, using only the question and the model's internal knowledge. They reported competitive performance against open-domain systems, however, later studies attributed these results to test-train overlap (Lewis et al., 2021), not inherent model knowledge. Wang et al. (2021) confirmed these findings, showing BART's (Lewis et al., 2020) limitations in memorisation and knowledge retrieval. Conversely, Brown et al. (2020) demonstrated GPT-3's high performance in factual QA. Peinl and Wirth (2023) built an English-only dataset (with questions on physics, math puzzles, metaphors, etc.) and focus on comparing the performance of a large number of language models. Recent studies have started to explore long-form QA (Amplayo et al., 2023), requiring more complex information use.

Multilinguality While the majority of language models are trained almost exclusively on English data, the exploration of their multilingual capabilities is an active field of research. Though their performance is often on par with existing state-of-the-art cross-lingual models and translation models (Winata et al., 2021), it increases further when explicitly trained on multilingual data (Lin et al., 2022). Shi et al. (2022) demonstrated the strong multilingual reasoning abilities of the models using chain-of-thought prompting on a mathematical task, even for low-resource languages. However, when Zhang et al. (2023) investigated similar behaviour, the model behaved in a translating manner, meaning performance can be affected by tasks where data cannot be explicitly translated. The closest work to ours is Sen et al. (2022) who built a multilingual QA dataset based on Wikipedia entities and with different question categories. They cover 9 different languages (4 of them overlap with ours) and presented baseline results including mT5 (Xue et al., 2021) language model and T5-CBQA (Roberts et al., 2020). We propose here an extension of an English dataset into a multilingual dataset, including 6 languages and present the performance of GPT-3.5, while also being interested in measuring the certainty when responding to such questions and how this relates to the change of accuracy across languages.

3 Methodology

3.1 Languages

Our analysis covers six languages with different amounts of resources available. Joshi et al. (2020) introduce a taxonomy to classify languages according to the amount of resources they have available on a scale of 0 (exceptionally limited resources) to 5 (quintessential rich-resource). Three of our analysed languages fall into the highest category (5): **English**, **German** and **Spanish**. **Dutch** and **Hindi** are categorised as Level 4: comparable to Level 5, but challenged by a lesser amount of labelled data. With **Amharic** we cover one Level 2 language, meaning a small amount of labelled datasets has been collected for it, but overall resources are very limited.

3.2 Dataset and task

We use a further modified version of the dataset used by Mielke et al. (2022). Theirs itself is a modified version of the TriviaQA dataset (Joshi et al., 2017). Originally a reading comprehension task, it features complex questions about trivia topics, that were intended to need cross-sentence reasoning to

	What planet orbits between Uranus and Pluto? *Gold answer:* Neptune
en	There is no planet that orbits between Uranus and Pluto.
am	የትኛው ፕላኔት ነው የኢንተርኔት ፕላኔት (Internet Protocol) ነው።
de	Es gibt keinen Planeten, der zwischen Uranus und Pluto kreist.
es	El planeta que orbita entre Urano y Plutón es Neptuno.
hi	मंगल ग्रह परिक्रमा करता है।
nl	Er is geen planeet die tussen Uranus en Pluto draait.

Example 1: Example answers where all, except Spanish are wrong and should have expressed uncertainty or lack of knowledge.

find answers.

To exclusively assess the knowledge encoded within the model's weights, Mielke et al. (2022) adapt the task to create a closed-book QA setting. All evidence documents associated with the questions were eliminated. They also removed the "disambiguation" suffix from the aliases originating from Wikipedia and employed these aliases to compile a set of permissible gold answers.

To create our dataset, we randomly extracted a subset of 1000 questions from the original training set utilised in their study. These questions were then translated into our target languages, specifically Amharic (am), German (de), Spanish (es), Hindi (hi), and Dutch (nl). English, German, Spanish and Dutch are written using the Latin script, while Amharic is written in Ge'ez script and Hindi in Devanagari script. For the translation process, we utilised the deep-translator library[2], which accessed Google Translate. The translations were validated during the subsequent annotation process. As a result, our closed-book QA dataset encompasses a total of 6000 question-answer pairs across the covered languages.

3.3 Model selection

For our analysis, we consider models that are capable of answering questions in a sentence format suitable for linguistic confidence analysis. Our initial consideration focuses on GPT-based models (`text-davinci-002`, `text-davinci-003`, `gpt-3.5-turbo`) (Brown et al., 2020), and publicly available open source models such as LLaMA (Touvron et al., 2023), BLOOM (Scao et al., 2023), and mT5 (Xue et al., 2021). We look at factors such as complexity of model setup, compute requirements, and language support in choosing which language model to investigate. Due to the computational cost involved in setting up publicly available base models, we instead opt for GPT-3.5[3]. All of our target languages except Amharic are explicitly listed as being part of GPT-3's training dataset[4]. Given that there is no transparent description of the full sources of GPT-3.5's training data, there is no guarantee that the model has not seen the language at all. Therefore we still decide to measure the performance of Amharic as zero-shot (or possibly few-shot) language probing. We specifically use the GPT3.5 variant `text-davinci-003` since it allows access to the log probabilities with its output. We require this score as a proxy to measure how confident the model is in its generated output sequence.

3.4 Annotation

The annotation scheme utilised in our study is derived from the methodology presented in Mielke et al. (2022). Each instance in the original dataset includes a question, a gold answer and a list of possible aliases to facilitate the annotator's job when assessing correctness (given that the generative model could realise a correct answer in different ways). During our annotation process, the first step was to validate that both the question and the correct gold answer were sensical and properly translated into each target language. Each question-answer pair was evaluated one by one by a native speaker, corrections were made to improve readability and keep the semantics of the original English question in case the annotator considered it adequate. As for the aliases, we left the original English and appended the translated aliases to the list of alternative correct answers to avoid confusions when e.g. translating Named Entities For example, if the original answer was the band *The Monkeys*, the correct answer should still be the original name of the band, not the translation *los monos*. Next, following the original guidelines, each automatically generated response was manually annotated according to the following criteria:

Linguistic confidence Labels are split into high (`HI`: confidently answers), low (`LO`: expresses uncertainty), and none (`DK`: admits not to know).

Correctness is divided fourfold, `Right` (correct answer and no incorrect additions), `Extra` (correct answer with added incorrect knowledge), `Wrong`

[2]https://github.com/nidhaloff/deep-translator

[3]For a detailed analysis of concerns involved in this choice, please see the Limitations section.

[4]github.com/openai/gpt-3/blob/master/dataset_statistics/languages_by_character_count.csv

(incorrect but not absurd answer), and `Other` (absurd/unrelated/no answer).

Not classifiable We add two labels to the Not classifiable class. The original had only `OT` (off-topic) in case the answer completely ignores the question. We add `NI` (not intelligible), the answer is not readable as a sentence e.g. due to incorrect syntax. Second, we add `CO` (Cut-off) for when the answer is too verbose and cut off before getting to the relevant part. For a fully annotated example see Appendix 8.

Due to the high cost associated with data collection, we only have one annotator per language, all have linguistic training and are both proficient in English and native speakers of their respective languages. Parallel annotation as such did not occur, however, all annotators were working with exactly the same questions (in their respective language), therefore a discussion was conducted among them regarding the edge cases, in order to share a similar decision-making process when judging them. Given that this dataset deals with factual answers, and that we followed a specific annotation process and strict guidelines, there was not much space for ambiguity: the annotator had to judge the answer based on the gold answers and possible aliases from the dataset. In case of doubt, annotators were also encouraged to search the web for confirming the correctness of each answer.

4 Results and Discussion

In this section, we report our findings on the performance of the model in terms of its accuracy, perceived confidence and their interplay. We also investigate difficulties overall and for specific languages. We look at 1000 samples for all languages.

4.1 Accuracy

As expected, English shows the highest correctness (83.05%) of answers, followed by German (77.65%). Interestingly, Spanish (69.99%) performs worse than Dutch (73.61%), even though it is the higher resource language. Model performance drops drastically for Hindi, at just 12.11%, and even more so for Amharic with nearly all answers being incorrect (only 0.53% correct).

We also look at automatic match-based evaluation, judging based on whether aliases appear in the generated response. Here we see high-performing languages lose performance, and low-performance ones gain, possibly influenced by keywords appearing in otherwise unintelligible answers.

	label	en	am	de	es	hi	nl
detailed labels	Right	**82.25**	0.53	**77.35**	**68.77**	12.56	**73.00**
	Wrong	16.85	**88.73**	19.24	24.92	**76.93**	23.86
	Extra	0.80	-	0.30	1.22	0.41	0.61
	NI	0.10	-	-	0.10	0.72	-
	OT	-	10.74	-	-	1.03	0.40
	CO	-	-	2.61	2.34	1.13	1.21
	Other	-	-	0.50	2.64	7.21	0.91
binary	Correct	83.05	0.53	77.65	69.99	12.98	73.61
	Incorrect	16.95	99.47	22.34	30.01	87.02	26.39
match	Correct	↓ 80.50	↑ 3.91	↓ 68.70	↓ 65.50	↑ 14.50	↓ 69.20
	Incorrect	19.50	96.09	31.30	34.50	85.50	30.80

Table 1: Normalised Correctness values. In case of no value, the label was not assigned. For binary labels, *Right* and *Extra* were merged into *Correct*, and the rest into *Incorrect*. For match-based labels, arrows indicate whether scores in- or decrease compared to human annotation.

4.2 Linguistic Confidence

Expressed confidence is generally high, with only a handful of answers indicating some level of uncertainty across all languages. Wrong answers can be seen as opportunities for the model to express uncertainty or admit lack of knowledge, however, Table 2 shows that, in most cases, such opportunities were missed. For example, the model is 99% confident in English while being 82.3% accurate, whereas it is also 99% in German while being only 77.4% accurate; one would expect at least a slight decrease in confidence for German outputs. An instance illustrating this can be found in Example 1. In this case, the model exhibits a high level of confidence in asserting the absence of a planet between Uranus and Pluto, despite the correct answer being Neptune. This indicates that the model needs further calibration and specific prompt engineering to express its confidence verbally.

	en	am	de	es	hi	nl
HI	**99.00**	27.75	**99.00**	**97.87**	**100.00**	**99.29**
LO	1.00	-	0.60	-	-	0.51
NI	-	**72.25**	-	-	-	-
CO	-	-	0.40	2.13	-	-
OT	-	-	-	-	-	0.20

Table 2: Normalised Linguistic Confidence values.

Correctness of Confident Answers Figure 1 shows the overlap of correct and high-confidence answers. Due to the high performance on languages like English, German or Dutch, the gap is smaller, but overall the results show a highly overconfident model, bettered only if performance catches up with its expressed confidence. Hindi shows a stark contrast in this regard, with 100% confident answers while only 12% are correct.

4.3 Correlations with Perplexity

Results revealed statistically significant correlations, ranging from weak to moderate, between perplexity and correctness across all languages except Hindi. Pearson correlation coefficients were computed for each language[5], yielding values ranging from $r = 0.23$, $p < .001$ (English) to $r = 0.40$, $p < .001$ (Amharic), suggesting potential for enhanced calibration. It is important to exercise caution when interpreting the results for Amharic due to the limited number of correct answers ($n < 10$).

Regarding the association between perplexity and confidence, the findings displayed variability. Notably, a significant yet weak correlation emerged solely in Spanish ($r = 0.25$, $p = .001$) and Dutch ($r = 0.10$, $p = .001$). Conversely, for English, German, Hindi, and Amharic, the p-values indicated the absence of a significant correlation. Thus, the relationship between perplexity and confidence appears less consistent across the languages tested.

4.4 Identification of Difficult Questions

We investigate patterns in the questions that the model tends to get correct/incorrect in each language. To do so, we compute n-grams, ranging from size 1 to 7, filtering out stop-words as well as instances with frequency less than 5 over the whole question set. Table A7 shows examples of 1-grams most related to correct and incorrect answers, per language respectively[6].

We observed certain patterns across languages. For instance, questions about "island" tend to be answered correctly in German, Spanish, and Dutch, while questions about "olympic" tend to receive incorrect answers in English, German, and Spanish. These patterns might indicate a knowledge gap within the model itself. However, we also found indications of language bias in knowledge access, as mentioned by Zhang et al. (2023). For example, the most relevant word for correct answers in English is "American," while in Dutch, the model often provides incorrect responses related to countries like "Russia" and "Britain."

[5]The Pearson correlation coefficients and p-values were calculated using scipy.stats.pearsonr from the SciPy library.

[6]Ngrams of size > 1 did not show any patterns

	% of answers in English	% correct in English	% correct overall
am	19.84	↑ 2.00	0.53
hi	18.90	↑ 44.00	12.56

Table 3: Percentages of answers that were given in English instead of the language of the question and how many of those were correct in comparison with the overall accuracy.

4.5 Lower-resource settings

As stated earlier, both Amharic and Hindi showed notably poor performance. However, there were distinct differences: while Hindi responses were incorrect but coherent, most of the Amharic responses were incomprehensible. English was used for 18.9% and 19.8% of all answers for Hindi and Amharic, respectively (see Table 3. Notably, only 2% of these English responses were correct for Amharic, while for Hindi, this proportion spiked to 44% - increasing by 31% compared to overall accuracy. Interestingly, while Hindi and Dutch are in the same resource class according to Joshi et al. (2020), the accuracy of Hindi as a non-Latin script language is significantly lower.

For the case of Amharic, the model still generated some valid words, although the meaning of full sentences was non-sensical. The few cases that were judged as correct, were because the model generated the right (English) named entity as an answer. This could mean that the model saw at least some Amharic text during training, but given the extremely limited amount of data, the model cannot make much sense of the prompts that are being submitted.

5 Conclusion

Our work highlights performance disparities in LLMs across languages and shows a prevalent cross-language expressed overconfidence in responses in a closed-book setting. These findings underscore the importance of nuanced, multilingual calibration in LLMs. Accordingly, we hope to spur further progress by releasing our multilingual dataset and annotations.

Limitations

In our study, we acknowledge several limitations associated with the use of GPT-3.5 by OpenAI. Firstly, there is a cost factor involved in utilising this model due to its computational requirements and access restrictions. Additionally, the exact details of the data sources used in training GPT-3.5 are unknown, which can raise concerns about potential biases or inaccuracies in the model's responses. Similarly, the closed nature of GPT-3.5. as a proprietary model means the inner workings and specifics of its architecture and training process are not fully disclosed, limiting transparency and the ability for independent verification.

Furthermore, it is important to note that (`text-davinci-003`) is scheduled for deprecation in January 2024[7]. This time-frame imposes challenges in replicating and verifying the results of our study in the future. It was announced after the completion of this study.

Regarding the annotation process, we acknowledge that the limited number of annotators (only one) may pose a limitation. While we employ expert annotators, a larger pool of annotators would have been beneficial, as it could have provided a broader range of perspectives and potentially increased the reliability of the annotations.

Acknowledgements

This research was partially funded by the Vrije Universiteit Amsterdam and the Netherlands Organisation for Scientific Research (NWO) via the *Spinoza* grant (SPI 63-260) awarded to Piek Vossen, the *Hybrid Intelligence Centre* via the Zwaartekracht grant (024.004.022), Huawei Finland through the DreamsLab project, and by the EU Horizon 2020 project InTaVia: In/Tangible European Heritage - Visual Analysis, Curation and Communication (http://intavia.eu) under grant agreement No. 101004825.

References

Reinald Kim Amplayo, Kellie Webster, Michael Collins, Dipanjan Das, and Shashi Narayan. 2023. Query refinement prompts for closed-book long-form QA. In *Proceedings of the 61st Annual Meeting of the Association for Computational Linguistics (Volume 1: Long Papers)*, pages 7997–8012, Toronto, Canada. Association for Computational Linguistics.

Lyle A Brenner, Derek J Koehler, Varda Liberman, and Amos Tversky. 1996. Overconfidence in probability and frequency judgments: A critical examination. *Organizational Behavior and Human Decision Processes*, 65(3):212–219.

Tom Brown, Benjamin Mann, Nick Ryder, Melanie Subbiah, Jared D Kaplan, Prafulla Dhariwal, Arvind Neelakantan, Pranav Shyam, Girish Sastry, Amanda Askell, et al. 2020. Language models are few-shot learners. *Advances in neural information processing systems*, 33:1877–1901.

Yangyi Chen, Lifan Yuan, Ganqu Cui, Zhiyuan Liu, and Heng Ji. 2023. A close look into the calibration of pre-trained language models. In *Proceedings of the 61st Annual Meeting of the Association for Computational Linguistics (Volume 1: Long Papers)*, pages 1343–1367, Toronto, Canada. Association for Computational Linguistics.

Chuan Guo, Geoff Pleiss, Yu Sun, and Kilian Q. Weinberger. 2017. On Calibration of Modern Neural Networks. In *Proceedings of the 34th International Conference on Machine Learning*, pages 1321–1330. PMLR.

Mandar Joshi, Eunsol Choi, Daniel Weld, and Luke Zettlemoyer. 2017. TriviaQA: A large scale distantly supervised challenge dataset for reading comprehension. In *Proceedings of the 55th Annual Meeting of the Association for Computational Linguistics (Volume 1: Long Papers)*, pages 1601–1611, Vancouver, Canada. Association for Computational Linguistics.

Pratik Joshi, Sebastin Santy, Amar Budhiraja, Kalika Bali, and Monojit Choudhury. 2020. The state and fate of linguistic diversity and inclusion in the NLP world. In *Proceedings of the 58th Annual Meeting of the Association for Computational Linguistics*, pages 6282–6293, Online. Association for Computational Linguistics.

Saurav Kadavath, Tom Conerly, Amanda Askell, Tom Henighan, Dawn Drain, Ethan Perez, Nicholas Schiefer, Zac Hatfield-Dodds, Nova DasSarma, Eli Tran-Johnson, Scott Johnston, Sheer El-Showk, Andy Jones, Nelson Elhage, Tristan Hume, Anna Chen, Yuntao Bai, Sam Bowman, Stanislav Fort, Deep Ganguli, Danny Hernandez, Josh Jacobson, Jackson Kernion, Shauna Kravec, Liane Lovitt, Kamal Ndousse, Catherine Olsson, Sam Ringer, Dario Amodei, Tom Brown, Jack Clark, Nicholas Joseph, Ben Mann, Sam McCandlish, Chris Olah, and Jared Kaplan. 2022. Language Models (Mostly) Know What They Know.

Lorenz Kuhn, Yarin Gal, and Sebastian Farquhar. 2023. Semantic Uncertainty: Linguistic Invariances for Uncertainty Estimation in Natural Language Generation.

Mike Lewis, Yinhan Liu, Naman Goyal, Marjan Ghazvininejad, Abdelrahman Mohamed, Omer Levy, Veselin Stoyanov, and Luke Zettlemoyer. 2020. BART: Denoising sequence-to-sequence pre-training

[7]https://platform.openai.com/docs/deprecations

for natural language generation, translation, and comprehension. In *Proceedings of the 58th Annual Meeting of the Association for Computational Linguistics*, pages 7871–7880, Online. Association for Computational Linguistics.

Patrick Lewis, Pontus Stenetorp, and Sebastian Riedel. 2021. Question and answer test-train overlap in open-domain question answering datasets. In *Proceedings of the 16th Conference of the European Chapter of the Association for Computational Linguistics: Main Volume*, pages 1000–1008, Online. Association for Computational Linguistics.

Sarah Lichtenstein and Baruch Fischhoff. 1977. Do those who know more also know more about how much they know? *Organizational Behavior and Human Performance*, 20(2):159–183.

Xi Victoria Lin, Todor Mihaylov, Mikel Artetxe, Tianlu Wang, Shuohui Chen, Daniel Simig, Myle Ott, Naman Goyal, Shruti Bhosale, Jingfei Du, Ramakanth Pasunuru, Sam Shleifer, Punit Singh Koura, Vishrav Chaudhary, Brian O'Horo, Jeff Wang, Luke Zettlemoyer, Zornitsa Kozareva, Mona Diab, Veselin Stoyanov, and Xian Li. 2022. Few-shot learning with multilingual generative language models. In *Proceedings of the 2022 Conference on Empirical Methods in Natural Language Processing*, pages 9019–9052, Abu Dhabi, United Arab Emirates. Association for Computational Linguistics.

Andrey Malinin and Mark Gales. 2022. Uncertainty Estimation in Autoregressive Structured Prediction. In *International Conference on Learning Representations*.

Sabrina J. Mielke, Arthur Szlam, Emily Dinan, and Y-Lan Boureau. 2022. Reducing conversational agents' overconfidence through linguistic calibration. *Transactions of the Association for Computational Linguistics*, 10:857–872.

René Peinl and Johannes Wirth. 2023. Evaluation of medium-large language models at zero-shot closed book generative question answering.

Adam Roberts, Colin Raffel, and Noam Shazeer. 2020. How much knowledge can you pack into the parameters of a language model? In *Proceedings of the 2020 Conference on Empirical Methods in Natural Language Processing (EMNLP)*, pages 5418–5426, Online. Association for Computational Linguistics.

Teven Le Scao, Angela Fan, Christopher Akiki, Ellie Pavlick, Suzana Ilić, Daniel Hesslow, Roman Castagné, Alexandra Sasha Luccioni, and François Yvon et al. 2023. Bloom: A 176b-parameter open-access multilingual language model.

Priyanka Sen, Alham Fikri Aji, and Amir Saffari. 2022. Mintaka: A complex, natural, and multilingual dataset for end-to-end question answering. In *Proceedings of the 29th International Conference on Computational Linguistics*, pages 1604–1619, Gyeongju, Republic of Korea. International Committee on Computational Linguistics.

Freda Shi, Mirac Suzgun, Markus Freitag, Xuezhi Wang, Suraj Srivats, Soroush Vosoughi, Hyung Won Chung, Yi Tay, Sebastian Ruder, Denny Zhou, Dipanjan Das, and Jason Wei. 2022. Language models are multilingual chain-of-thought reasoners.

Chenglei Si, Zhe Gan, Zhengyuan Yang, Shuohang Wang, Jianfeng Wang, Jordan Boyd-Graber, and Lijuan Wang. 2023. Prompting gpt-3 to be reliable. In *International Conference on Learning Representations (ICLR)*.

Chenglei Si, Chen Zhao, Sewon Min, and Jordan L. Boyd-Graber. 2022. Re-Examining Calibration: The Case of Question Answering. In *Conference on Empirical Methods in Natural Language Processing*.

Vicki L. Smith and Herbert H. Clark. 1993. On the course of answering questions. *Journal of Memory and Language*, 32(1):25–38.

Hugo Touvron, Thibaut Lavril, Gautier Izacard, Xavier Martinet, Marie-Anne Lachaux, Timothée Lacroix, Baptiste Rozière, Naman Goyal, Eric Hambro, Faisal Azhar, et al. 2023. Llama: Open and efficient foundation language models. *arXiv preprint arXiv:2302.13971*.

Cunxiang Wang, Pai Liu, and Yue Zhang. 2021. Can generative pre-trained language models serve as knowledge bases for closed-book QA? In *Proceedings of the 59th Annual Meeting of the Association for Computational Linguistics and the 11th International Joint Conference on Natural Language Processing (Volume 1: Long Papers)*, pages 3241–3251, Online. Association for Computational Linguistics.

Genta Indra Winata, Andrea Madotto, Zhaojiang Lin, Rosanne Liu, Jason Yosinski, and Pascale Fung. 2021. Language models are few-shot multilingual learners. In *Proceedings of the 1st Workshop on Multilingual Representation Learning*, pages 1–15, Punta Cana, Dominican Republic. Association for Computational Linguistics.

Linting Xue, Noah Constant, Adam Roberts, Mihir Kale, Rami Al-Rfou, Aditya Siddhant, Aditya Barua, and Colin Raffel. 2021. mt5: A massively multilingual pre-trained text-to-text transformer.

Xiang Zhang, Senyu Li, Bradley Hauer, Ning Shi, and Grzegorz Kondrak. 2023. Don't trust gpt when your question is not in english.

Kaitlyn Zhou, Dan Jurafsky, and Tatsunori Hashimoto. 2023. Navigating the Grey Area: Expressions of Overconfidence and Uncertainty in Language Models.

A Appendix

A.1 Average Perplexity

	en	am	de	es	hi	nl
HI	**0.87**	0.78	**0.89**	**0.88**	**0.88**	**0.88**
LO	0.81	-	0.82	-	-	0.84
NI	-	**0.87**	-	-	-	-
CO	-	-	**0.89**	0.86	-	-
OT	-	-	-	-	-	0.85

Table A 4: Average perplexity per confidence label

	en	am	de	es	hi	nl
RIGHT	**0.88**	**0.88**	**0.90**	**0.89**	**0.88**	**0.89**
WRONG	0.82	0.86	0.86	0.86	**0.88**	0.84
EXTRA	0.84	-	0.87	0.84	0.87	0.90
NI	0.75	-	-	0.86	0.91	-
OT	-	0.69	-	-	0.78	0.83
CO	-	-	0.88	0.87	0.87	0.86
OTHER	-	-	0.86	0.84	**0.87**	0.84

Table A 5: Average perplexity per correctness label

Difficulty with Wh-Questions We investigate the performance, according to the binary correctness labels, for different Wh-question, for each language, and across languages, as shown in Table 6. For this, we first search for Wh keywords in the English corpus, and select the corresponding translated questions.

The highest performance is achieved by "What" and "How" questions, while "Who", "Where" and "Which" have similar performances[8].

	en	am	de	es	hi	nl	total
Who (110)	84.5	1.0	84.4	70	12.0	74.3	54.9
What (219)	85.3	0.5	84.1	72.8	13.5	76.0	57.2
Where (8)	87.5	0.0	75	71.4	0.0	75.0	51.1
When (1)	0.0	0.0	0.0	0.0	-	0.0	0.0
Which (193)	78.7	0.7	75.9	66.3	11.9	71.5	53.2
How (27)	81.4	0.0	66.6	80	20	70.3	55.8

Table A 6: Accuracy on "Correct" class, per type of WH-question, Sample size in parenthesis.

[8]We exclude "When" due to the low sample size

lang	1-gram	%correct	%incorrect	1-gram	%correct	%incorrect
en	american	96.0	4.0	years	42.9	57.1
	known	95.0	5.0	half	50.0	50.0
	capital	94.7	5.3	olympic	50.0	50.0
am	የሚታወቀው (known)	16.7	83.3	የትኛው (which one)	1.5	98.5
	በፊት (past)	16.7	83.3	ከተማ (city)	2.2	97.8
	የነበረው (which was)	16.7	83.3	ዋና (main)	3.6	96.4
de	gegründet (founded)	93.8	6.2	olympischen (olympic)	25.0	75.0
	insel (island)	92.3	7.7	einzigen (single)	33.3	66.7
	rolle (role)	91.7	8.3	vereinigten (united)	42.9	57.1
es	escribió (wrote)	95.7	4.3	olímpico (olympic)	16.7	83.3
	principal (main)	94.1	5.9	actual (current)	33.3	66.7
	isla (island)	93.3	6.7	tres (three)	33.3	66.7
hi	मृत्यु (death)	50.0	50.0	सबसे (most)	3.8	96.2
	बार (times)	42.9	57.1	शहर (city)	4.2	95.8
	लिखा (written)	42.9	57.1	भूमिका (role)	7.7	92.3
nl	speelde (played)	95.4	4.6	verscheen (appeared)	28.6	71.4
	hoofdstad (capital)	94.4	5.6	rusland (Russia)	33.3	66.7
	eiland (island)	92.9	7.1	brittannië (Britain)	42.9	57.1

Table A 7: Top 1-grams most related to correct (left) and incorrect (right) answers, per language respectively. English translations in parenthesis.

Who was Britain's youngest Olympian at the 2008 games?
Correct answer: TOM DALEY
Possible aliases: Tom Daley, Rob Daley, Thomas Daley, Tom Daly

Linguistic Confidence	Correctness	Generated response
HI	RIGHT	Tom Daley was Britain's youngest Olympian at the 2008 games..
	EXTRA	Tom Daley, who was a figure skater at the 2008 games.
	WRONG	That's Mo Farah.
	OTHER	In 2008, China hosted the Olympics for the first time.
LO	RIGHT	I think it was Tom Daley.
	EXTRA	I think at the London games in 2008, the youngest Olympian was Tom Daly.
	WRONG	Not sure, maybe Ellie Simmonds.
	OTHER	I guess the games were a success that year.
DK	RIGHT	I do not know, but I think it might have been Thomas Daley.
	EXTRA	I don't know what the Olympics are, but it could be Tom Daley?
	WRONG	I don't know what the Olympics are, but it could be Tom Daley?
	OTHER	No clue, but did you know that London hosted the Olympics in 2012?
OT		Swimming is a very demanding sport!
NI		Olympics of can 3 can 2008 2008 2008 2008
CO		The Olympics are such a fascinating event. Every four years, athletes from all over the world gather to compete in a variety of sports. It's not just about who wins the gold, silver, or bronze, but also about personal stories of perseverance, resilience, and determination. Speaking of personal stories, the 2008 Olympic Games held

Table A 8: Examples of all categories in the annotation scheme.

Visual Question Generation in Bengali

Mahmud Hasan, Labiba Islam, Jannatul Ferdous Ruma
Tasmiah Tahsin Mayeesha and **Rashedur M. Rahman**
North South University
{mahmud.hasan03,labiba.islam,jannatul.ruma,
tasmiah.tahsin,rashedur.rahman}@northsouth.edu

Abstract

The task of Visual Question Generation (VQG) is to generate human-like questions relevant to the given image. As VQG is an emerging research field, existing works tend to focus only on resource-rich language such as English due to the availability of datasets. In this paper, we propose the first Bengali Visual Question Generation task and develop a novel transformer-based encoder-decoder architecture that generates questions in Bengali when given an image. We propose multiple variants of models - (i) image-only: baseline model of generating questions from images without additional information, (ii) image-category and image-answer-category: *guided* VQG where we condition the model to generate questions based on the answer and the category of expected question. These models are trained and evaluated on the translated VQAv2.0 dataset. Our quantitative and qualitative results establish the first state of the art models for VQG task in Bengali and demonstrate that our models are capable of generating grammatically correct and relevant questions. Our quantitative results show that our image-cat model achieves a BLUE-1 score of 33.12 and BLEU-3 score of 7.56 which is the highest of the other two variants. We also perform a human evaluation to assess the quality of the generation tasks. Human evaluation suggests that image-cat model is capable of generating goal-driven and attribute-specific questions and also stays relevant to the corresponding image.

1 Introduction

Visual Question Generation (VQG) is an emerging research field in both Computer Vision and Natural Language Processing. The task of VQG simply uses an image and other side information (e.g. answers or answer categories) as input and generates meaningful questions related to the image. Tasks like cross-modal Visual Question Answering (VQA) (Antol et al., 2015; Cadene et al., 2019; Peng et al., 2019; Jiang et al., 2020; Guo et al., 2022), Video Captioning (VC) (Chen et al., 2019), Image Captioning (IC) (Vinyals et al., 2015; Karpathy and Fei-Fei, 2017; Xu et al., 2015), and Multimodal Machine Translation (Specia et al., 2016; Elliott et al., 2017; Barrault et al., 2018; Caglayan et al., 2019) are the recent advances in the AI community. While the majority of visuo-lingual tasks tend to focus on VQA, a few recent approaches have been proposed, focusing on the under-researched multi-modal task of VQG. VQG is a more creative and particularly challenging problem than VQA, because the generated questions need to be relevant, semantically coherent and comprehensible to the diverse contents of the given image.

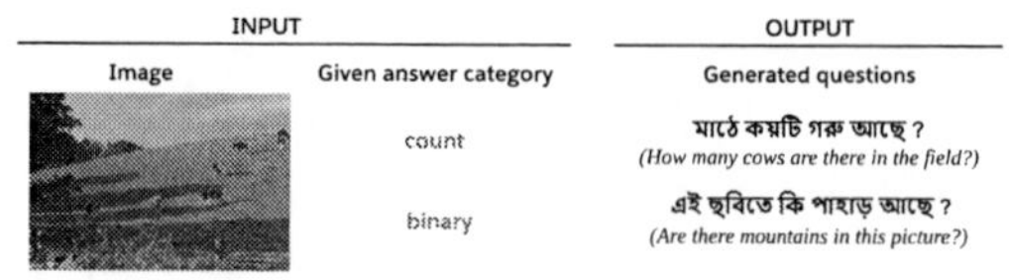

Figure 1: Examples of Bengali VQG Predictions with category of answers as additional information.

Existing studies on Visual Question Generation (VQG) have been primarily focused on languages that have ample resources, such as English. While some VQA research have been conducted in low-resource languages like Hindi (Gupta et al., 2020), Bengali (Islam et al., 2022), Japanese (Shimizu et al., 2018), and Chinese (Gao et al., 2015), limitations have been identified specifically in the context of Bengali language. While Bengali language has some recent work on reading comprehension based question answering (Mayeesha et al., 2021; Aurpa et al., 2022) and visual question answering (Islam et al., 2022; Rafi et al., 2022), there has been no research conducted for VQG task specifically in Bengali language.

To obtain meaningful questions, some VQG

Proceedings of the Workshop on Multimodal, Multilingual Natural Language Generation and Multilingual WebNLG Challenge (MM-NLG 2023), pages 10–19
September 12, 2023 ©2023 Association for Computational Linguistics

methods have either augmented the input including additional information such as answer categories, objects in image and expected answers (Pan et al., 2019; Krishna et al., 2019; Vedd et al., 2022). Pan et al. (2019) used ground truth answer with the image as an input, underscoring it to be an effective approach to produce non-generic questions. Krishna et al. (2019) stated that knowing the answers beforehand simply defeats the purpose of generating realistic questions since the main purpose of generating a question is to attain an answer. Instead, they introduced a variational auto-encoder model, which uses the concept of latent space, providing answer categories to generate relevant questions. Vedd et al. (2022), recently, proposed a guiding approach with three variant families that conditions the generative process to focus on specific chosen properties of the input image for generating questions. Inspired by previous work, we also use additional information such as answer and answer categories in our experiments. To summarize, the main contributions of our paper are the following:

- In our study, we introduce the first visual question generation system that leverages the power of Transformer-based encoder-decoder architecture for the low resource Bengali language.
- We conduct experiments of multiple variants considering only the image and also additional information as input such as answers and answer categories.
- We evaluate our novel VQG system with well-established text generation evaluation metrics and report our results as the state of the art in Visual Question Generation in Bengali.
- We perform a human evaluation on our generations to assess the quality and the relevance of the questions.

2 Related Works

The advent of visual understanding has been made possible due to continuous research in question answering and the availability of large-scale Visual Question Answering (VQA) datasets (Antol et al., 2015; Johnson et al., 2017; Mostafazadeh et al., 2017). In the past few years, many methods have been proposed to increase the model's performance for a VQG task. Earlier studies (Xu et al., 2015; Jain et al., 2017; Mostafazadeh et al., 2016; Serban et al., 2016; Vijayakumar et al., 2018; Ren et al., 2015) have explored the task of visual question generation through Recurrent Neural Network (RNN), Generative Adversarial Network (GAN), and Variational Auto-Encoder (VAE) which either followed algorithmic rule-based or learning-based approach.

In the visual-language domain, the first VQG paper proposed by Mostafazadeh et al. (2016) introduced question-response generation that takes meaningful conversational dialogues as input to generate relevant questions. Zhang et al. (2017) used an LSTM-based encoder-decoder model that automates the generation of meaningful questions with question types to be highly diverse. Motivated by the discriminator setting in GAN, Fan et al. (2018) formulated a visual natural question generation task that learns two non-generic textual characteristics from the perspective of content and linguistics producing non-deterministic and diverse outputs. Whereas, Jain et al. (2017) followed the VAE paradigm along with LSTM networks instead of GAN to generate large set of diverse questions given an image-only input. During inference, their obtained results nevertheless required the use of ground truth answers. To defeat this non-viable scenario, Krishna et al. (2019) proposed a VAE model that uses the concept of latent variable and requires information from the target, i.e. answer categories, as input with the image during inference. Similarly, Vedd et al. (2022) follows the concept of latent variable, however, their proposed model architecture explores VQG from the perspective of guiding, which involves two variant families, explicit and two types of implicit guiding approach. Our work is closely related to their explicit guiding method excluding the use of latent space. Recently, Scialom et al. (2020) proposed a BERT-gen model which is capable of generating texts either in mono or multi-modal representation from out of the box pre-trained encoders.

3 Methodology

In this section, we introduce our transformer based Bengali Visual Question Generation models which can generate meaningful non-generic questions when shown an image along with additional textual information. Our VQG problem is designed as follows: Given an image $\tilde{i} \in I$, where I denotes a set of images, decode a question q. For each image $\tilde{i}$, we also have access to textual utterances, such as ground truth answer and answer categories. Note,

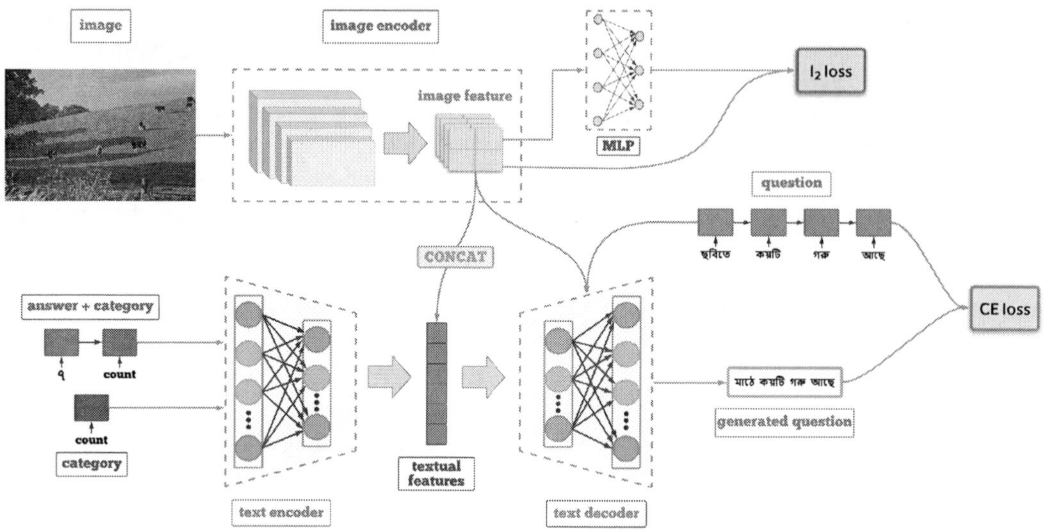

Figure 2: Architecture of the Bengali VQG Model: Given an image, we first extract image features using an image encoder (CNN). Concatenated form answer and category (`image-ans-cat`) or only category (`image-cat`) are given as input to the text encoder to obtain textual features which are then concatenated with the obtained image features. Then, this concatenated form of vision and textual modalities combined with target questions are given as inputs to the decoder question generation in Bengali. Finally, we optimize the CE and MSE loss.

we will use terms "answer category" and "category" interchangeably throughout the paper. In our work, we used answer categories from (Krishna et al., 2019) that take 1 out of 16 categorical variables to indicate the type of questions asked. For example, if our model wants to understand answers of "রং (*color*)" category, then it should generate a question "এটা কি রঙের বাস ? (*What color is the bus?*)".

Our baseline is an $image - only$ model with no additional textual information like answer or category. We present further two variants both of which shares the same architecture but takes different inputs in training. We feed two different textual information to our model during training. The first model is $image - ans - cat$ that feeds the concatenated ground truth answer and category to the encoder and is concatenated with the image features. The second model is $image - cat$ that takes only the relevant answer category as input to the encoder. In both of the versions, the input image is reconstructed to maximize information between the image and encoded outputs.

Vocabulary: We construct vocabulary considering all the textual utterances: questions, answers and answer categories. Our vocabulary has a total of 7081 entries including the special tokens. We use word level tokenization. We set a default length of 20 token to each of the questions and 5 to each of the answers. In table 1, we see as maximum length of question in our training dataset is 22 and validation is 21 tokens long, we choose 20 to be the default length. Questions longer than default are truncated and the shorter ones are padded with special <pad> token.

Image Encoder: Given an image $\tilde{i}$, we can extract image features, $f \in \mathbb{R}^{B \times 300}$ where B is batch size. Our image encoder is a ResNet-18 pretrained CNN model, which is a convolutional neural network with 72-layer architecture consisting 18 deep layers (He et al., 2016). Once obtaining these features, they are passed to a fully connected layer followed by a batch normalization layer. Specifically, given f from image $\tilde{i}$: $i = BatchNorm(f) \in \mathbb{R}^{B \times 300}$.

Encoder: We build a Transformer encoder (Vaswani et al., 2017) and use Bengali pretrained GloVe (Global Vectors for Word Representation) word vectors (Sarkar, 2019) as the embedding layer of the text encoder. Next, we provide answer or answer categories and image features f as input to the text encoder. Note that, *image-cat* variant only takes answer category c as its input during training and *image-ans-cat* takes concatenated version of answer and category, $[a; c]$ (; operator represents concatenation) as seen in figure 2. For *image-ans-cat* variant, a concatenated version of answer and category $[a; c]$ is passed through the embedding layer and projected out as context, $C_{img+ans+cat} = embedding([a; c]) \in \mathbb{R}^{B \times T \times 300}$ where, B is batch size and T is the length of the $[a; c]$. For the *image-cat* variant, we only pass the category, c and similarly generate a context $C_{img+cat} = embedding(c) \in \mathbb{R}^{B \times T \times 300}$, where T is the length of c.

Additionally, we generate padding masks on answer and category $[a; c]_m = generate - mask([a; c]) \in \mathbb{R}^{B \times 1 \times T}$ to avoid <pad> tokens being processed by the encoder as well as the decoder. Same operation is performed on category input c and a masked category is generated c_m. The *image-cat* model takes context, C and masked category c_m as input to the encoder to encode textual feature representation: $S = encoder(C_{img+cat}, c_m) \in \mathbb{R}^{B \times T \times 300}$. We follow the same procedure for the *image-ans-cat* model, where now encoder takes the context, $C_{img+ans+cat}$ and masked concatenated answer and category, $[a; c]_m$.

These textual feature representation S from the encoder are then concatenated to the input image features $i \in \mathbb{R}^{B \times 300}$, thus, representing our final encoder outputs as the concatenation (; operator) of textual and vision modality: $X = [S; i] \in \mathbb{R}^{B \times T \times 300}$ where B is the batch size and T is length of S.

Decoder: Our decoder is a Transformer decoder that also uses GloVe embeddings. Following sequence-to-sequence causal decoding practices, our decoder receives encoder outputs from text encoder and ground truth questions during training. We, initially, extract `<start>` (Start of Sequence) token from encoder outputs which is then taken to the GPU. Each target question is concatenated with a `<start>` token, forming a tensor.

In our decoder we follow similar steps as we did in our text encoder. We take ground truth questions q and generate target context: $C_q \in \mathbb{R}^{B \times T \times 300}$ and question masks: $q_m \in \mathbb{R}^{B \times 1 \times 300}$. Before, we pass the target context, C_q to the decoder, we concatenate it with the same image features i that were passed as input to the encoder previously. The final target context can be denoted by $Q = [C_q; i] \in \mathbb{R}^{B \times T \times 300}$. Finally, the decoder takes the encoder outputs X from the text encoder, the concatenated target context Q and the source mask ($[a; c]_m$ or c_m) depending on the model variant and target question q_m in the form of a tuple. Our decoder is represented as following: $\hat{q} = Decoder(X, Q)$ where the decoder outputs a generated question $\hat{q}$.

4 Experiments

4.1 Datasets

To collect all relevant information for the VQG task in Bengali, we use the VQA v2.0 (Antol et al., 2015) dataset consisting of 443.8K questions from 82.8K images in the training dataset, and 214.4K questions from 40.5K images for validation dataset. From the annotations of previous work (Krishna et al., 2019), 16 categories were derived from the top 500 answers. The top 500 answers cover around 82% of the total VQA v2.0 dataset (Antol et al., 2015). The annotated categories include objects (e.g. "বিড়াল cat", "ফুল flower", attributes (e.g. "ঠান্ডা cold", "পুরাতন old)", color ("লাল red", "বাদামী brown"), etc.

	Train	Val
Number of Questions	184100	124795
Number of Images	40800	28336
Max Length of Question (by words)	22	21
Min Length of Question (by words)	1	1
Avg Length of Question (by words)	4	4

Table 1: Analysis of the dataset.

Previously in Bengali machine translation research (Hasan et al., 2020) , Google translate was found to be competitive with machine translation models trained in Bengali corpora. In another work on Bengali question answering (Mayeesha et al., 2021), synthetic dataset translated by Google translate was again used for creating Bengali question answering models. Due to Bengali being a low resource language, there has been no available VQG dataset. So we translated the VQA v2.0 (Antol et al., 2015) with Google translate following previous works. We maintained the same partitioning as the original dataset. Due to computational constraints we translated a smaller subset of the training and the validation set. We translate the initial 220K questions and answers for training and 150K questions and answers for validation set in Bengali using GoogleTrans library. In table 1, we see out of 220K training and 150K validation questions, 184K training and 124K validation questions were used. It is because these sets of questions map to top 500 answers in the dataset and we could not use questions and answers that had no mappings to the 16 categories. In figure 3, we can see the samples of our dataset. The 16 categories in our dataset are following in English - *"activity", "animal", "attribute", "binary", "color", "count", "food", "location", "material", "object", "other", "predicate", "shape', "spatial", "stuff", "time"*.

Image	Category	Question	Answer
	count	কয়টি আমেরিকান পতাকা আছে ? *(How many American flags are there?)*	১ *(1)*
	object	মাটিতে কি আছে ? *(What is on the ground?)*	ঘাস *(grass)*
		কেন্দ্রে কোন ধরনের ভবন দেখা যায় ? *(What type of building is seen on the center?)*	গির্জা *(church)*
	binary	ঝরনা কি বড় ? *(Is the shower large?)*	হ্যাঁ *(yes)*
		গামছা ঝুলানো আছে ? *(Is there towel hanging?)*	হ্যাঁ *(yes)*

Figure 3: Samples from our dataset

4.2 Training and Optimization

Our transformer based encoder-decoder architecture is a variation of explicit guiding variant established by (Vedd et al., 2022) where object labels, image captions and object detected features were used as guiding information. However, we only use answer categories and answers as additional information in our work. Instead of BERT (Devlin et al., 2019) we use Bengali Glove embeddings (Pennington et al., 2014; Sarkar, 2019) for encoding text. We use less number of layers, attention heads and our embedding dimensions and hidden state dimensions are also reduced due to computational constraints. Similar to work done by (Krishna et al., 2019) we use the concept of answer category as our primary textual information and attempt to generate questions that are conditioned towards a specific category.

In summary, we begin by first passing the image through a Convolutional Neural Network (CNN) to attain a high dimensional encoded representation of image features, i. The image features are passed through an MLP (Multi-layer Perceptron) layer to get a vector representation of reconstructed image features, i_r. Our architecture takes an image and additional information in the form of a concatenated answer and category $[a; c]$ or answer category c as input. We feed these input to our text encoder which then generates the textual S and concatenates the textual S and vision modality representations i. Our decoder takes the concatenated form of target context Q, the encoder outputs X, and generates the predicted question, $\hat{q}$ as shown in equation 1.

During training, we optimize the L_q between the predicted $\hat{q}$ and target question q. Additionally, we try to reconstruct the input image from the encoded output, X and minimize the l_2 loss between the reconstructed image features, i_r and the input image features i to maximize mutual information between the input image features and the encoder outputs as mentioned in equation 2.

$$\hat{q} = Decoder([S; i], [C_q; i]) \tag{1}$$

$$\begin{aligned} L_q &= CrossEntropy(\hat{q}, q) \\ L_i &= ||i - i_r||_2 \end{aligned} \tag{2}$$

4.3 Inference

During inference, except the `image-only` variant, both model variants are provided with only answer category (e.g. " রঙ (*color*)", "বৈশিস্ট্য (*attribute*)", "গননা (*count*"), etc.) alongside an image during inference, because providing answers to the model would violate the realistic scenario (Krishna et al., 2019; Vedd et al., 2022). As a result our model is kept under a realistic inference setting by not providing an answer as input during inference.

4.4 Evaluation Metrics

In our experiments, we followed well established language modelling evaluation metrics BLEU: (Papineni et al., 2002), CIDEr (Vedantam et al., 2015), METEOR (Lavie and Agarwal, 2007), and ROUGE-L (Lin, 2004).

4.5 Implementation details

We use a pretrained ResNet18 as our image encoder to encode image features. Both of our transformer based encoder and decoder uses glove embeddings. We set our transformer encoder and decoder with the following setting: number of layers = 4, number of attention heads = 4, embedding dimension = 300, hidden dimension = 300 and filter size = 300. The model trains a total number of 13000 steps, with a learning rate of 0.003 and batch size of 64. We have implemented our model with pytorch. We expect to release our code and translated dataset publicly at https://github.com/mahmudhasankhan/vqg-in-bengali

		466137	85187	82846	349926	82259	567390
Ground Truths		প্লেট কি সাদা ? (Is the plate white?)	এটা কি মার্কিন যুক্তরাষ্ট্রে ? (Is this in the USA?)	পটভূমিতে কতগুলো ইটের ভবন আছে ? (How many brick buildings are in the background?)	ফ্রিসবি কি রঙ ? (What color is the Frisbee?)	আবহাওয়া কেমন ? (What is the weather like?)	প্লেটে কি আছে ? (What is on the plate?)
Image + Ans + Cat	Given Category :	binary	other	count	color	attribute	object
	Given Answer :	হ্যাঁ (yes)	না (no)	২ (2)	সাদা (white)	ঠাণ্ডা (cold)	হ্যাঁ (yes)
	Generated Question :	এই প্রাণী কি পান ? (What do these animals drink?)	এটা কি ইংরেজি ভাষাভাষী দেশ ? (Is it an English speaking country?)	এটা কি রৌদ্রোজ্জ্বল দিন ? (Is it a sunny day?)	এই ঘটনা কি ? (What is this event?)	এই ছবিতে কি তুষার আছে ? (Is there snow in this picture?)	পিৎজা কি টুকরা করা আছে ? (Is the pizza sliced?)
Image + Cat	Given Category :	binary	other	count	color	attribute	object
	Generated Question :	টেডি বিয়ার কি বিক্রয়ের জন্য ? (Are teddy bears for sale?)	চিহ্ন গুলো কোন ভাষায় লেখা ? (What language are the signs written in?)	বাসে কয়টি জানালা আছে ? (How many windows are there in the bus?)	দলের ইউনিফর্ম কি রং ? (What color is the team's uniform?)	পাহাড়ে কি বরফের তাপমাত্রা ঠাণ্ডা ? (Is the temperature of ice cold in the mountains?)	প্লেটের আকৃতি কি ? (What is the shape of the plate?)

Figure 4: Qualitative Examples. Ground truths are target questions for both models.

Model	BLEU 1	BLEU 2	BLEU 3	CIDEr	METEOR	ROUGE-L
ablations						
image-only	34.84	8.04	3.98	10.62	17.14	36.56
text-only	28.05	7.57	3.65	18.72	19.10	29.68
without-image-recon	11.59	4.85	2.08	26.61	12.34	31.43
variants						
image-cat	33.12	**13.52**	**7.56**	22.76	17.18	36.12
image-ans-cat	32.97	11.80	3.82	18.63	18.63	36.90

Table 2: Evaluation results of model variants and ablations.

4.6 Model Ablations

We experiment with a series of ablations performed on our model such as `image-only` does not include text encoder. Inversely, `text-only` model does not have image encoder. With respect to `without-image-recon`, we avoid optimizing the reconstruction l_2 loss between the reconstructed image features and input image features. As for our model variants, `image-cat` and `image-ans-cat`, the entire architecture remains intact.

5 Results

5.1 Quantitative Results

We test our model variants except with only categorical information because giving answer to a model beforehand would be unrealistic. We tried to figure out which textual input is more significant and leads to better results. Firstly, our model ablations justify our model architecture as such our intact architecture outperforms all the ablations in BLEU-2 and BLEU-3 (see Table 2). Our baseline `image-only` model achieves a BLEU-3 score of 3.98 which is higher than `image-ans-cat` variant. Moreover, we find that in some metrics `image-cat` model outperforms the `image-ans-cat` model and in some metrics stay ahead marginally. As seen in table 2, `image-cat` model achieves a BLEU-3 score of 7.56 that is almost 4 points ahead of both `image-only` and `image-ans-cat` model. Moreover, we notice that `image-cat` model also performs marginally better in CIDEr metrics. However, both the variants show similar performance on other evaluation metrics except for METEOR and ROUGE-L metric where `image-ans-cat` variant performs slightly better. In comparison to (Vedd et al., 2022) for experiments in explicit image-category setting for English, our BLEU-1 score is 33.12 while for English we see a score of 40.8 with a 7.68 difference, however, BLEU-2 and BLEU-3 scores have higher differences. However, for METEOR in English, the score is 20.8 while our `image-cat` model scores 17.18 with a 3.62 difference only and for ROUGE the English score is 43.0 while we score 36.12 with a 6.88 point difference. Similar experiments on guided visual generation have not been performed for other languages or Bengali to our knowledge, so we compare only

Model	Experiment	
	1	2
image-cat	47.5%	40%
image-ans-cat	30%	37.5%

Table 3: Human evaluation result of our model variants.

with English. While our scores are lower than English, we train on smaller and translated dataset for computational and data annotation related constraints. Based on the quantitative results we can come to a conclusion that categorical information shows better results overall. In the next section, we see the qualitative results where we shall see that categorical information conditions the `image-cat` variant to generate category specific questions i.e. goal driven, attribute specific questions rather than generic questions.

5.2 Qualitative Results

In figure 4, we can compare the generated questions from our model variants with the reference ground truth question and answer category more illustratively. Questions generated from the `image-cat-ans` model although are grammatically and semantically correct but in some cases are not conditioned towards the given category. For example, in image 82846, although the question is grammatically correct, however, the generated question does not follow the given category which is "count". We see similar behavior for images 349926 and 82259 where questions are grammatically correct and relevant to the image but do not follow the category. In contrast, the `image-cat` model perfectly conditions its questions towards the given category. The questions are not only grammatically and semantically valid but also follow the given categorical information. The questions from the `image-cat` model generates goal driven, non-generic and category oriented questions. To understand why this variant of VQG performs well although having less side information during training, is likely due to the fact that in validation step both variants only take category side information. Therefore, the `image-cat` learns better than `image-ans-cat`.

Additionally, we notice that both variants are able to decode the semantic information from the input image as well. Both variants can rightly identify the objects and features present in the images.

5.3 Human Evaluation

We conducted a human evaluation to understand the quality of the generated questions similar to work done in (Vedd et al., 2022). In our experiments, we ask three annotators to evaluate our generated questions with two questions. There was no annotator overlap where two annotators annotated the same question. We evaluate category wise question generation by comparing two of our model variants, `image-cat` and `image-ans-cat`.

In *Experiment 1*, known as the Visual Turing Test, we present annotators with an image, a ground truth question, and a model-generated question. The task of annotators is to discern which question, among the two, they think is produced by the model. *Experiment 2* involves displaying an image to the annotators along with a question generated by the model. Subsequently, the annotators are asked to decide whether the generated question seems relevant to the given image. For each of the experiments we annotate 40 generations for each models, resulting in 80 annotations per experiment. The complete results of our evaluation is listed in table 3.

In *Experiment 1*, the result of our `image-cat` model outperforms the `image-ans-cat` variant fooling humans about 47.5% of the time. In a Visual Turing Test, if a model is capable of generating human-like questions, it is expected that its performance would reach approximately 50%. Although close to the desired score of 50%, the `image-cat` variant represents a promising advancement in surpassing the Visual Turing Test. We evaluate *Experiment 2* on both our model variants where the `image-ans-cat` model shows a percentage score of 37.5%, outperforming the `image-cat` model. It is possible that providing the answer with the image and the category helps in generating more relevant questions.

6 Conclusion

We proposed the first VQG work in Bengali and presented a novel transformer based encoder-decoder architecture that generates questions in

Bengali when shown an image and a given answer category. In our work, we presented two variants of our architecture: `image-cat` and `image-ans-cat` that differs from what input they receive during training. Both of the variants generate a question based on answer category as guiding information from an image. However, due to having two different input combinations, `image-cat` performs marginally better in terms of quantitative scores, however, generates goal driven, specific questions conditioned towards the categorical information it receives. In contrast, the `image-ans-cat` model although generating grammatically valid questions fail to learn about answer categories. Future work could analyze the impact of using more modern CNN architectures and newer pretrained models to generate questions from images.

7 Acknowledgement

This work was funded by the Faculty Research Grant [CTRG-22-SEPS-07], North South University, Bashundhara, Dhaka 1229, Bangladesh

References

Stanislaw Antol, Aishwarya Agrawal, Jiasen Lu, Margaret Mitchell, Dhruv Batra, C. Lawrence Zitnick, and Devi Parikh. 2015. Vqa: Visual question answering. In *Proceedings of the IEEE International Conference on Computer Vision (ICCV)*.

Tanjim Taharat Aurpa, Richita Khandakar Rifat, Md Shoaib Ahmed, Md. Musfique Anwar, and A. B. M. Shawkat Ali. 2022. Reading comprehension based question answering system in bangla language with transformer-based learning. *Heliyon*, 8(10):e11052.

Loïc Barrault, Fethi Bougares, Lucia Specia, Chiraag Lala, Desmond Elliott, and Stella Frank. 2018. Findings of the third shared task on multimodal machine translation. In *Proceedings of the Third Conference on Machine Translation: Shared Task Papers*, pages 304–323, Belgium, Brussels. Association for Computational Linguistics.

Remi Cadene, Corentin Dancette, Hedi Ben younes, Matthieu Cord, and Devi Parikh. 2019. Rubi: Reducing unimodal biases for visual question answering. In *Advances in Neural Information Processing Systems*, volume 32. Curran Associates, Inc.

Ozan Caglayan, Pranava Madhyastha, Lucia Specia, and Loïc Barrault. 2019. Probing the need for visual context in multimodal machine translation. In *Proceedings of the 2019 Conference of the North American Chapter of the Association for Computational Linguistics: Human Language Technologies, Volume 1 (Long and Short Papers)*, pages 4159–4170, Minneapolis, Minnesota. Association for Computational Linguistics.

Shaoxiang Chen, Ting Yao, and Yu-Gang Jiang. 2019. Deep learning for video captioning: A review. In *Proceedings of the Twenty-Eighth International Joint Conference on Artificial Intelligence, IJCAI-19*, pages 6283–6290. International Joint Conferences on Artificial Intelligence Organization.

Jacob Devlin, Ming-Wei Chang, Kenton Lee, and Kristina Toutanova. 2019. BERT: pre-training of deep bidirectional transformers for language understanding. In *Proceedings of the 2019 Conference of the North American Chapter of the Association for Computational Linguistics: Human Language Technologies, NAACL-HLT 2019, Minneapolis, MN, USA, June 2-7, 2019, Volume 1 (Long and Short Papers)*, pages 4171–4186. Association for Computational Linguistics.

Desmond Elliott, Stella Frank, Loïc Barrault, Fethi Bougares, and Lucia Specia. 2017. Findings of the second shared task on multimodal machine translation and multilingual image description. In *Proceedings of the Second Conference on Machine Translation*, pages 215–233, Copenhagen, Denmark. Association for Computational Linguistics.

Zhihao Fan, Zhongyu Wei, Siyuan Wang, Yang Liu, and Xuanjing Huang. 2018. A reinforcement learning framework for natural question generation using bi-discriminators. In *Proceedings of the 27th International Conference on Computational Linguistics*, pages 1763–1774, Santa Fe, New Mexico, USA. Association for Computational Linguistics.

Haoyuan Gao, Junhua Mao, Jie Zhou, Zhiheng Huang, Lei Wang, and Wei Xu. 2015. Are you talking to a machine? dataset and methods for multilingual image question answering. In *Proceedings of the 28th International Conference on Neural Information Processing Systems - Volume 2*, NIPS'15, page 2296–2304, Cambridge, MA, USA. MIT Press.

Yangyang Guo, Liqiang Nie, Zhiyong Cheng, Qi Tian, and Min Zhang. 2022. Loss re-scaling vqa: Revisiting the language prior problem from a class-imbalance view. *Trans. Img. Proc.*, 31:227–238.

Deepak Gupta, Pabitra Lenka, Asif Ekbal, and Pushpak Bhattacharyya. 2020. A unified framework for multilingual and code-mixed visual question answering. In *Proceedings of the 1st Conference of the Asia-Pacific Chapter of the Association for Computational Linguistics and the 10th International Joint Conference on Natural Language Processing*, pages 900–913, Suzhou, China. Association for Computational Linguistics.

Tahmid Hasan, Abhik Bhattacharjee, Kazi Samin, Masum Hasan, Madhusudan Basak, M. Sohel Rahman, and Rifat Shahriyar. 2020. Not low-resource anymore: Aligner ensembling, batch filtering, and new datasets for Bengali-English machine translation. In *Proceedings of the 2020 Conference on Empirical Methods in Natural Language Processing (EMNLP)*, pages 2612–2623, Online. Association for Computational Linguistics.

Kaiming He, Xiangyu Zhang, Shaoqing Ren, and Jian Sun. 2016. Deep residual learning for image recognition. In *2016 IEEE Conference on Computer Vision and Pattern Recognition (CVPR)*, pages 770–778.

S M Shahriar Islam, Riyad Ahsan Auntor, Minhajul Islam, Mohammad Yousuf Hossain Anik, A. B. M. Alim Al Islam, and Jannatun Noor. 2022. Note: Towards devising an efficient vqa in the bengali language. In *ACM SIGCAS/SIGCHI Conference on Computing and Sustainable Societies (COMPASS)*, COMPASS '22, page 632–637, New York, NY, USA. Association for Computing Machinery.

U. Jain, Z. Zhang, and A. Schwing. 2017. Creativity: Generating diverse questions using variational autoencoders. In *2017 IEEE Conference on Computer Vision and Pattern Recognition (CVPR)*, pages 5415–5424, Los Alamitos, CA, USA. IEEE Computer Society.

H. Jiang, I. Misra, M. Rohrbach, E. Learned-Miller, and X. Chen. 2020. In defense of grid features for visual question answering. In *2020 IEEE/CVF Conference on Computer Vision and Pattern Recognition (CVPR)*, pages 10264–10273, Los Alamitos, CA, USA. IEEE Computer Society.

J. Johnson, B. Hariharan, L. van der Maaten, L. Fei-Fei, C. Zitnick, and R. Girshick. 2017. Clevr: A diagnostic dataset for compositional language and elementary visual reasoning. In *2017 IEEE Conference on Computer Vision and Pattern Recognition (CVPR)*, pages 1988–1997, Los Alamitos, CA, USA. IEEE Computer Society.

Andrej Karpathy and Li Fei-Fei. 2017. Deep visual-semantic alignments for generating image descriptions. *IEEE Transactions on Pattern Analysis and Machine Intelligence*, 39(4):664–676.

R. Krishna, M. Bernstein, and L. Fei-Fei. 2019. Information maximizing visual question generation. In *2019 IEEE/CVF Conference on Computer Vision and Pattern Recognition (CVPR)*, pages 2008–2018, Los Alamitos, CA, USA. IEEE Computer Society.

Alon Lavie and Abhaya Agarwal. 2007. METEOR: An automatic metric for MT evaluation with high levels of correlation with human judgments. In *Proceedings of the Second Workshop on Statistical Machine Translation*, pages 228–231, Prague, Czech Republic. Association for Computational Linguistics.

Chin-Yew Lin. 2004. ROUGE: A package for automatic evaluation of summaries. In *Text Summarization Branches Out*, pages 74–81, Barcelona, Spain. Association for Computational Linguistics.

Tasmiah Tahsin Mayeesha, Abdullah Md Sarwar, and Rashedur M. Rahman. 2021. Deep learning based question answering system in bengali. *Journal of Information and Telecommunication*, 5(2):145–178.

Nasrin Mostafazadeh, Chris Brockett, Bill Dolan, Michel Galley, Jianfeng Gao, Georgios Spithourakis, and Lucy Vanderwende. 2017. Image-grounded conversations: Multimodal context for natural question and response generation. In *Proceedings of the Eighth International Joint Conference on Natural Language Processing (Volume 1: Long Papers)*, pages 462–472, Taipei, Taiwan. Asian Federation of Natural Language Processing.

Nasrin Mostafazadeh, Ishan Misra, Jacob Devlin, Margaret Mitchell, Xiaodong He, and Lucy Vanderwende. 2016. Generating natural questions about an image. In *Proceedings of the 54th Annual Meeting of the Association for Computational Linguistics (Volume 1: Long Papers)*, pages 1802–1813, Berlin, Germany. Association for Computational Linguistics.

Liangming Pan, Wenqiang Lei, Tat-Seng Chua, and Min-Yen Kan. 2019. Recent advances in neural question generation.

Kishore Papineni, Salim Roukos, Todd Ward, and Wei-Jing Zhu. 2002. Bleu: a method for automatic evaluation of machine translation. In *Proceedings of the 40th Annual Meeting of the Association for Computational Linguistics*, pages 311–318, Philadelphia, Pennsylvania, USA. Association for Computational Linguistics.

Gao Peng, Haoxuan You, Zhanpeng Zhang, Xiaogang Wang, and Hongsheng Li. 2019. Multi-modality latent interaction network for visual question answering. In *2019 IEEE/CVF International Conference on Computer Vision (ICCV)*, pages 5824–5834.

Jeffrey Pennington, Richard Socher, and Christopher Manning. 2014. GloVe: Global vectors for word representation. In *Proceedings of the 2014 Conference on Empirical Methods in Natural Language Processing (EMNLP)*, pages 1532–1543, Doha, Qatar. Association for Computational Linguistics.

Mahamudul Hasan Rafi, Shifat Islam, S. M. Hasan Imtiaz Labib, SM Sajid Hasan, Faisal Muhammad Shah, and Sifat Ahmed. 2022. A deep learning-based bengali visual question answering system. In *2022 25th International Conference on Computer and Information Technology (ICCIT)*, pages 114–119.

Mengye Ren, Ryan Kiros, and Richard S. Zemel. 2015. Exploring models and data for image question answering. In *Proceedings of the 28th International Conference on Neural Information Processing Systems - Volume 2*, NIPS'15, page 2953–2961, Cambridge, MA, USA. MIT Press.

Sagor Sarkar. 2019. https://github.com/sagorbrur/glove-bengali.

Thomas Scialom, Patrick Bordes, Paul-Alexis Dray, Jacopo Staiano, and Patrick Gallinari. 2020. What bert sees: Cross-modal transfer for visual question generation. In *International Conference on Natural Language Generation*.

Iulian Vlad Serban, Alberto García-Durán, Caglar Gulcehre, Sungjin Ahn, Sarath Chandar, Aaron Courville, and Yoshua Bengio. 2016. Generating factoid questions with recurrent neural networks: The 30M factoid question-answer corpus. In *Proceedings of the 54th Annual Meeting of the Association for Computational Linguistics (Volume 1: Long Papers)*, pages 588–598, Berlin, Germany. Association for Computational Linguistics.

Nobuyuki Shimizu, Na Rong, and Takashi Miyazaki. 2018. Visual question answering dataset for bilingual image understanding: A study of cross-lingual transfer using attention maps. In *Proceedings of the 27th International Conference on Computational Linguistics*, pages 1918–1928, Santa Fe, New Mexico, USA. Association for Computational Linguistics.

Lucia Specia, Stella Frank, Khalil Sima'an, and Desmond Elliott. 2016. A shared task on multimodal machine translation and crosslingual image description. In *Proceedings of the First Conference on Machine Translation: Volume 2, Shared Task Papers*, pages 543–553, Berlin, Germany. Association for Computational Linguistics.

Ashish Vaswani, Noam Shazeer, Niki Parmar, Jakob Uszkoreit, Llion Jones, Aidan N Gomez, Ł ukasz Kaiser, and Illia Polosukhin. 2017. Attention is all you need. In *Advances in Neural Information Processing Systems*, volume 30. Curran Associates, Inc.

Ramakrishna Vedantam, C. Lawrence Zitnick, and Devi Parikh. 2015. Cider: Consensus-based image description evaluation. In *2015 IEEE Conference on Computer Vision and Pattern Recognition (CVPR)*, pages 4566–4575.

Nihir Vedd, Zixu Wang, Marek Rei, Yishu Miao, and Lucia Specia. 2022. Guiding visual question generation. In *Proceedings of the 2022 Conference of the North American Chapter of the Association for Computational Linguistics: Human Language Technologies*, pages 1640–1654, Seattle, United States. Association for Computational Linguistics.

Ashwin K Vijayakumar, Michael Cogswell, Ramprasath R. Selvaraju, Qing Sun, Stefan Lee, David Crandall, and Dhruv Batra. 2018. Diverse beam search: Decoding diverse solutions from neural sequence models.

O. Vinyals, A. Toshev, S. Bengio, and D. Erhan. 2015. Show and tell: A neural image caption generator. In *2015 IEEE Conference on Computer Vision and Pattern Recognition (CVPR)*, pages 3156–3164, Los Alamitos, CA, USA. IEEE Computer Society.

Kelvin Xu, Jimmy Lei Ba, Ryan Kiros, Kyunghyun Cho, Aaron Courville, Ruslan Salakhutdinov, Richard S. Zemel, and Yoshua Bengio. 2015. Show, attend and tell: Neural image caption generation with visual attention. In *Proceedings of the 32nd International Conference on International Conference on Machine Learning - Volume 37*, ICML'15, page 2048–2057. JMLR.org.

Shijie Zhang, Lizhen Qu, Shaodi You, Zhenglu Yang, and Jiawan Zhang. 2017. Automatic generation of grounded visual questions. In *Proceedings of the 26th International Joint Conference on Artificial Intelligence*, pages 4235–4243, United States of America. Association for the Advancement of Artificial Intelligence (AAAI). International Joint Conference on Artificial Intelligence 2017, IJCAI 2017 ; Conference date: 19-08-2017 Through 25-08-2017.

Keeping an Eye on Context: Attention Allocation over Input Partitions in Referring Expression Generation

Simeon Schüz and **Sina Zarrieß**
Bielefeld University
{simeon.schuez,sina.zarriess}@uni-bielefeld.de

Abstract

In Referring Expression Generation, model inputs are often composed of different representations, including the visual properties of the intended referent, its relative position and size, and the visual context. Yet, the extent to which this information influences the generation process of black-box neural models is largely unclear. We investigate the relative weighting of target, location, and context information in the attention components of a Transformer-based generation model.[1] Our results show a general target bias, which, however, depends on the content of the generated expressions, pointing to interesting directions for future research.

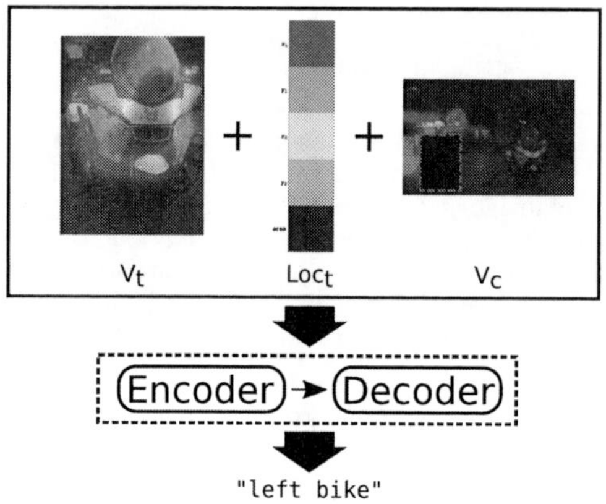

Figure 1: Input for our REG model. Input vectors are concatenations of visual (V_t) and location (Loc_t) features for targets and visual context features (V_c). We examine the relative attention weights of each partition.

1 Introduction

Context is crucial in multimodal language generation tasks such as Referring Expression Generation (REG), as descriptions for visible entities not only depend on their own appearance but also on their surroundings (e.g. Yu et al. 2016). For REG, this is especially evident, as the same expression can unambiguously describe an object in one context but be misleading in others (Schüz et al., 2023).

To this end, it has become a common practice to provide neural generation models for multimodal REG not only with visual representations for the target itself but also with information about its location and size and the visual context it appears in (see Figure 1). However, due to their black-box nature, it is not entirely clear to which extend state-of-the-art neural REG models take all of these representations into consideration. While ablation studies show how context information contribute to model performance (Yu et al., 2016; Zarrieß and Schlangen, 2018), they provide limited insight into how it is processed and to what extend it is relevant for e.g. lexical decisions.

Similar questions arise in other vision & language (V&L) tasks such as image captioning, where recent work has looked into analyzing the internal attention mechanisms of generation models (e.g. Ilinykh and Dobnik 2021, 2022). However, as the respective models usually take global images as input, analyses are mostly concerned with attention distribution *within* those representations rather than *across* different parts of the input. For REG, some authors use attention heatmaps as a method of model introspection (Tanaka et al., 2019; Liu et al., 2020; Sun et al., 2022), but without analyzing the patterns in detail.

As a first step for deeper investigations of how contextual information is processed in REG models, we quantify how attention is allocated over the partitioned inputs in a simple REG model. In more detail, we examine the model's relative focus on different parts of the input during inference, i.e. representations of the visual appearance of the referential target, its location in the image and the visual context it appears in. We analyze the attention weights on these input partitions both globally

[1] Code and models for this project are available at: https://github.com/clause-bielefeld/REG-Input-Partitions

Proceedings of the Workshop on Multimodal, Multilingual Natural Language Generation and Multilingual WebNLG Challenge (MM-NLG 2023), pages 20–27
September 12, 2023 ©2023 Association for Computational Linguistics

and for a subset of generated tokens to see if the weighting is affected by the expression content. To the best of our knowledge, no dedicated studies have yet been conducted on how attention is allocated across input partitions in REG models (but see Tanaka et al. 2019, who discuss this for a single example). Our results indicate that contextual information is utilized by the model in linguistically meaningful ways, highlighting promising directions for further research.

2 Background

Referring Expression Generation In REG, the goal is to generate descriptions for entities, which allow their identification in a given context (Reiter and Dale, 2000). Based on symbolic representations of objects in a given domain, classic work focused on rule-based approaches for determining *distinguishing* sets of attribute-value pairs, which identify a target by ruling out all other objects, cf. Krahmer and van Deemter 2012 for a survey.

In recent years, advances in neural modeling and vision and language corpora such as RefCOCO (Kazemzadeh et al., 2014) enabled REG set-ups based on real-world images. Neural REG models generally resemble architectures from e.g. image captioning, but are adapted in different ways to increase the discriminativeness of generated expressions (Schüz et al., 2023). This includes simulations of listener behaviour embedded in training objectives (Mao et al., 2016), comprehension modules (Luo and Shakhnarovich, 2017), reinforcement agents (Yu et al., 2017) or decoding strategies (Schüz and Zarrieß, 2021), but also supplementing model inputs with additional information.

For this, some works propose *visual comparisons* to encode differences in appearance between targets and context objects (Yu et al., 2016, 2017; Tanaka et al., 2019; Kim et al., 2020; Liu et al., 2020), whereas others directly use representations of the global image as context (Mao et al., 2016; Luo and Shakhnarovich, 2017; Zarrieß and Schlangen, 2018; Panagiaris et al., 2020, 2021). In addition to visual context, many approaches provide their models with the relative position and size of the target in the image (Mao et al., 2016; Yu et al., 2016, 2017; Liu et al., 2017; Luo and Shakhnarovich, 2017; Li and Jiang, 2018; Tanaka et al., 2019; Kim et al., 2020; Panagiaris et al., 2020; Liu et al., 2020). To be used as model inputs, different representations are usually concatenated, i.e. the inputs are composed of partitions of visual target and context features as well as location information.

Attention Analysis in V&L In recent years, attention mechanisms (Bahdanau et al., 2015; Luong et al., 2015) have become a cornerstone in generative V&L tasks like image captioning (Xu et al. 2015; Lu et al. 2016; Anderson et al. 2018; Herdade et al. 2019; Huang et al. 2019; Cornia et al. 2020; Pan et al. 2020, among many others, cf. Zohourian-shahzadi and Kalita 2021). Despite some cautious remarks (Jain and Wallace, 2019), attention is used as a method for model introspection (e.g. Clark et al. 2019; Voita et al. 2019; Vig 2019 for text and Cao et al. 2020, 2022; Ilinykh and Dobnik 2021, 2022 for V&L settings). While recent REG approaches build on Transformer (Vaswani et al., 2017) architectures with attention as the key component (Panagiaris et al., 2021; Sun et al., 2022), the inner workings of the attention modules have only been studied in qualitative terms (Tanaka et al. 2019; Liu et al. 2020; Sun et al. 2022). Here, we perform a quantitative analysis of attention allocation in a simple Transformer-based REG model.

3 Experiments

3.1 Model

We implement a simple REG model which is based on an existing implementation for image captioning.[2] Following the general architecture in Vaswani et al. (2017), our model consists of transformer encoder and decoder and is largely comparable to the REG model in Panagiaris et al. (2021), but without self-critical sequence training and layer-wise connections between encoder and decoder. Unlike e.g. Mao et al. (2016), who enforce informativeness during training, we train our model with Cross Entropy Loss (cf. Limitations Section).

The model takes as input a concatenated feature vector $[V_t; Loc_t; V_c]$ where V_t is the visual representation of the target region, Loc_t is a vector of length 5 with the corner coordinates of the target bounding box and its area relative to the whole image, and V_c is the visual representation of the image context, i.e. the global image with the target bounding box masked out (cf. Figure 1). For both V_t and V_c the respective parts of the image are scaled to 224×224 resolution (keeping the original ratio and masking out the padding) and

[2] https://github.com/saahiluppal/catr

encoded with ResNet-101 (He et al., 2015), resulting in representations with 196 features (14×14) and embedding size 2048 for both target and context. Before being passed to the model encoder, V_t, Loc_t and V_c are concatenated into a sequence of 397 features ($196 + 5 + 196$). When generating an expression like *left bike* in Figure 1, we store one set of attention weights per input from the encoder self-attention component and one set per generated token from the decoder cross-attention component. In line with the input structure, the weights can be decomposed into partitions applying to V_t, Loc_t and V_c, with 196, 5 and 196 values, respectively.

3.2 Data

We use RefCOCO and RefCOCO+ (Kazemzadeh et al., 2014) for training and evaluation. Both are based on MSCOCO images (Lin et al., 2014) and contain references to the same objects, but the location attributes *left* and *right*, which are ubiquitous in RefCOCO, have been prohibited in RefCOCO+. The original test splits are separated for references to humans (*TestA*) and other objects (*TestB*). We combine both splits in our attention analysis but provide detailed results in the appendix.

3.3 Evaluation

Generation Quality To estimate the general generation capabilities of our models we rely on BLEU (Papineni et al., 2002), CIDEr (Vedantam et al., 2014) and METEOR (Banerjee and Lavie, 2005) as established metrics for automatic evaluation. However, we note that these metrics have been designed for other tasks and have limited utility for evaluating the overarching task objective in REG, i.e. identifying the intended referent.

Attention Allocation To examine attention allocation, we compare the summed attention weights directed to the target and its location and context for both the encoder (self-attention) and decoder (cross-attention) multi-head attention components. Importantly, we have different sample sizes for encoder and decoder, as the attention weights are calculated once per input for the encoder and once per inference step for the autoregressive decoder.

First, we compute α_t, α_l and α_c as the cumulative attention weights directed to V_t, Loc_t and V_c, respectively. For this, we calculate the sum of the attention weights assigned to each input partition, normalized such that $\alpha_t + \alpha_l + \alpha_c = 1$. As the dimensionality of V_l is considerably lower, we also

	$BLEU_1$	$BLEU_2$	CIDEr	METEOR
TestA	49.7	30.7	92.0	19.5
TestB	51.9	30.0	127.7	22.1
TestA+	24.4	13.6	80.3	12.3
TestB+	20.6	8.9	61.0	10.0

Table 1: Automatic Quality Metrics for RefCOCO TestA / TestB and RefCOCO+ TestA+ / TestB+.

	RefCOCO			RefCOCO+		
	α_t	α_l	α_c	α_t	α_l	α_c
Encoder	.55	.04	.40	.57	.01	.42
$\alpha_{norm-t/l/c}$	.21	.63	.16	.39	.32	.29
Decoder	.58	.03	.39	.64	.02	.34
$\alpha_{norm-t/l/c}$	.32	.49	.19	.42	.38	.20

Table 2: Relative cumulative attention to the target (α_t), location (α_l) and context partitions (α_c) of inputs. $\alpha_{norm-t/l/c}$ scores are normalized by the respective dimensionality of V_t, Loc_t and V_c.

report normalized scores α_{norm-t}, α_{norm-l} and α_{norm-c}, where we first divide the raw cumulative scores by the number of features in each partition.

Second, to investigate the respective influence of visual target and context features more closely, we quantify the attention difference between α_t and α_c as $\Delta_{t,c}$. As we exclude α_l here, we normalize the target and context scores such that $\alpha_t + \alpha_c = 1$. We then calculate $\Delta_{t,c} = \alpha_t - \alpha_c$, i.e. $0 < \Delta_{t,c} \leq 1$ if there is relative focus on the target, $-1 \leq \Delta_{t,c} < 0$ if there is relative focus on the context, and $\Delta_{t,c} = 0$ when both parts of the input are equally weighted. We also test whether target and context are weighted differently by the decoder when head or subordinate nouns are generated. In the referential noun phrases, head nouns generally represent the class label of the target and are therefore hypothesized to relate to V_t more clearly. To select nouns and determine NP heads in generated expressions, we rely on the POS tagger and dependency parser from the spaCy library.[3]

4 Results and Discussion

BLEU, CIDEr and METEOR are reported in Table 1. Although our scores fall below e.g. Panagiaris et al. (2021),[4] we note that our models are able to generate well-formed expressions with reasonable

[3]https://spacy.io/

[4]The discrepancies between RefCOCO and RefCOCO+ as well as the respective TestA and TestB splits can be also observed in other work on multimodal REG, cf. Section 2.

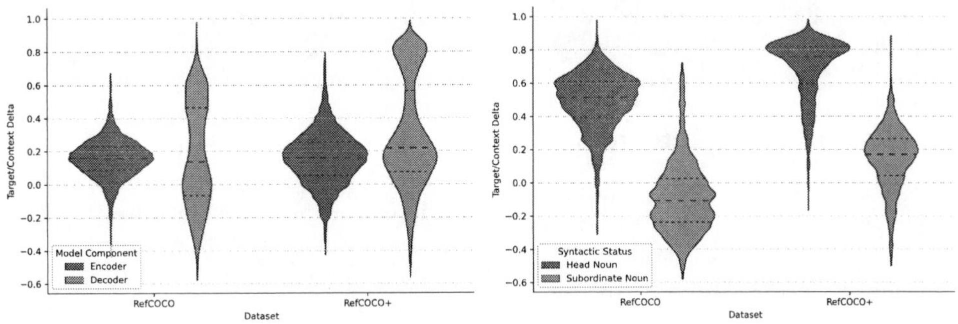

(a) $\Delta_{t,c}$ for Encoder and Decoder (all tokens)

(b) Decoder $\Delta_{t,c}$ for head and subordinate nouns

Figure 2: Target-Context Deltas ($\Delta_{t,c}$), inner lines denote quartiles. Left: Global distribution, averaged over all inputs (encoder) and generated tokens (decoder). Right: Decoder $\Delta_{t,c}$ for head and subordinate nouns.

	RefCOCO	RefCOCO+
Encoder	.16	.16
Decoder	.18	.30
Decoder / N_{head}	.49	.69
Decoder / N_{sub}	-.09	.15

Table 3: Mean target-context deltas ($\Delta_{t,c}$) for RefCOCO and RefCOCO+. *Decoder /* N_{head} and N_{sub} refer to deltas for generated NP-head or subordinated nouns.

similarity to the ground-truth annotations.

Table 2 shows the mean α_t, α_l and α_c scores for RefCOCO and RefCOCO+, as well as their dimension-normalized counterparts. Without normalizing for dimensionality, target features receive most attention in all cases, in line with the intuition that visual features of the referential target are the primary source of information for generating referring expressions. Loc_t features are consistently ranked last by a large margin. However, this changes if scores are normalized by their dimensionality: In this case, α_{norm-l} surpasses α_{norm-c} for both datasets and even α_{norm-t} for RefCOCO. The large differences between both datasets with respect to α_{norm-l} could be partly due to the location attributes *left* and *right*, which are highly common in RefCOCO but excluded in RefCOCO+.

Regarding the relative focus on target and context partitions, the mean $\Delta_{t,c}$ scores in Table 3 again show a general bias toward the target for both datasets, especially for decoder attention. Between datasets, the encoder scores are nearly identical, but the RefCOCO+ decoder is more biased to the target. Figure 2 (a) provides a more detailed view of the delta distribution: For both datasets, the median values of encoder and decoder are similar, but the decoder distributions extend more toward both extrema. This indicates that decoder attention shifts between target and context features during generation, possibly depending on which parts of the input are relevant for the generated tokens.

To investigate this in more detail, we report decoder deltas for generated nouns in Table 3 and Figure 2 (b), broken down by their syntactic status (head or subordinate noun in the referential noun phrase). For both datasets, mean scores and illustrations clearly show that there is a strong bias toward the target partition of the input when generating head nouns, supporting the intuition that information from this part of the inputs is particularly relevant for generating the class label for the referential target. However, the plots also reveal cases where context is given notable attention weight.

Overall, while generally biased towards the visual target features, our models allocate substantial attention weights to all input partitions. The increased target bias for head nouns and the high α_{norm-l} scores for RefCOCO indicate that attention allocation is sensitive to the respective relevance of different input partitions during the generation process. Importantly, as encoder and decoder are connected serially in our architecture, attention allocation in the decoder might be affected by attention biases in the encoder. Against this background, questions arise about the role of residual connections as well as layer-wise connections between encoder and decoder in the style of Panagiaris et al. (2021) for processing contextual information, which we leave for future work.

5 Conclusion and Future Directions

In this paper, we investigated attention allocation across input partitions for a simple REG model. Our results show that the model attends to all sources of information, albeit with a general bias towards the target. In addition, our models show systematic differences between encoder and decoder attention across datasets, as well as sensitivity to the meaning of the generated tokens.

Importantly, this study only represents a small step toward a more thorough understanding of the significance of different types of information in REG. One limitation of this work is that our models are not explicitly optimized for the general objective of the REG task, i.e., unambiguously identifying the referential target (see Limitations Section). Consequently, as regarding for possible distractors is crucial for this, we see great potential in investigating how different approaches to increase the pragmatic informativeness of generated expressions (cf. Section 2) affect the relative weighting of input partitions. Along with this, given the multifaceted role of situational context for REG (Schüz et al., 2023), future work should take a closer look at attention allocation over semantic units in the visual context, e.g. to see whether objects with certain classes or relations to the target are weighted more or less during generation.

Limitations

We identify three main limitations in our study:

First, as our models are trained using Cross Entropy Loss as a target function, they have not been optimized for the general objective in the REG task and therefore may not be able to reflect certain pragmatic influences on attention allocation. We plan to address this weakness in future studies.

Second, the spaCy POS taggers and dependency parsers are prone to errors on RefCOCO and RefCOCO+ annotations, in part because they often do not consist of fully formulated sentences. This is a potential problem for selecting nouns from generated expressions and identifying the heads of noun phrases (although samples have shown that this still works reasonably well in practice).

Finally, as previous studies have found that large V&L models encode different kinds of information in different attention layers (e.g. Ilinykh and Dobnik 2021), a comprehensive investigation of attention allocation in Transformer-based generation models would require a comparison between different layers and heads of the multi-head attention modules. Likewise, further state-of-the-art explanation techniques for Transformer-based models (e.g. Abnar and Zuidema 2020; Mohebbi et al. 2023) could be instructive with respect to our research question. Due to time and space constraints, we leave this for future studies.

References

Samira Abnar and Willem Zuidema. 2020. Quantifying attention flow in transformers. In *Proceedings of the 58th Annual Meeting of the Association for Computational Linguistics*, pages 4190–4197, Online. Association for Computational Linguistics.

Peter Anderson, Xiaodong He, Chris Buehler, Damien Teney, Mark Johnson, Stephen Gould, and Lei Zhang. 2018. Bottom-up and top-down attention for image captioning and visual question answering. In *2018 IEEE/CVF Conference on Computer Vision and Pattern Recognition*. IEEE.

Dzmitry Bahdanau, Kyunghyun Cho, and Yoshua Bengio. 2015. Neural machine translation by jointly learning to align and translate. In *3rd International Conference on Learning Representations, ICLR 2015, San Diego, CA, USA, May 7-9, 2015, Conference Track Proceedings*.

Satanjeev Banerjee and Alon Lavie. 2005. METEOR: An automatic metric for MT evaluation with improved correlation with human judgments. In *Proceedings of the ACL Workshop on Intrinsic and Extrinsic Evaluation Measures for Machine Translation and/or Summarization*, pages 65–72, Ann Arbor, Michigan. Association for Computational Linguistics.

Feiqi Cao, Soyeon Caren Han, Siqu Long, Changwei Xu, and Josiah Poon. 2022. Understanding attention for vision-and-language tasks. In *Proceedings of the 29th International Conference on Computational Linguistics*, pages 3438–3453, Gyeongju, Republic of Korea. International Committee on Computational Linguistics.

Jize Cao, Zhe Gan, Yu Cheng, Licheng Yu, Yen-Chun Chen, and Jingjing Liu. 2020. Behind the scene: Revealing the secrets of pre-trained vision-and-language models. In *Computer Vision – ECCV 2020*, pages 565–580. Springer International Publishing.

Kevin Clark, Urvashi Khandelwal, Omer Levy, and Christopher D. Manning. 2019. What does BERT look at? an analysis of BERT's attention. In *Proceedings of the 2019 ACL Workshop BlackboxNLP: Analyzing and Interpreting Neural Networks for NLP*, pages 276–286, Florence, Italy. Association for Computational Linguistics.

Marcella Cornia, Matteo Stefanini, Lorenzo Baraldi, and Rita Cucchiara. 2020. Meshed-memory transformer for image captioning. In *2020 IEEE/CVF Conference on Computer Vision and Pattern Recognition (CVPR)*. IEEE.

Kaiming He, Xiangyu Zhang, Shaoqing Ren, and Jian Sun. 2015. Deep residual learning for image recognition.

Simao Herdade, Armin Kappeler, Kofi Boakye, and Joao Soares. 2019. *Image Captioning: Transforming Objects into Words*. Curran Associates Inc., Red Hook, NY, USA.

Lun Huang, Wenmin Wang, Jie Chen, and Xiao-Yong Wei. 2019. Attention on attention for image captioning. In *2019 IEEE/CVF International Conference on Computer Vision (ICCV)*. IEEE.

Nikolai Ilinykh and Simon Dobnik. 2021. What does a language-and-vision transformer see: The impact of semantic information on visual representations. *Frontiers in Artificial Intelligence*, 4.

Nikolai Ilinykh and Simon Dobnik. 2022. Attention as grounding: Exploring textual and cross-modal attention on entities and relations in language-and-vision transformer. In *Findings of the Association for Computational Linguistics: ACL 2022*, pages 4062–4073, Dublin, Ireland. Association for Computational Linguistics.

Sarthak Jain and Byron C. Wallace. 2019. Attention is not Explanation. In *Proceedings of the 2019 Conference of the North American Chapter of the Association for Computational Linguistics: Human Language Technologies, Volume 1 (Long and Short Papers)*, pages 3543–3556, Minneapolis, Minnesota. Association for Computational Linguistics.

Sahar Kazemzadeh, Vicente Ordonez, Mark Matten, and Tamara Berg. 2014. ReferItGame: Referring to objects in photographs of natural scenes. In *Proceedings of the 2014 Conference on Empirical Methods in Natural Language Processing (EMNLP)*, pages 787–798, Doha, Qatar. Association for Computational Linguistics.

Jungjun Kim, Hanbin Ko, and Jialin Wu. 2020. CoNAN: A complementary neighboring-based attention network for referring expression generation. In *Proceedings of the 28th International Conference on Computational Linguistics*, pages 1952–1962, Barcelona, Spain (Online). International Committee on Computational Linguistics.

Emiel Krahmer and Kees van Deemter. 2012. Computational generation of referring expressions: A survey. *Computational Linguistics*, 38(1):173–218.

Xiangyang Li and Shuqiang Jiang. 2018. Bundled object context for referring expressions. *IEEE Transactions on Multimedia*, 20(10):2749–2760.

Tsung-Yi Lin, Michael Maire, Serge Belongie, James Hays, Pietro Perona, Deva Ramanan, Piotr Dollár, and C. Lawrence Zitnick. 2014. Microsoft coco: Common objects in context. In *Computer Vision – ECCV 2014*, pages 740–755, Cham. Springer International Publishing.

Jingyu Liu, Liang Wang, and Ming-Hsuan Yang. 2017. Referring expression generation and comprehension via attributes. In *2017 IEEE International Conference on Computer Vision (ICCV)*. IEEE.

Jingyu Liu, Wei Wang, Liang Wang, and Ming-Hsuan Yang. 2020. Attribute-guided attention for referring expression generation and comprehension. *IEEE Transactions on Image Processing*, 29:5244–5258.

Jiasen Lu, Caiming Xiong, Devi Parikh, and Richard Socher. 2016. Knowing when to look: Adaptive attention via a visual sentinel for image captioning.

R. Luo and Gregory Shakhnarovich. 2017. Comprehension-guided referring expressions. *2017 IEEE Conference on Computer Vision and Pattern Recognition (CVPR)*, pages 3125–3134.

Thang Luong, Hieu Pham, and Christopher D. Manning. 2015. Effective approaches to attention-based neural machine translation. In *Proceedings of the 2015 Conference on Empirical Methods in Natural Language Processing*, pages 1412–1421, Lisbon, Portugal. Association for Computational Linguistics.

Junhua Mao, J. Huang, A. Toshev, Oana-Maria Camburu, A. Yuille, and Kevin Murphy. 2016. Generation and comprehension of unambiguous object descriptions. *2016 IEEE Conference on Computer Vision and Pattern Recognition (CVPR)*, pages 11–20.

Hosein Mohebbi, Willem Zuidema, Grzegorz Chrupała, and Afra Alishahi. 2023. Quantifying context mixing in transformers. In *Proceedings of the 17th Conference of the European Chapter of the Association for Computational Linguistics*, pages 3378–3400, Dubrovnik, Croatia. Association for Computational Linguistics.

Yingwei Pan, Ting Yao, Yehao Li, and Tao Mei. 2020. X-linear attention networks for image captioning. In *2020 IEEE/CVF Conference on Computer Vision and Pattern Recognition (CVPR)*. IEEE.

Nikolaos Panagiaris, Emma Hart, and Dimitra Gkatzia. 2020. Improving the naturalness and diversity of referring expression generation models using minimum risk training. In *Proceedings of the 13th International Conference on Natural Language Generation*, pages 41–51, Dublin, Ireland. Association for Computational Linguistics.

Nikolaos Panagiaris, Emma Hart, and Dimitra Gkatzia. 2021. Generating unambiguous and diverse referring expressions. *Computer Speech & Language*, 68:101184.

Kishore Papineni, Salim Roukos, Todd Ward, and Wei-Jing Zhu. 2002. Bleu: a method for automatic evaluation of machine translation. In *Proceedings of the 40th Annual Meeting of the Association for Computational Linguistics*, pages 311–318, Philadelphia, Pennsylvania, USA. Association for Computational Linguistics.

Ehud Reiter and Robert Dale. 2000. *Building natural language generation systems*. Cambridge University Press, Cambridge, U.K. New York.

Simeon Schüz and Sina Zarrieß. 2021. Decoupling pragmatics: Discriminative decoding for referring expression generation. In *Proceedings of the Reasoning and Interaction Conference (ReInAct 2021)*, pages 47–52, Gothenburg, Sweden. Association for Computational Linguistics.

Simeon Schüz, Albert Gatt, and Sina Zarrieß. 2023. Rethinking symbolic and visual context in referring expression generation. *Frontiers in Artificial Intelligence*, 6.

Mengyang Sun, Wei Suo, Peng Wang, Yanning Zhang, and Qi Wu. 2022. A proposal-free one-stage framework for referring expression comprehension and generation via dense cross-attention. *IEEE Transactions on Multimedia*, pages 1–1.

M. Tanaka, Takayuki Itamochi, K. Narioka, Ikuro Sato, Y. Ushiku, and T. Harada. 2019. Generating easy-to-understand referring expressions for target identifications. *2019 IEEE/CVF International Conference on Computer Vision (ICCV)*, pages 5793–5802.

Ashish Vaswani, Noam Shazeer, Niki Parmar, Jakob Uszkoreit, Llion Jones, Aidan N. Gomez, Lukasz Kaiser, and Illia Polosukhin. 2017. Attention is all you need.

Ramakrishna Vedantam, C. Lawrence Zitnick, and Devi Parikh. 2014. Cider: Consensus-based image description evaluation.

Jesse Vig. 2019. A multiscale visualization of attention in the transformer model. In *Proceedings of the 57th Annual Meeting of the Association for Computational Linguistics: System Demonstrations*, pages 37–42, Florence, Italy. Association for Computational Linguistics.

Elena Voita, David Talbot, Fedor Moiseev, Rico Sennrich, and Ivan Titov. 2019. Analyzing multi-head self-attention: Specialized heads do the heavy lifting, the rest can be pruned. In *Proceedings of the 57th Annual Meeting of the Association for Computational Linguistics*, pages 5797–5808, Florence, Italy. Association for Computational Linguistics.

Kelvin Xu, Jimmy Ba, Ryan Kiros, Kyunghyun Cho, Aaron Courville, Ruslan Salakhudinov, Rich Zemel, and Yoshua Bengio. 2015. Show, attend and tell: Neural image caption generation with visual attention. 37:2048–2057.

Licheng Yu, Patrick Poirson, Shan Yang, Alexander C. Berg, and Tamara L. Berg. 2016. Modeling context in referring expressions. In *Computer Vision – ECCV 2016*, pages 69–85, Cham. Springer International Publishing.

Licheng Yu, Hao Tan, Mohit Bansal, and Tamara L Berg. 2017. A joint speaker-listener-reinforcer model for referring expressions. In *Computer Vision and Pattern Recognition (CVPR)*, volume 2.

Sina Zarrieß and David Schlangen. 2018. Decoding strategies for neural referring expression generation. In *Proceedings of the 11th International Conference on Natural Language Generation*, pages 503–512, Tilburg University, The Netherlands. Association for Computational Linguistics.

Zanyar Zohourianshahzadi and Jugal K. Kalita. 2021. Neural attention for image captioning: review of outstanding methods. *Artificial Intelligence Review*, 55(5):3833–3862.

A Appendix

	TestA	TestB	TestA+	TestB+
Encoder	.19	.12	.22	.09
Decoder	.16	.21	.34	.26
Decoder / N_{head}	.50	.48	.69	.69
Decoder / N_{sub}	-.07	-.10	.22	.07

Table 4: Mean target-context deltas ($\Delta_{t,c}$) for RefCOCO and RefCOCO+. *Decoder / N_{head}* and N_{sub} refer to the deltas when generating NP-head or subordinated nouns.

A.1 Data, Implementation and Training Details

As described in Section 3, we trained our models on RefCOCO and RefCOCO+.[5] Both datasets consist of about 140k expressions for 50k objects in 20k images, out of which 42k objects in 17k images are assigned to the train splits.

Our model configurations for RefCOCO and RefCOCO+ are identical: In both cases, the model has 6 encoder and 6 decoder layers with 8 attention heads, a hidden dimension of 256, a feedforward dimension of 2048, and a total of $\sim$ 84,000,000 parameters. Our initial learning rate is set to 0.0001 for the transformer encoder and decoder, and 0.00001 for the pre-trained ResNet-101 backbone. We trained our models on an Nvidia RTX A40. The RefCOCO model was trained for 5 and the RefCOCO+ model for 7 epochs, with each epoch lasting approximately 2 hours.

[5] https://github.com/lichengunc/refer

	TestA			TestB			TestA+			TestB+		
Encoder	.57	.05	.38	.54	.04	.42	.60	.02	.38	.54	.01	.45
$\alpha_{norm-t/l/c}$	.21	.65	.14	.22	.60	.18	.37	.40	.24	.42	.22	.35
Decoder	.56	.04	.40	.59	.02	.38	.65	.02	.32	.62	.02	.36
$\alpha_{norm-t/l/c}$	.28	.54	.18	.36	.44	.20	.40	.42	.18	.44	.34	.23

Table 5: Relative cumulative attention to the target (α_t), location (α_l) and context partitions (α_c) of inputs. $\alpha_{norm-t/l/c}$ scores are normalized by the respective dimensionality of V_t, Loc_t and V_c.

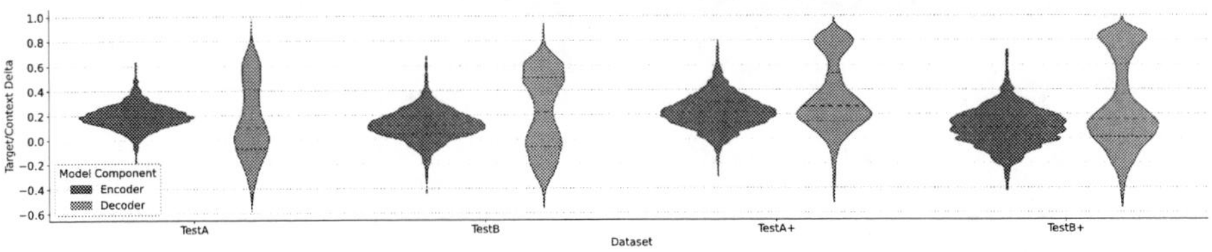

(a) $\Delta_{t,c}$ for Encoder and Decoder (all tokens)

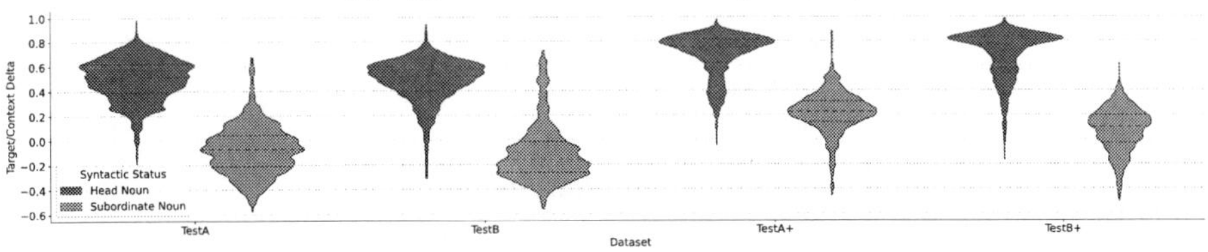

(b) Decoder $\Delta_{t,c}$ for head and subordinate nouns

Figure 3: Target-Context Deltas ($\Delta_{t,c}$) for all splits in RefCOCO (TestA / TestB) and RefCOCO+ (TestA+, TestB+), inner lines denote quartiles. Top: Global distribution, averaged over all inputs (encoder) and generated tokens (decoder). Bottom: Decoder $\Delta_{t,c}$ for head and subordinate nouns.

A.2 Results for Individual Test Splits

In our attention analysis, we have combined the TestA and TestB splits of RefCOCO and RefCOCO+ for greater clarity. Table 5 shows the α_t, α_l and α_c scores as well as their normalized counterparts for each test split. In Table 4 we report and visualize target context deltas ($\Delta_{t,c}$) for the individual test splits (visualized in Figure 3).

These results are largely consistent with the findings in Section 4: Visual target features receive the most attention, but location features score high when normalized by partition size. With respect to target-context deltas, decoder attention exhibits greater variance, and there is strong target bias for generated head nouns.

Are language-and-vision transformers sensitive to discourse? A case study of ViLBERT

Ekaterina Voloshina [†] and **Nikolai Ilinykh** [*] [†] and **Simon Dobnik** [*] [†]
[*]Centre for Linguistic Theory and Studies in Probability (CLASP),
Department of Philosophy, Linguistics and Theory of Science (FLoV),
[†]University of Gothenburg, Sweden
gusvolek@student.gu.se,
nikolai.ilinykh@gu.se, simon.dobnik@gu.se

Abstract

Language-and-vision models have shown good performance on tasks such as image-caption matching and caption generation. However, it is challenging for such models to generate *pragmatically* correct captions, which adequately reflect what is happening in one or several images. Here we explore to what extent contextual language-and-vision models are sensitive to different discourses, both textual and visual. In particular, we employ one of the multi-modal transformers (ViLBERT) and test if it can match descriptions and images, differentiating them from distractors of different degree of similarity that are sampled from different visual and textual contexts. We place our evaluation in the multi-sentence and multi-image setup, where images and sentences are expected to form a single narrative structure, e.g. discourse. We show that the model can distinguish different situations but it is not sensitive to differences within one narrative structure. We also demonstrate that the model's performance depends on the task itself, for example, the effect of what modality remains unchanged in non-matching pairs or how similar non-matching pairs are to the original pairs.

1 Introduction

Large language models are considered "black boxes" as it is often hard to explain their predictions. Therefore, it is essential to evaluate such models on tasks different from downstream applications to see if they have acquired necessary knowledge, including linguistic knowledge, during the pre-training process (Liu et al., 2019; Belinkov, 2022; Elazar et al., 2021). Moreover, model performance on linguistic tasks has been shown to correlate with downstream applications (Saphra, 2021). Although the models have been tested on morphology, semantics, and syntax (Conneau et al., 2018; Warstadt et al., 2020; Taktasheva et al., 2021; Stańczak et al., 2022; Maudslay and Cotterell, 2021; Lasri et al., 2022), little has been done on the evaluation of discourse (Hong et al., 2020; Liang et al., 2022). Models such as GPT-3 are good at generating long, coherent sequences but they are often not sensitive to intents or communicative purposes that the narratives are written with (Ruis et al., 2022).

In this work, we focus on the evaluation of the sensitivity of multi-modal models to *discourse*. We understand discourse as contextual information defined by the situation of communication connected to social and cultural background. Discourse can be **local** defined by individual items such as an utterance or an image or **narrative** defined by a sequence of several items. Discourse meaning includes but is not limited to:

- **Textual discourse**: linguistic relations and dependencies that exist between linguistic units across words in a single utterance;
- **Visual discourse**: images represent parts of reality by being focused on specific situations involving entities and events among all that are visually available;
- **Situation-level discourse**: operates at a level of larger structures such as narratives and requires world knowledge and awareness of the social context.

As we are interested in how a language-and-vision model in general captures all three components of discourse outlined above and to investigate the effects and the role of discourse on the generation of text across different discourses, for experiments we evaluate a single multi-modal transformer, ViLBERT (Lu et al., 2019), that was trained on a (simple) discourse task of image-text matching. This is also one of the first transformer-based models with a cross-modal alignment pre-training objective. For the data we use the Visual Storytelling dataset (VIST) (Huang et al., 2016) which

Proceedings of the Workshop on Multimodal, Multilingual Natural Language Generation and Multilingual WebNLG Challenge (MM-NLG 2023), pages 28–38
September 12, 2023 ©2023 Association for Computational Linguistics

consists of descriptions of images at two different levels of annotation and therefore discourses: *descriptions-in-isolation* and *stories-in-sequence*. While *descriptions-in-isolation* were collected following standard instructions for image captioning in MS-COCO (Lin et al., 2014) (for example, annotators have to name all important parts, i.e. *local discourse*), for *stories-in-sequence* crowd workers were asked to write a story about a sequence of images (*narrative discourse*, see Figure 1). *Stories-in-sequence* do not tend to name objects in images but rather connect images to a coherent situation, and therefore we expect them to be more challenging for a language-and-vision model.

We assume that during pre-training a model acquires the knowledge of situation described by a specific image-text pair. Since we understand discourse as a situation itself rather than a sequence of images, we adapt a standard image-caption matching task to our experiments by creating different perturbations, i. e. non-matching pairs that we call **distractors**, by permuting data in several ways, across stories and within one story. We investigate the model's abilities of grounding discourse at different levels:

1. Can a language-and-vision model perform *visual grounding of individual descriptive captions* when non-matching images or captions are taken from different situations?

2. Can a language-and-vision model perform *story visual grounding*, i. e. ground captions that are parts of a narrative but there is a mismatch between images or captions and the situation?

3. Can a language-and-vision model understand the narrative structure, i. e. the model can detect if two parts of the same story form a coherent whole?

In the first two cases we are testing the model's ability to identify distractors across different stories and situations, hence testing the model's ability to identify *local discourse*. In the third case, we are testing the model's ability to identify distractors within the same narrative and hence we are testing the model's ability to identify *narrative discourse*.

We introduce a new method of constructing evaluation tasks for language-and-vision models. We then analyse the role of different discourse structures and different modalities on the performance on our tasks. Our results reveal details about the behaviour of large multi-modal transformer for a setup that is beyond simple image-text matching.

2 Related Work

Little has been done on evaluating models' knowledge of discourse. For language models Ettinger (2020) shows that BERT produces pragmatically incorrect outputs as it does not take into account broader context. Most of the previous work on discourse evaluation of BERT and BERT-like models was focused on local discourse structures. For example, Nie et al. (2019) evaluate models on explicit discourse relations expressed with conjunctions. Chen et al. (2019) propose a benchmark for model evaluation on different discourse tasks such as prediction of implicit discourse relations based on the Penn Discourse Treebank annotation (Prasad et al., 2008), discourse coherence, and others. Araujo et al. (2021) attempt to improve the results on discourse tasks from DiscoEval by changing the pre-training objective of models. Recently, Hong et al. (2023a) introduced a dataset for image-based story generation and proposed a character-based story generation model that is evaluated based on the coherence of generated texts.

Multimodal models were shown to ground semantic and syntactic knowledge. Ilinykh and Dobnik (2022a) provide results that the models ground both semantic and syntactic relations. Parcalabescu et al. (2021) argue that models can ground objects but struggle with interdependence relations. Most of the work on discourse evaluation of language-and-vision models focuses on downstream tasks such as Visual Question Answering (VQA) and Visual Coreference. Bernardi and Pezzelle (2021) provide an overview of VQA systems and their challenges related to reasoning, language ambiguity etc. Several studies address the problem of discourse-coherent image generation. Takmaz et al. (2020) introduce a generation mechanism that produces captions grounded not only in the visual context but also in the established common ground. Alikhani et al. (2020) improve the quality of generated captions by feeding models with additional information on the types of connections between two clauses. Ilinykh and Dobnik (2022b) show how different decoding strategies for image captioning reflect discourse structure in comparison to reference captions.

As for existing image-caption datasets, Alikhani

and Stone (2019) argue that existing datasets do not reflect all possible coherence types and are limited in the word usage. However, even existing datasets are challenging for models, as (Alikhani et al., 2023) show models such as CLIP or ViLBERT do not capture differences in coherence relations. However, recently discourse has started to receive increased attention in the research community, including development of new approaches to building discourse datasets (Hong et al., 2023b).

3 Models

We examine ViLBERT (Vision-and-Language BERT) (Lu et al., 2019), a dual-stream multi-modal BERT-based model. Unlike single-stream models that encode both modalities at the same time, dual-stream models initially represent each modality separately. These models then learn cross-modal grounding which should include some knowledge of discourse structure, depending on the context in which data was collected. ViLBERT performs well on the image-text matching task and it is frequently used in the studies of multi-modality. One important feature of ViLBERT is that its text module's parameters are initialised with BERT. In comparison, LXMERT (Tan and Bansal, 2019), a very similar model to ViLBERT, learns its text module from scratch. Although there are more recent transformers trained for different discourse contexts we focus on a transformer that was trained on a simple referring context (the properties of which are well-known to us) in order to investigate how well the knowledge of that discourse transfers to other (more complex) discourses. We expect that the performance of a model will vary depending on how well its pre-training objective(s) and datasets that it was trained on match the visual storytelling task.

ViLBERT was trained on three objectives: masked language modelling, image region masking, and an image-text matching task. In the latter task, the model has to predict if a given sequence of tokens consisting of a visual input (an image) and a language input (a caption) match or do not match. This objective helps the model to ground descriptions in images and differentiate them from non-matching counter-parts. This task therefore also involves learning about contextual sensitivity of descriptions to discourse and therefore, provided that non-matching items are controlled, we see it as a suitable task for our investigation.

We test the ViLBERT model from VOLTA (Bugliarello et al., 2021), a framework that provides the code base for several transformer-based language-and-vision encoders and allows working with custom datasets. The model takes a set of pre-processed features: masked sentences, token ids, visual features, image location, masked images with regions of interest and their object labels. Textual features are generated by the BERT tokeniser[*] that returns a sequence of token ids. To extract image features, we use the Caffe VG Faster R-CNN implementation (Anderson et al., 2018)[†]. The model extracts 36 proposal boxes with features of dimension 2048 and object labels. We do not mask any tokens or regions as we only focus on one output head of ViLBERT that predicts if an image and a text match.

4 Data

For experiments we use images and descriptions from the Visual Storytelling Dataset (VIST) (Huang et al., 2016). The dataset includes stories from 10,117 Flickr albums containing 210,819 images split into train (80%), dev (10%), and test (10%) samples. Stories reflect narrative structure and sentences are linked with discourse relations. An example of a story taken from the dataset is illustrated in Figure 1.

Although there are other datasets that include narrative captions, such as RecipeQA (Yagcioglu et al., 2018), we choose VIST as it includes several types of captions, which allows us to look at different discourse structures. The dataset includes three levels of description annotation, *descriptions-in-isolation, descriptions-in-sequence*[‡], and *stories-in-sequence*, by crowd-workers hired through Amazon's Mechanical Turk. For *stories-in-sequence* a worker selected at least 5 images and wrote a story about them. Then, another worker received the same images and wrote their story. For *descriptions-in-isolation* workers followed the instructions of image captioning tasks from MS COCO (Lin et al., 2014). For each album, 5 stories were collected, and for each image 3 workers wrote *descriptions-in-isolation*. Not to repeat images, we limit our data to only one annotation.

We expect that the first type of captions,

[*] `https://huggingface.co/bert-base-cased`

[†] `https://github.com/airsplay/py-bottom-up-attention`

[‡] According to the authors of the dataset, this layer of annotation has been lost.

Desc-in-Isolation	A black frisbee is sitting on top of a roof.	A man playing soccer outside of a white house with a red door.	The boy is throwing a soccer ball by the red door.	A soccer ball is over a roof by a frisbee in a rain gutter.	Two balls and a frisbee are on top of a roof.
Desc-in-Sequence	A roof top with a black frisbee laying on the top of the edge of it.	A man is standing in the grass in front of the house kicking a soccer ball.	A man is in the front of the house throwing a soccer ball up.	A blue and white soccer ball and black Frisbee are on the edge of the roof top.	Two soccer balls and a Frisbee are sitting on top of the roof top.
Story-in-Sequence	**A discus got stuck up on the roof.**	**Why not try getting it down with a soccer ball?**	**Up the soccer ball goes.**	**It didn't work so we tried a volley ball.**	**Now the discus, soccer ball, and volleyball are all stuck on the roof.**

Figure 1: A story from the VIST dataset with three different layers of annotations: *descriptions-in-isolation*, *descriptions-in-sequence*, and *stories-in-sequence*.

descriptions-in-isolation, is more descriptive, in other words, annotators tend to mention objects on a picture rather than describe events. *Stories-in-sequence*, on the other hand, might not be directly related to pictures, and annotators can omit some information that could be extracted from visual context. Hence, two types of annotation reflect different types of image-text coherence.

5 Experimental setup

We run three experiments based on type of descriptions in VIST and whether descriptions were considered as a part of local or narrative discourse as shown in Table 1.

Captions	Local discourse	Narrative discourse
Descriptions-in-isolation	Experiment I	-
Stories-in-sequence	Experiment II	Experiment III

Table 1: Summary of experiments

In Experiment I and II we test the model on the image-caption matching task where items are selected in one of five different conditions according to which distractors are selected (Figure 2). In addition to a random assignment (condition 5) we also use similarity scores to control for different degree of distraction (conditions 1–4). To every item we match either a caption or an image with one of highly similar or dissimilar captions or images from the entire dataset. For each condition we create a separate dataset that consists of both matching and non-matching pairs. In Experiment III, we create distractors by selecting randomly an image or a caption from the same story. In every experiment, we test the model on each item (image or caption) *twice*: with its original caption or image and with its non-matching version and the task of the model is to identify a match or mismatch. In that way, we make our evaluation datasets balanced and this setup allows us to compare scores for match or mismatch across different setups.

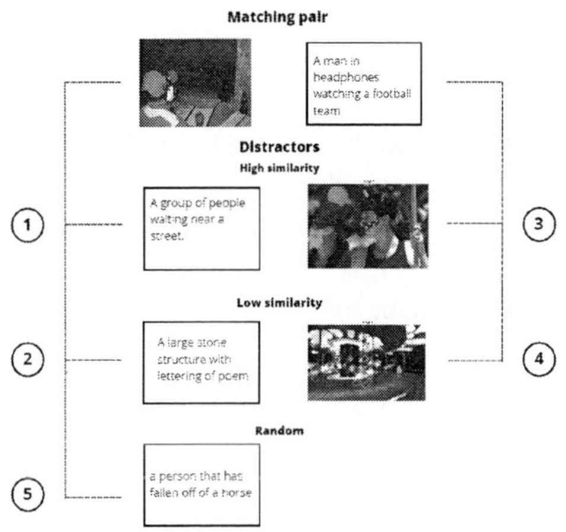

Figure 2: The dataset construction based on different similarities scores and modalities. The 5th condition repeats the procedure of assigning random captions in the pre-training objective of ViLBERT.

For constructing non-matching pairs based on similarity, we extract textual and visual representations of original descriptions or images and calculate pairwise scores between each dataset item of the same type with cosine similarity. We then take the upper quartile of the distribution of similarity scores as a threshold for high similarity items and the lower quartile as a threshold for low similar-

Distractors	High Similarity	Low similarity
Textual	0.92	0.95
Visual	0.94	0.95

Table 2: The overall performance on the image-caption matching task with *descriptions-in-isolation* based on accuracy on a balanced dataset. The accuracy of the baseline on random distractor descriptions is **0.94**.

ity items. For details see Appendix A. For each item, we construct lists of items with high and low similarity distractors from which we select items randomly. This way, we make our data more diverse as the same distractor is only used in one comparison task.

To extract representations for texts we use the Hugging Face implementation of BERT (Devlin et al., 2018) [§]. For image representations we use ResNet-101 (He et al., 2016), a deep residual network based on a CNN architecture. We choose these models since these are used by most language-and-vision transformers.

6 Results

6.1 Experiment I: Local discourse and descriptions in isolation

Here we test the model on images and their descriptions by distracting it with out-of-story captions permuted according to the five conditions outlined in Figure 2. Distractors are selected according to the modality (text or vision), the degree of similarity (high or low) or they are picked randomly.

The model shows high performance on *descriptions-in-isolation*: in all five conditions the accuracy is greater than 0.9 (Table 2).[¶] As for differences in similarity, the model performs better when distinguishing distractors of low similarity, possibly because such items are easier to differentiate. In terms of the modality, the difference in performance is observed only with high similarity distractors: the performance is slightly lower with textual distractors compared to visual distractors. This indicates the sensitivity of the model to changes in text where individual words carry high information content and, possibly, this result might also be indicative that the model is relying on text much more than on vision. This is a well-known challenge for multi-modal architectures – models are known to ground text in images better than images in text (Agrawal et al., 2018; Thomason et al., 2019; Ilinykh et al., 2022). In general, we cannot see a large difference in the results of the experiment under all five conditions.

[§]https://huggingface.co/bert-base-uncased

[¶]Note that since both classes are balanced accuracy is a suitable measure here.

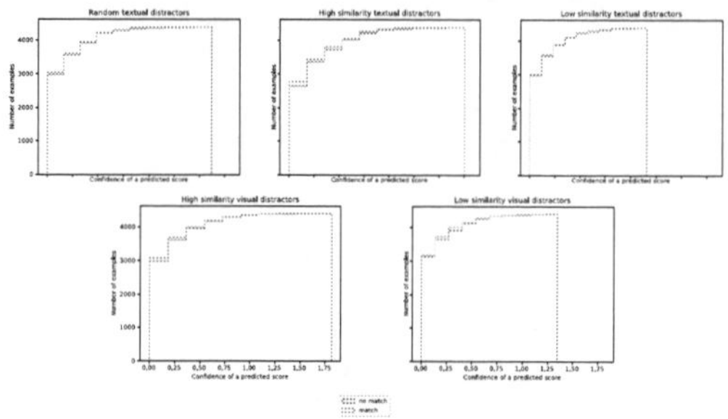

Figure 3: The confidence of the model in predicting a correct answer (match / no match) in an image-caption matching task for *descriptions-in-isolation*.

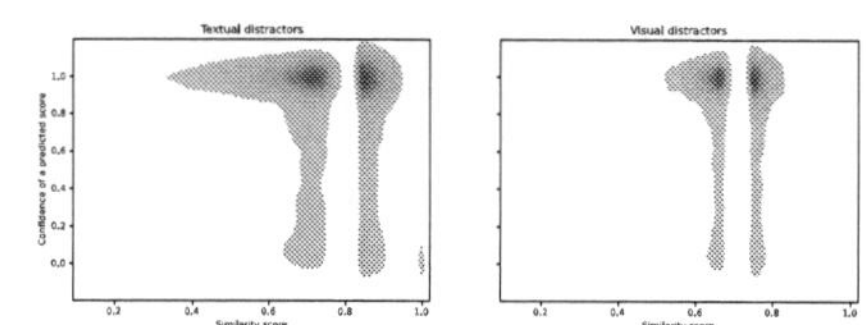

Figure 4: The relation between similarity scores and the model's confidence on correct answers for matching distractors for *descriptions-in-isolation*.

To understand the uncertainty of the model when predicting a match or non-match we look at its predictions on individual classes. If the model is confident in its predictions, predictions will be evenly distributed as the classes are balanced. Differences in performance on individual classes might reveal any differences in model uncertainty in cases involving high and low similarity distractors or between textual or visual distractors.

Figure 3 demonstrates that a predominant majority of the examples can be classified with high confidence. There is almost no difference between the different conditions except for random distractors where the model is less confident on non-matching labels than in the other four conditions. Figure 4 illustrates the relationship between similarity scores of distractors and confidence of the model. For a large number of examples the model is confident in identifying distractors of both high and low similarity. However, we can see that in the range of similarity scores where two classes meet the confidence drops on both classes with some examples. This is also the range where most of the examples lie. When examples are more dissimilar the model retains high confidence.

Distractors	Condition	T-test
Similarity	captions: similar vs dis-similar	<0.001
	images: similar vs dis-similar	<0.001
Modality	similar: captions vs images	<0.001
	dis-similar: captions vs images	0.8

Table 3: The p-values of a *Student t-test* on model performance scores on *descriptions-in-isolation* using different distractors.

Finally, to demonstrate any differences between distractors in terms of degree of similarity or modality we run a *Student t-test* on prediction scores for non-matching examples. The results of the tests are summarised in Table 3 and indicate a significant difference in model's performance on different distractor types in three out of four cases. The t-test found no significant difference between dissimilar captions vs images. In the remaining cases, distractors of different types have a different effect on the model's performance.

6.2 Experiment II: Local discourse and stories in sequence

Distractors	High Similarity	Low similarity
Textual	0.78	0.85
Visual	0.81	0.85

Table 4: The overall performance on the image-caption matching task with *stories-in-sequence* based on accuracy on accuracy on a balanced dataset. The results on random distractor descriptions are **0.82**.

We implement the same experimental setup for *stories-in-sequence* to test the model's sensitivity to local discourse structure on captions that were originally part of a narrative. As seen in Table 4, the results are worse than on *descriptions-in-isolation*. The model performs slightly better on dissimilar distractors than on similar distractors. Modality matters for similar distractors, images are more easily identifiable than captions.

In Figure 5 we take a closer look at the model's confidence on predicting matches or mismatches. Overall, the model is quite certain in its predictions. The majority of cases are identified with high confidence scores. The model is more uncertain in matching distractors than true examples. Note however, that the confidence on true examples is less distributed with random distractors compared to distractors created with our similarity scores

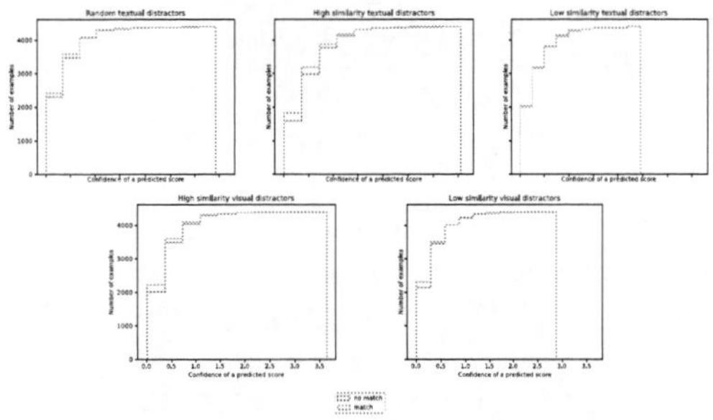

Figure 5: The confidence of the model in predicting a correct answer (match /no match) in an image-caption matching task for *stories-in-sequence*.

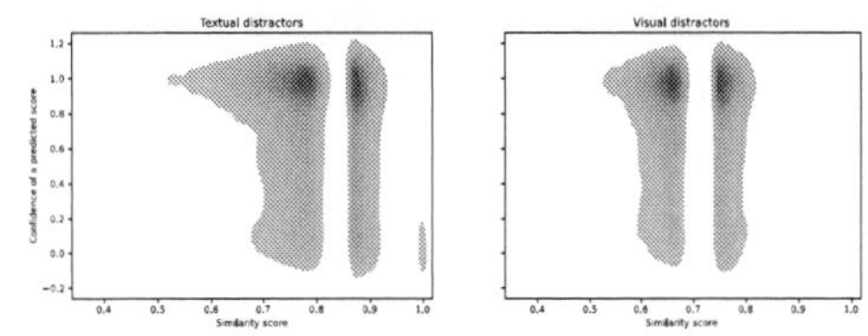

Figure 6: The relation between similarity scores and the model's confidence on correct answers for matching distractors for *stories-in-sequence*.

which indicates that the task we created is more difficult. Figure 6 shows the relation between similarity scores and the model confidence for matching distractors. The trends are similar to the ones reported for *descriptions-in-isolation*.

Table 5 shows a Student t-test of the model's performance identifying distractors of different kinds. The results are identical to the ones obtained for *descriptions-in-isolation* condition.

Distractors	Condition	T-test
Similarity	captions: similar vs dis-similar	<0.001
	images: similar vs dis-similar	<0.001
Modality	similar: captions vs images	<0.001
	dis-similar: captions vs images	0.08

Table 5: The p-values of a *Student t-test* on model performance scores on *stories-in-sequence* using different distractors.

6.3 Experiment III: narrative discourse and stories-in-sequence

The last task includes image-caption matching of sentences from the *stories-in-sequence* annotation layer where distractors are randomly sampled from the same story. The results can be seen in Table 6. Unlike in the previous experiments the model's performance is higher on textual distractors than on visual distractors. A possible reason might be that images within one story are more similar than cap-

Distractors	Random
Textual	0.63
Visual	0.6

Table 6: The overall performance on the image-caption matching task with *stories-in-sequence*. Distractors are randomly sampled from the same story.

tions but also our earlier observation that images are less informative for the model than texts. Another reason might be the way *stories-in-sequence* are collected. Some workers were not the ones who combined pictures in stories and were only asked to write a story about a pre-chosen sequence of images. Different crowd-workers would have different perspectives and understanding of sequences of images, resulting that in some cases more descriptions are focused on creating coherent storyline rather than referring to images.

In comparison to Experiment II where *stories-in-sequence* were used but were taken from different stories, the performance here drops by 0.2 which indicates that the model struggles identifying distractors from the same story. As the same entities appear across the sequence of a story the model struggles to capture causal relations that could identify items from different parts of a story. Moreover, as seen in Figure 7, the model finds it harder to identify distractors than true labels: more than 1,500 distractors out of 2,500 are identified as true labels. Furthermore, the model does not only predict wrong answers but it gives high confidence scores to false positives (low confidence in the distractor label means high confidence in the true label). Overall, we can conclude that the model is struggling in identifying distractors from the narrative discourse.

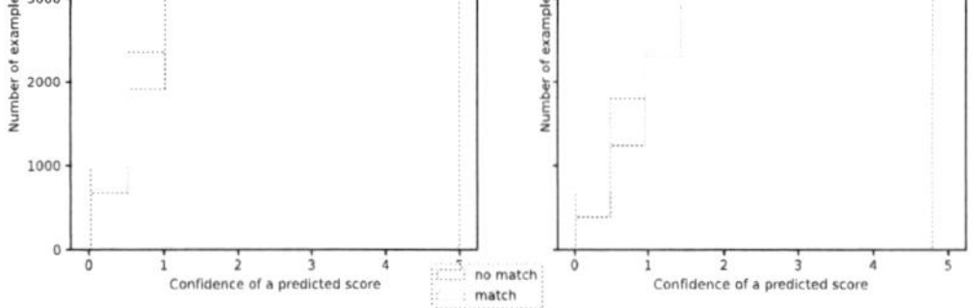

Figure 7: The confidence of the model in predicting a correct answer (match / no match) in an image-caption matching task for *stories-in-sequence*.

7 Discussion

7.1 The impact of non-matching discourse

Overall, for *local discourse* the evaluation results show that the model was not particularly challenged by distractors with high similarity, especially for *descriptions-in-isolation*. In other words, the model distinguishes different situations well regardless whether descriptions or images of the situations are close in similarity or not. However, for *stories-in-sequence*, the performance of the model on distractors of high similarity was slightly lower than those with distractors of low similarity. Table 5 confirms that this drop in performance is statistically significant. Here, the model can distinguish between two completely different situations but is less sensitive in identifying similar entities (whether textual or visual) in different situations.

Descriptions-in-isolation contain captions that are more grounded in images as they were not created as a part of narrative. For example, they refer to entities and their attributes and how they are related in images. On the other hand, *stories-in-sequence* are more abstract in the sense that they are more grounded in the narrative of the story. In such captions, annotators rely on visual attention of an interpreter to match the story with the images but such information which is part of human cognitive processing ability is not explicitly expressed in the data. Crowd-workers had different communication intents while writing these annotations. The model has thus less information to ground descriptions in images.

The differences between *descriptions-in-isolation* and *stories-in-sequence* on the local discourse task could be also due to the fact that the model was pre-trained on captions that were also produced in isolation although they were from a different dataset (Conceptual Captions rather than VIST).

7.2 The role of modalities

It has been shown that models rely more on the textual modality in its predictions than on the visual modality (Frank et al., 2021). Our results from Experiments I and II reveal the same tendency. The results on experiments where image distractors were tested are better on *descriptions-in-isolation* and *stories-in-sequence*. It is more difficult for the model to identify a mismatch between an image and a distractor caption than a mismatch between a caption and a distractor image. The distribution of similarity scores indicates that images are less diverse than captions. A correct caption will be more informative for the model to find sufficient information in the image to make a decision.

In Experiment III, however, the model performs better on textual distractors meaning that having a correct image is more informative to identify a mismatch of textual distractors. This means that here captions are more similar to each other which could be explained by the fact that they create a story narrative whereas images are different snapshots of the situations involved.

7.3 Are transformers sensitive to discourse?

The model shows better performance on captions taken from different stories than on ones taken from the same story which means that the model is less sensitive to distinctions made within a narrative. The model is good at capturing even fine-grained differences but the performance degrades when it is presented with more abstract captions that are grounded more in the narrative than in an image. It could be related to different types of image-text coherence (Alikhani et al., 2023) since in *stories-in-sequence* information that overlaps with visual context could be omitted. It makes the image-caption matching task more complicated for the model and reflects that the model struggles with complex coherence relations. However, taking into account the biases of the dataset, such as some sequences could have stronger visual discourse and otherwise, it is a complicated issue whether the model is not sensitive to visual, textual, or situation-level discourse.

However, the performance of the model on distractors sampled from the same story is still better than a random baseline which for a balanced binary classification task is 0.5. Looking at the example in Figure 1 we see that the story mentions the same objects, but the sentences in the story are not interchangeable so there is some discourse information there that the model can utilise. In other words, the model can differentiate different situations but it struggles with identifying fine-grained pragmatic distinctions through form alone when all items come from the same story.

8 Conclusion

In this work we examined whether a language-and-vision model is sensitive to discourse structure at different levels of granularity of distractors, random, similar and dissimilar to control for the difficulty of the task. We focused on local and narrative discourse in the task of image-caption matching which is one of the pre-training objectives of multimodal models. We ran three experiments on ViLBERT under different conditions using data from the Visual Storytelling dataset where images are collected into stories. The dataset has several layers of annotation including captions of images in isolation and captions of images in stories in sequence.

In Experiment I we test ViLBERT's image-caption matching performance on the captions of images in isolation under five different conditions with different distractors, random, similar and dissimilar. We observe that the model performs better than 90% in all cases.

In Experiment II we take the *stories-in-sequence* annotation level and test them for local discourse matching against distractors from different stories. The results drop by 0.1 in comparison with the previous experiment which shows that captions that are part of a narrative are harder to distinguish from captions from different narratives. However, the model still achieves high performance and has therefore learnt to distinguish the differences in local discourse structure by identifying from other local discourses.

In Experiment III we focus on *stories-in-sequence* discourses where distracting items are sampled from the same story. The model's performance drops to 0.6. The model assigns false positives to the matching class with high confidence and therefore finds it challenging to distinguish items from the same story discourse that refer to the same entities but over a sequence of relations. The model is more successful in distinguishing between different entities and situations as shown by Experiment I and II.

The effect of dis/similarity of distractors becomes more pronounced when the nature of discourse becomes more challenging. Overall, such behaviour of the model is expected since it has never been trained on captions that come from stories in sequence. While this might be achieved through fine-tuning which we will attempt in our future work it also raises a more profound question about the nature of semantic knowledge captured in large models. On the one hand, the models are exposed to contextual discourse knowledge while they are trained since *all* descriptions are made within some context. On the other hand, their performance quickly degrades when the nature of the context changes. Understanding the discourse context is therefore important both at the level of data creation and at the level of utilisation of pre-trained models. It is important to note that our results should be considered relative to the dataset and the model we investigated and variations are expected based on the contexts in which the model was trained and the contexts it is applied to. Assessing the similarities between discourses (even by expert linguists) may not be straightforward as parameters may not be directly observable or known.

In our future work, we are planning to expand our methods to other language-and-vision models, such as single-stream models, and other narrative discourse datasets, such as RecipeQA, which is an example of naturally created narrative in comparison with crowd-sourced VIST dataset.

Acknowledgments

Ilinykh and Dobnik were supported by a grant from the Swedish Research Council (VR project 2014-39) for the establishment of the Centre for Linguistic Theory and Studies in Probability (CLASP) at the University of Gothenburg. All authors would like to thank reviewers for their comments.

References

Aishwarya Agrawal, Dhruv Batra, Devi Parikh, and Aniruddha Kembhavi. 2018. Don't just assume; look and answer: Overcoming priors for visual question answering. In *2018 IEEE Conference on Computer Vision and Pattern Recognition, CVPR 2018, Salt Lake City, UT, USA, June 18-22, 2018*, pages 4971–4980. Computer Vision Foundation / IEEE Computer Society.

Malihe Alikhani, Baber Khalid, and Matthew Stone. 2023. Image–text coherence and its implications for multimodal ai. *Frontiers in Artificial Intelligence*, 6.

Malihe Alikhani, Piyush Sharma, Shengjie Li, Radu Soricut, and Matthew Stone. 2020. Clue: Cross-modal coherence modeling for caption generation. *arXiv preprint arXiv:2005.00908*.

Malihe Alikhani and Matthew Stone. 2019. "caption" as a coherence relation: Evidence and implications. In *Proceedings of the Second Workshop on Shortcomings in Vision and Language*, pages 58–67, Minneapolis, Minnesota. Association for Computational Linguistics.

Peter Anderson, Xiaodong He, Chris Buehler, Damien Teney, Mark Johnson, Stephen Gould, and Lei Zhang. 2018. Bottom-up and top-down attention for image captioning and visual question answering. In *CVPR*.

Vladimir Araujo, Andrés Villa, Marcelo Mendoza, Marie-Francine Moens, and Alvaro Soto. 2021. Augmenting BERT-style models with predictive coding to improve discourse-level representations. *arXiv preprint arXiv:2109.04602*.

Yonatan Belinkov. 2022. Probing classifiers: Promises, shortcomings, and advances. *Computational Linguistics*, 48(1):207–219.

Raffaella Bernardi and Sandro Pezzelle. 2021. Linguistic issues behind visual question answering. *Language and Linguistics Compass*, 15(6):elnc3–12417.

Emanuele Bugliarello, Ryan Cotterell, Naoaki Okazaki, and Desmond Elliott. 2021. Multimodal pretraining unmasked: A meta-analysis and a unified framework of vision-and-language BERTs. *Transactions of the Association for Computational Linguistics*, 9:978–994.

Mingda Chen, Zewei Chu, and Kevin Gimpel. 2019. Evaluation benchmarks and learning criteria for discourse-aware sentence representations. *arXiv preprint arXiv:1909.00142*.

Alexis Conneau, German Kruszewski, Guillaume Lample, Loïc Barrault, and Marco Baroni. 2018. What you can cram into a single vector: Probing sentence embeddings for linguistic properties. *arXiv preprint arXiv:1805.01070*.

Jacob Devlin, Ming-Wei Chang, Kenton Lee, and Kristina Toutanova. 2018. BERT: Pre-training of deep bidirectional transformers for language understanding. *arXiv preprint arXiv:1810.04805*.

Yanai Elazar, Shauli Ravfogel, Alon Jacovi, and Yoav Goldberg. 2021. Amnesic probing: Behavioral explanation with amnesic counterfactuals. *Transactions of the Association for Computational Linguistics*, 9:160–175.

Allyson Ettinger. 2020. What BERT is not: Lessons from a new suite of psycholinguistic diagnostics for language models. *Transactions of the Association for Computational Linguistics*, 8:34–48.

Stella Frank, Emanuele Bugliarello, and Desmond Elliott. 2021. Vision-and-language or vision-for-language? on cross-modal influence in multimodal transformers. *arXiv preprint arXiv:2109.04448*.

Kaiming He, Xiangyu Zhang, Shaoqing Ren, and Jian Sun. 2016. Deep residual learning for image recognition. In *Proceedings of the IEEE conference on computer vision and pattern recognition*, pages 770–778.

Xudong Hong, Asad Sayeed, Khushboo Mehra, Vera Demberg, and Bernt Schiele. 2023a. Visual Writing Prompts: Character-Grounded Story Generation with Curated Image Sequences. *Transactions of the Association for Computational Linguistics*, 11:565–581.

Xudong Hong, Asad Sayeed, Khushboo Mehra, Vera Demberg, and Bernt Schiele. 2023b. Visual writing prompts: Character-grounded story generation with curated image sequences. *Transactions of the Association for Computational Linguistics*, 11:565–581.

Xudong Hong, Rakshith Shetty, Asad Sayeed, Khushboo Mehra, Vera Demberg, and Bernt Schiele. 2020. Diverse and relevant visual storytelling with scene graph embeddings. In *Proceedings of the 24th Conference on Computational Natural Language Learning (CoNLL 2020)*, pages 420–430, Online. ACL.

Ting-Hao Huang, Francis Ferraro, Nasrin Mostafazadeh, Ishan Misra, Aishwarya Agrawal, Jacob Devlin, Ross Girshick, Xiaodong He, Pushmeet Kohli, Dhruv Batra, et al. 2016. Visual storytelling. In *Proceedings of the 2016 conference of the North American chapter of the association for computational linguistics: Human language technologies*, pages 1233–1239.

Nikolai Ilinykh and Simon Dobnik. 2022a. Attention as grounding: Exploring textual and cross-modal attention on entities and relations in language-and-vision transformer. In *Findings of the Association for Computational Linguistics: ACL 2022*, pages 4062–4073.

Nikolai Ilinykh and Simon Dobnik. 2022b. Do Decoding Algorithms Capture Discourse Structure in Multi-Modal Tasks? A Case Study of Image Paragraph Generation. In *Proceedings of the 2nd Workshop on Natural Language Generation, Evaluation, and Metrics (GEM)*, pages 480–493, Abu Dhabi, United Arab Emirates (Hybrid). Association for Computational Linguistics.

Nikolai Ilinykh, Yasmeen Emampoor, and Simon Dobnik. 2022. Look and answer the question: On the role of vision in embodied question answering. In *Proceedings of the 15th International Conference on Natural Language Generation*, pages 236–245.

Karim Lasri, Tiago Pimentel, Alessandro Lenci, Thierry Poibeau, and Ryan Cotterell. 2022. Probing for the usage of grammatical number. *arXiv preprint arXiv:2204.08831*.

Percy Liang, Rishi Bommasani, Tony Lee, Dimitris Tsipras, Dilara Soylu, Michihiro Yasunaga, Yian Zhang, Deepak Narayanan, Yuhuai Wu, Ananya Kumar, et al. 2022. Holistic evaluation of language models. *arXiv preprint arXiv:2211.09110*.

Tsung-Yi Lin, Michael Maire, Serge Belongie, James Hays, Pietro Perona, Deva Ramanan, Piotr Dollár, and C Lawrence Zitnick. 2014. Microsoft COCO: Common objects in context. In *Computer Vision–ECCV 2014: 13th European Conference, Zurich, Switzerland, September 6-12, 2014, Proceedings, Part V 13*, pages 740–755. Springer.

Nelson F Liu, Matt Gardner, Yonatan Belinkov, Matthew E Peters, and Noah A Smith. 2019. Linguistic knowledge and transferability of contextual representations. *arXiv preprint arXiv:1903.08855*.

Jiasen Lu, Dhruv Batra, Devi Parikh, and Stefan Lee. 2019. ViLBERT: Pretraining task-agnostic visiolinguistic representations for vision-and-language tasks. *Advances in neural information processing systems*, 32.

Rowan Hall Maudslay and Ryan Cotterell. 2021. Do syntactic probes probe syntax? experiments with jabberwocky probing. *arXiv preprint arXiv:2106.02559*.

Allen Nie, Erin Bennett, and Noah Goodman. 2019. DisSent: Learning sentence representations from explicit discourse relations. In *Proceedings of the 57th Annual Meeting of the Association for Computational Linguistics*, pages 4497–4510.

Letitia Parcalabescu, Michele Cafagna, Lilitta Muradjan, Anette Frank, Iacer Calixto, and Albert Gatt. 2021. Valse: A task-independent benchmark for vision and language models centered on linguistic phenomena. *arXiv preprint arXiv:2112.07566*.

Rashmi Prasad, Nikhil Dinesh, Alan Lee, Eleni Miltsakaki, Livio Robaldo, Aravind K Joshi, and Bonnie L Webber. 2008. The Penn Discourse TreeBank 2.0. In *LREC*.

Laura Ruis, Akbir Khan, Stella Biderman, Sara Hooker, Tim Rocktäschel, and Edward Grefenstette. 2022. Large language models are not zero-shot communicators. *arXiv*, arXiv:2210.14986 [cs.CL]:1–45.

Naomi Saphra. 2021. *Training dynamics of neural language models*. Doctoral thesis, School of Informatics, University of Edinburgh, Edinburg, UK.

Karolina Stańczak, Edoardo Ponti, Lucas Torroba Hennigen, Ryan Cotterell, and Isabelle Augenstein. 2022. Same neurons, different languages: Probing morphosyntax in multilingual pre-trained models. *arXiv preprint arXiv:2205.02023*.

Ece Takmaz, Mario Giulianelli, Sandro Pezzelle, Arabella Sinclair, and Raquel Fernández. 2020. Refer, reuse, reduce: Generating subsequent references in visual and conversational contexts. *arXiv preprint arXiv:2011.04554*.

Ekaterina Taktasheva, Vladislav Mikhailov, and Ekaterina Artemova. 2021. Shaking syntactic trees on the sesame street: Multilingual probing with controllable perturbations. *arXiv preprint arXiv:2109.14017*.

Hao Tan and Mohit Bansal. 2019. LXMERT: Learning cross-modality encoder representations from transformers. In *Proceedings of the 2019 Conference on Empirical Methods in Natural Language Processing and the 9th International Joint Conference on Natural Language Processing (EMNLP-IJCNLP)*, pages 5100–5111, Hong Kong, China. Association for Computational Linguistics.

Jesse Thomason, Daniel Gordon, and Yonatan Bisk. 2019. Shifting the baseline: Single modality performance on visual navigation & QA. In *Proceedings of the 2019 Conference of the North American Chapter of the Association for Computational Linguistics: Human Language Technologies, Volume 1 (Long and Short Papers)*, pages 1977–1983, Minneapolis, Minnesota. Association for Computational Linguistics.

Alex Warstadt, Alicia Parrish, Haokun Liu, Anhad Mohananey, Wei Peng, Sheng-Fu Wang, and Samuel R Bowman. 2020. BLiMP: The benchmark of linguistic minimal pairs for english. *Transactions of the Association for Computational Linguistics*, 8:377–392.

Semih Yagcioglu, Aykut Erdem, Erkut Erdem, and Nazli Ikizler-Cinbis. 2018. Recipeqa: A challenge dataset for multimodal comprehension of cooking recipes. *arXiv preprint arXiv:1809.00812*.

A Study of similarity scores in Conceptual Captions and Visual Storytelling Datasets

We use similarity scores for constructing our tasks for the model. However, the dataset can be biased and this will affect the similarity scores needed for construction of tasks for the first two experiments. As seen in Figure 8, the similarity scores between images or texts vary between 0.6 and 0.9. Since these scores are not interpretable, i.e. we cannot compare their relative differences across modalities, we compare their distribution with the distribution in the Conceptual Captions dataset that language-and-vision models are trained on. Figure 8 shows that the distribution of similarities of captions is similar in the two datasets, although image similarities have a slightly narrower distribution in the VIST dataset. In other words, they are less diverse. This may lead to the model struggling to distinguish similar images, as they are more similar than in the pre-training data.

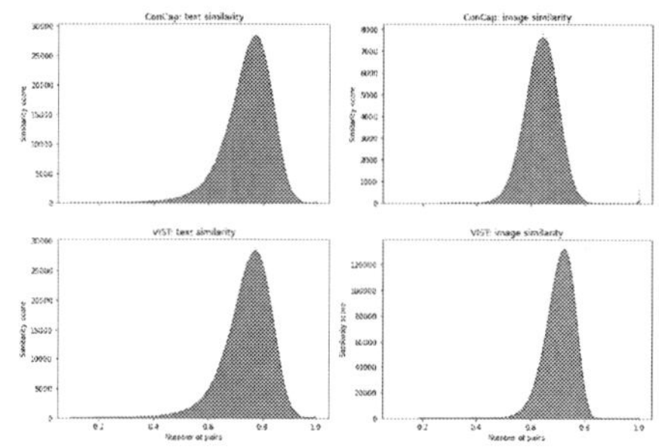

Figure 8: The distribution of similarity scores for captions and images for the Conceptual Captions (ConCap) and the Visual Storytelling dataset (VIST).

Using Large Language Models for Zero-Shot Natural Language Generation from Knowledge Graphs

Agnes Axelsson and **Gabriel Skantze**
Division of Speech, Music and Hearing (TMH) / Lindstedtsvägen 24
KTH Royal Institute of Technology / Stockholm, Sweden
agnaxe@kth.se and skantze@kth.se

Abstract

In any system that uses structured knowledge graph (KG) data as its underlying knowledge representation, KG-to-text generation is a useful tool for turning parts of the graph data into text that can be understood by humans. Recent work has shown that models that make use of pretraining on large amounts of text data can perform well on the KG-to-text task, even with relatively little training data on the specific graph-to-text task. In this paper, we build on this concept by using large language models to perform zero-shot generation based on nothing but the model's understanding of the triple structure from what it can read. We show that ChatGPT achieves near state-of-the-art performance on some measures of the WebNLG 2020 challenge, but falls behind on others. Additionally, we compare factual, counter-factual and fictional statements, and show that there is a significant connection between what the LLM already knows about the data it is parsing and the quality of the output text.

1 Introduction

For any system that presents verbal information to users, whether that information is in the form of text or audio, it can be useful to generate the system's speech or text from a consistent underlying knowledge representation based on structured data. A commonly used data representation is **knowledge graphs** (KGs), where information is stored as *properties* or *relations* tying *entities* together (Hogan et al., 2021). The combination of a property, its source and its target is referred to as a **triple** (Lassila and Swick, 1999; Hogan et al., 2021). KGs as an underlying structured data representation have been used to allow systems to tell narrative information (Colas et al., 2022), to retrieve information in chatbots (Zhou et al., 2020) or recommender systems (Shao et al., 2021), and to reason about the grounding status of the information in terms of what the user currently knows (Axelsson and Skantze, 2020).

Traditionally, template-based approaches for generating text from knowledge graphs have been sufficient for confined dialogue domains (Konstas and Lapata, 2013; Duma and Klein, 2013; Perera and Nand, 2015). An alternative is to train a data-driven end-to-end generation model, but a limiting factor is the relative lack of human-labelled data for the task. The WebNLG datasets produced for the challenges in 2017 (Gardent et al., 2017a) and 2020 (Castro Ferreira et al., 2020) are relatively small, and although recent progress has been made on producing much larger datasets (Colas et al., 2022), methods for natural language generation from knowledge graphs have generally had to work around the absence of large datasets.

Recently, approaches that use pretraining on large amounts of non-KG-related text data, which is then finetuned on the KG-to-text task, have shown promising results (Kale and Rastogi, 2021; Colas et al., 2022; Li et al., 2021a; Yang et al., 2020; Ke et al., 2021). Such models can learn and extrapolate from patterns in the text data to the KG data that the model has never seen before. The logical endpoint of such an approach is to simply rely on the pretraining, and not use any finetuning at all. In this paper, we perform a partial evaluation of this approach by using large language models (LLMs) to generate text from knowledge graph data, zero-shot.

A known problem with natural language generation through language models is that the output – the text generated by the method – is not guaranteed to match the input – the specification for what should be generated (Ji et al., 2023). When such models over-generate, it is often referred to as **hallucinations** (Alkaissi and McFarlane, 2023; Ji et al., 2023). Both under-generation and hallucinatory over-generation can result in systems producing unwanted content, potentially disastrously so.

Proceedings of the Workshop on Multimodal, Multilingual Natural Language Generation and Multilingual WebNLG Challenge (MM-NLG 2023), pages 39–54
September 12, 2023 ©2023 Association for Computational Linguistics

Since LLMs rely on pretraining, their language generation competence will to some extent stem from the facts expressed in the pretraining data. Thus, the expression of the facts expressed in the KG triples could to some extent be helped by this inherent knowledge. While this could be advantageous when generating text from factual triples, a potential side-effect could be increased hallucinations, or that it could be harder for the LLM to generate from triples that express counter-factual or fictional knowledge. Thus, it is important to also gain an understanding of the ability of LLMs to perform the KG-to-text task, and not only evaluate their performance on factual triples.

In this paper, we present an evaluation of zero-shot KG-to-text natural language generation using LLMs. We address the following questions:

1. How do LLMs perform on KG-to-text tasks such as the WebNLG 2020 challenge (Castro Ferreira et al., 2020)?
2. How does the factualness of the KG triples (being factual, counter-factual, or fictional) affect the capability of the LLM to express arbitrary knowledge graph information, in terms of:
   (a) Grammar and coherence?
   (b) Coverage of the triples?
   (c) Hallucinations (overgeneration)?

In this paper, we will be using OpenAI's ChatGPT LLM (gpt-3.5-turbo). It should be noted that since the data used for training ChatGPT has not been disclosed, we cannot guarantee that it has not seen the WebNLG data used in Section 3. At the time when this study was conducted, we were not aware of any open-source LLMs with comparable performance to closed-source LLMs on these types of NLG tasks. However, our follow-up analysis in Section 4 is based on newly collected data for which KG-to-text references should not have existed in any LLM's training set.

2 Background

2.1 Knowledge graphs

The concept of representing human knowledge as a graph in a computer dates at least as far back as work by Schneider (1973), but did not grow into their modern relevance until work by Google and competitors in the early 2010s (Hogan et al., 2021). Ehrlinger and Wöß (2016) consider the difference between older and more recent use of KGs to lie primarily in how the data is collected – at a large scale, using automated tools, rather than handcrafted, as in earlier work. WikiData (Vrandečić and Krötzsch, 2014), a knowledge graph run by the WikiMedia foundation and editable by the public, is what Hogan et al. (2021) call a *property graph*, where each entity and edge can be annotated with an arbitrary set of key-value pairs.

Common to all types of knowledge graphs described by Hogan et al. (2021) is that entities, the nodes of the graph, are connected by relations. In Wikidata, the relations are called **properties** (Vrandečić and Krötzsch, 2014) (unrelated to *property graphs* as defined by Hogan et al. (2021)), terminology which we will use throughout this paper. A property, its source and its target combined are a **triple** (Lassila and Swick, 1999; Ding et al., 2005).

2.2 KG-to-text synthesis

The process of converting data represented as knowledge graphs into text is sometimes referred to as **graph to text** (Schmitt et al., 2020; Song et al., 2021), or **KG to text** (Schmitt et al., 2021; Wang et al., 2019). The term **Data-to-Text** typically refers to a more general group of tasks of which KG-to-text is part (Nan et al., 2021; Yin and Wan, 2022; Ji et al., 2023). Competitions like the WebNLG 2020 challenge contained tracks for both KG-to-text and text-to-KG (Castro Ferreira et al., 2020), but this paper only considers the KG-to-text task.

On small, restricted domains with structured data, examples of data-to-text generation with the use of prewritten templates can be found from the 1980s in the work by Kukich (1983) (stock market reports), and in the work of Goldberg et al. (1994) (weather forecasts). An early modern example of database-to-text synthesis is the work by Konstas and Lapata (2013), who used statistical rules to turn database entries into text through the use of rhetorical structure theory trees, which the system could generate from data, effectively generating its own templates. Patterns for converting individual knowledge graph triples into verb phrase templates are sometimes referred to as **lexicalisation** (Perera and Nand, 2015; Gardent et al., 2017a).

A problem with template-based approaches like the ones by Kukich (1983); Goldberg et al. (1994); Konstas and Lapata (2013) is that the templates may not be applicable outside of a specific domain of synthesised text. Duma and Klein (2013) and

Perera and Nand (2015) developed systems for generating lexicalisation templates from text data, but Duma and Klein (2013) found that their approach performed significantly worse than human-written reference text, and Perera and Nand (2015) found that their approach had varying performance depending on the domain of the text.

KG-to-text includes microplanning Levelt (1989), and surface realisation, referring expression generation and content selection must all be done simultaneously to produce a legible result (Gardent et al., 2017a,b). The 2017 WebNLG challenge was set up to evaluate KG-to-text models on English triple-to-text data. A novel dataset was collected specifically for the challenge. The top performing models were a bidirectional LSTM-based template extraction model and a rule-based transducer model (Gardent et al., 2017b).

The WebNLG 2020 challenge added Russian data to the KG-to-text task, and additionally had more triple data as a whole. On the English KG-to-text task (Castro Ferreira et al., 2020), the top-performing competitor was Amazon AI Shanghai's $\mathcal{P}^2$ model, which used an intermediate representation to first break down the requested triples into a plan, which a second model based on the T5 pretrained language model by Raffel et al. (2020) then turned into more coherent text (Guo et al., 2020). In second place, Ohio State University's OSU Lab presented a model that was pretrained on the T5 transformer model for English (Kale and Rastogi, 2021) to compensate for the relatively small amount of triple data to train on in the WebNLG dataset (Li et al., 2020).

Schmitt et al. (2020) proposed a parallel graph-to-text and text-to-graph model. While no gold standard human-written data existed as a baseline with which to compare the output of the graph-to-text model, the authors found that unsupervised training performed "nearly on par" with supervised training on BLEU, METEOR and CHRF++ measures compared to the text output of a baseline. The authors also found the text output by their own model was more readable than the baseline (Schmitt et al., 2020), but no structured evaluation was done on this factor

As a follow-up, Schmitt et al. (2021) proposed a Transformer-based architecture for graph-to-text generation where each relation in the graph is encoded in context with the other relations and entities in the graph. The resulting model performed favourably on BLEU, METEOR and CHRF++ measures compared to previous work on the WebNLG dataset (Schmitt et al., 2021; Gardent et al., 2017a; Castro Ferreira et al., 2020).

Koncel-Kedziorski et al. (2022) applied Transformer models to the abstracts of scientific articles. Four models that got differing amounts of information about the contents of the abstract of the article were prompted to write an abstract. The GraphWriter model that was fed with both the title of the article and a knowledge graph-based representation of the contents of the abstract was rated more highly by human annotators than other models which got more limited information, although the gold standard human-written abstract was considered the best in 64% of the cases (Koncel-Kedziorski et al., 2022).

Recently, Colas et al. (2022) presented the Event-Narrative dataset, which contains excerpts from EventKG matched with text from Wikipedia describing the event narrated by the knowledge graph data. While the authors could not manually validate their full dataset, which contains over 650 000 knowledge graph triples, a smaller annotation of 500 randomly sampled sets of triples with their corresponding Wikipedia text suggested that around 96% of both entities and relations are present in the text, with errors mostly appearing where Wikipedia and the underlying knowledge graph disagree about the nature of an event (Colas et al., 2022). The authors also provided benchmarks for models trained on the dataset, with the pretrained BART (Lewis et al., 2020) model performing the best on BLEU, ChrF++ and BERT measures, while GraphWriter (Koncel-Kedziorski et al., 2022) performed the best on CIDEr, METEOR and ROUGE.

In Axelsson and Skantze (2023), we proposed an approach where knowledge graph triples in a text form were fed to GPT-3, synthesised into sentences one-by-one using a few-shot approach, and then merged into one or more sentences of fluent text with a secondary prompt that summarises the sentences generated by the first step. While the approach worked for the presenting robot we used in that project, we did not evaluate specifically the graph-to-text synthesis, and this paper follows up on that aspect.

Recent work by Yuan and Färber (2023) applied ChatGPT to the WebNLG 2017 challenge, similar to our approach in Section 3. The authors additionally use the AGENDA dataset from Koncel-

Kedziorski et al. (2019). Yuan and Färber use a linearisation approach proposed by Ribeiro et al. (2019) to create a consistent representation of the graph data in text form to pass to the LLM as a prompt. The results are compared to the best-performing models from WebNLG 2017 (Gardent et al., 2017b), but both ChatGPT and GPT-3 perform relatively poorly on most measures. For ChatGPT, this appears to partially be because the LLM generates large amounts of hallucinated text beyond what it is prompted to synthesise.

2.3 NLG evaluation metrics

Numerous metrics have been proposed for evaluating KG-to-text output. *Bleu*, short for *bilingual evaluation understudy*, is a text similarity measure that combines n-gram precision score and a penalty for overly short candidates (Papineni et al., 2002). In WebNLG 2020, *Bleu NLTK* refers to Bleu extended with a specific smoothing algorithm referred to by the authors as *smoothing 3* (Chen and Cherry, 2014; Castro Ferreira et al., 2020). METEOR is a harmonic mean of precision and recall on stemmed words between the candidate and reference, with slight priority on recall, which also rewards candidates for matching large spans of the candidates word-by-word (Banerjee and Lavie, 2005). TER, short for *Translation Edit Rate*, counts the number of word shifts, insertions, substitutions and removals that must be performed to transform the candidate into a reference (Olive, 2005; Snover et al., 2006). CHRF is a weighted average of character 6-gram precision and recall between a reference and a candidate (Popović, 2015); CHRF++ is an extension to that measure which also considers word unigrams and bigrams (Popović, 2017).

BERTScore, henceforth simply BERT, uses contextual word embeddings to calculate the similarity between the meaning expressed by a candidate sentence and a reference, not necessarily requiring them to use the same words (Zhang et al., 2020). BLEURT is a BERT-based similarity metric that attempts to predict how a human annotator would rate the candidate compared to the reference, using the vector-based meaning encoding returned by BERT (Devlin et al., 2019; Sellam et al., 2020).

3 Applying LLMs to the WebNLG 2020 challenge

In the WebNLG 2020 Challenge, participants trained models to learn the transformation of sets of KG triples to natural language text. Graph-to-text data was provided for English and Russian (Castro Ferreira et al., 2020). The English-ALL test set contains 1779 sets of between 1 and 7 triples, each paired with up to five examples of human-written reference text that expresses those triples. The training set is not relevant to this paper, as zero-shot KG-to-text by definition does not perform training on the specific task. Models trained on the training set and evaluated on the test set (for which only the triples and no reference text were public until the end of the challenge) were ranked by METEOR score, with Bleu, Bleu-NLTK, TER, ChrF++, BERT and BLEURT scores also available for reference. The challenge organisers provided official evaluation scripts for evaluating hypotheses on the test set[1]. While recalculating the numbers for the other participants in Table 1, the BLEURT numbers we got were notably lower than those seen in Castro Ferreira et al. (2020) for all systems, but the internal order was the same.

The full Russian test set consisted of 1102 sets of between 1 and 7 triples, each paired with up to 7 references. While the reference text was written in Russian, the triple data was written in English, including both the labels of relations and the names of entities. Participants were ranked by the same automated metrics as for English, detailed above, except that the BLEURT measure was omitted (Castro Ferreira et al., 2020).

3.1 WebNLG 2020 LLM prompt

We chose OpenAI's *gpt-3.5-turbo* (ChatGPT) LLM for use in our KG-to-text process. The WebNLG 2020 dataset comes with preformatted triples in text form that we could pass relatively unchanged to our prompt (Castro Ferreira et al., 2020). We generated text for this dataset by appending the triples, newline-separated, to a prompt that told the LLM to briefly express only what it was given.

A preprocessing step was also included where the labels of entities in the prompt were filtered to remove underscore characters and replace them with spaces – if this was not done, ChatGPT tended to reproduce the underscores in its output. For Russian data, the prompt was modified to state that the output was to be given in Russian. Our full prompts are listed in Appendix B.

Team	BLEU	BLEU NLTK	METEOR	CHRF++	TER	BERT Prec.	BERT Recall	BERT F1	BLEURT
Amazon AI (Shanghai)	**0.539**	**0.535**	**0.417**	**0.690**	**0.406**	**0.960**	**0.957**	**0.958**	**0.47**
OSU Neural NLG	0.535	0.532	0.414	0.688	0.416	0.958	0.955	0.956	0.45
FBConvAI	0.526	0.523	0.413	0.686	0.423	0.957	0.955	0.956	0.46
bt5	0.517	0.517	0.411	0.679	0.435	0.955	0.954	0.954	0.43
ChatGPT	0.424	0.417	0.409	0.671	0.533	0.948	0.955	0.951	0.42
NUIG-DSI	0.517	0.514	0.403	0.669	0.417	0.959	0.954	0.956	0.45
cuni-ufal	0.503	0.500	0.398	0.666	0.435	0.954	0.950	0.951	0.39
DANGNT-SGU	0.407	0.405	0.393	0.646	0.511	0.940	0.946	0.943	0.27
CycleGT	0.445	0.432	0.387	0.637	0.479	0.949	0.949	0.948	0.40
RALI - Université de Montréal	0.402	0.393	0.386	0.634	0.504	0.944	0.944	0.944	0.28
TGen	0.509	0.482	0.384	0.636	0.454	0.952	0.947	0.949	0.36
Baseline-FORGE2020	0.405	0.396	0.373	0.621	0.517	0.946	0.941	0.943	0.26
Huawei Noah's Ark Lab	0.395	0.387	0.372	0.613	0.536	0.935	0.937	0.935	0.10
Baseline-FORGE2017	0.378	0.371	0.364	0.606	0.553	0.933	0.928	0.930	0.20
NILC	0.319	0.313	0.350	0.545	0.629	0.920	0.922	0.920	0.12
UPC-POE	0.391	0.379	0.337	0.579	0.564	0.933	0.927	0.929	0.08
ORANGE-NLG	0.382	0.376	0.335	0.571	0.577	0.920	0.920	0.920	-0.09

Table 1: Results when applying ChatGPT to the WebNLG 2020 English-ALL task. Note that ORANGE-NLG garnered slightly worse numbers in all metrics compared to Castro Ferreira et al. (2020) when we re-ran the evaluation scripts.

3.2 Results on the WebNLG 2020 dataset

The 1779 English and 1102 Russian prompts of the WebNLG 2020 test set, as described in Section 3, were expressed with *gpt-3.5-turbo* using the process described in Section 3.1. We present the results for English in Table 1, with every listed participant from Castro Ferreira et al. (2020) shown alongside ChatGPT. The table is ordered by METEOR as in the original challenge.

Beyond METEOR, ChatGPT performs less well on other measures, ranking slightly above the FORGE2020 baseline for BLEU and BLEU-NLTK, and below it for TER (note that higher TER values are worse). The relatively low BLEU and BLEU-NLTK scores and high TER – measures that reward exact word matches – but competitive METEOR and BLEURT scores, imply that ChatGPT consistently produces text that expresses roughly the same semantic content as the reference translations, using roughly the same stemmed words as the reference translations, but in orders and in forms (tenses, inflections) that are not expected from the reference translations.

ChatGPT's results for Russian were significantly worse than for English, obtaining a METEOR score of 0.403. This is below the FORGE2020 baseline which obtained a METEOR score of 0.467. The full results table for Russian is included in Appendix A.

[1]https://github.com/WebNLG/WebNLG-Text-to-triples/tree/master

Finally, it should be noted that we do not have access to the training data for ChatGPT, and we therefore cannot know whether the results of other models in the WebNLG 2020 challenge were part of the training. Thus, the results seen in Table 1 may be artificially inflated.

4 Evaluating the effects of KG factualness

As stated in the introduction, the LLM's pretraining on (mostly) factual data might influence its ability to generate text from the KG triples, if these are not also factual. To evaluate this effect, we chose to synthesise our own data through WikiData. This allowed us to retain metadata about the classes and types of entities in the graphs, limit and specify the types of properties that would be included in our triple set, and additionally guarantee that the LLM would not have seen the data during its training (which, as was noted above, cannot be guaranteed for the WebNLG 2020 test set).

We sampled the WikiData API for random small subgraphs of knowledge graph triples centered around an entity that represents a human. To further make sure that our generated text represented knowledge that was reasonably interesting to humans and representative of information that could appear in information text or a presentation, we manually created a list of 184 property identifiers that occured often in connection to humans[2]. Our prompts represented connected graphs; there was

[2]This list of properties is attached as a supplementary file.

always a path from any entity in our prompts to all other entities in the same prompt. We will call data sampled in this way **factual**, although it is possible that some triples are incorrect, either through vandalism or mistakes by the authors of the data.

4.1 Fictionalisation and counterfactualisation

For each *factual* graph sampled according to the method described in Section 4, we applied substitutions to the names of the entities in the graph to produce two new graphs with identical structure but different entities. By retaining the graph structure but changing the entities contained in the graph, we could create prompts that expressed knowledge that would contradict the information stored in the LLM's parameters, or create prompts that we could guarantee would not match factual information stored in the LLM's parameters.

To produce what we call a **fictional** graph, we separately asked GPT-3 to generate fictional examples of the WikiData types present in the graph[3]. To produce **counterfactual** graphs, entities were randomly replaced with a different example of the same WikiData class sampled from WikiData. To reduce the number of cases where humans were stated to have died before they were born, we also sorted dates so that the earliest date in the original graphs always corresponded to the earliest date in the substituted graphs.

A small example graph with all three sets of labels seen at the same time can be seen in Figure 1. The **factual** data is marked in bold on top in each entity, with **fictional** in the middle, marked in italics, and **counterfactual** on the bottom. Note that our date sorting approach did not affect events and entities *named* after a date, which allows the counterfactual graph in Figure 1 to state that someone who was born in 1975 also participated in a sporting event in 1970.

4.2 WikiData LLM prompt

To express our WikiData dataset, we used a two-step prompt structure rather than the one-step method shown in Section 3.1. This prompt was originally set up to be able to control the theme-rheme structure of the generated text – note that this is not relevant to the analysis presented here, and that we also do not evaluate potential performance differences between the two types of prompts.

For expressing knowledge graph data sampled from WikiData, we converted each edge in the graph into a string *Source / Property / Target*. *Source* and *Target* represented the WikiData labels of the entities or constants at both ends of the property. *Property* was the WikiData label of the property connecting the two entities. If the property was *Godparent*, *Mother*, *Father* or *Child*, we changed the label into *Has godparent*, *Has mother*, *Has father*, or *Has child*, respectively, as pilot testing found that both crowdworkers and ChatGPT often confused the intended direction of those properties.

Once all properties in the graph had been turned into a string according to the above process, we then passed the first triple to ChatGPT via a prompt that asked it to convert that triple into exactly one sentence; the remaining triples were then passed to the LLM in a second prompt using the context of the previous prompt and the model's previous response to ask it to insert the remaining triples into the text. The returned text from this second step was used as the KG-to-text output. An example prompt instantiated with graph data from Figure 1 is included in Appendix C.1.

4.3 Evaluation on sampled WikiData KG triples

We generated a total of 70 sets of prompts containing 7 triples, each representing a connected graph with seven edges (properties). The choice of seven triples matches the largest graphs in the WebNLG dataset. The three conditions (factual, fictional or counterfactual as described in Section 4) gave us a total of 210 graphs. Text was then generated for these graphs according to the process described in Section 4.2.

4.3.1 Results for grammar and coherence

Through Amazon's Mechanical Turk, we asked three annotators for each of our 210 graphs to evaluate the generated text for grammar and coherence (similarly to Li et al. (2021b)), using two sliders. The Grammar slider had one end stating "*The grammar in the text is extremely poor. It is not written in well-formed English.*" and the other stating "*The grammar in the text is perfect. It is written in well-formed English.*". The Coherence slider stated "*It is incoherent. The different parts of the text do not lead into each other.*" on one end and "*It is highly coherent. The different parts of the text flow well into each other.*" on the other. To submit their responses, participants had to indicate whether they

[3] See Appendix D for this prompt.

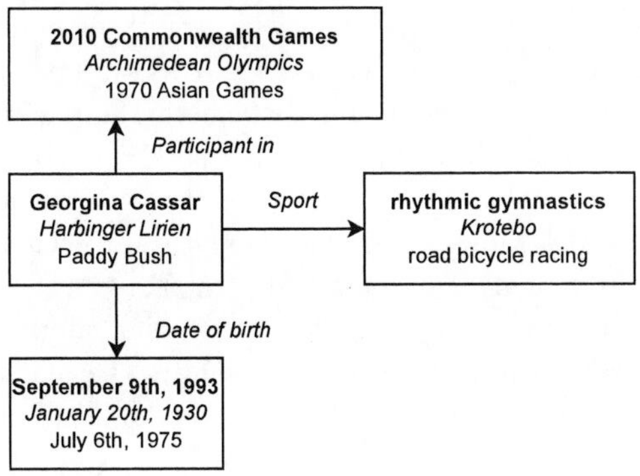

Figure 1: An example graph with three edges representing **factual** claims about its root entity. Fictional and counterfactual substitutions are listed as the second (in italics) and third (plain) row, respectively, of each entity (box).

understood that the task was not aboud the factual accuracy of the text but rather how well it matches the prompt; three annotators indicated they did not understand this and their evaluations were thus discarded. The average ratings by condition are listed in Table 2. The crowdworkers were paid $0.2 per prompt they rated. 34 unique crowdworkers participated, ranking an average of 18.5 prompts (SD = 20.0, min = 1, max = 83).

Condition	Avg. coherence	Avg. gramm.*
Factual	72.0%	71.6%
Fictional	67.6%	68.8%
Counterf.†	69.7%	71.1%

Table 2: Average ratings of coherence and grammaticity by condition. Unlike our CLMM analysis presented in Section 4.3.1, this table does not take the random factor of annotator identity into account. $\star$: *Grammaticity*. $\dagger$: *Counterfactual.*

To evaluate the given ratings of grammaticity and coherence, we set up two Cumulative Link Mixed Models (CLMMs) to treat the ratings as an ordinal measure (Agresti, 2012; Christensen, 2019). A recent study of how linear mixed models can be applied to scales of this type can be found by Howcroft and Rieser (2021). The factualness was treated as a fixed factor, with the identity of the annotator treated as a random factor. For grammaticity, the null model was not significantly different ($p = .0969$) from the model considering condition as a fixed factor, and as such we could not reject the null hypothesis that grammaticity was the same across all three conditions.

Condition	Present	Absent	Hallucinated
Factual	471	2	17
Counterf.†	470	8	12
Fictional	468	13	9

Table 3: The number of triples annotated as present, absent and hallucinated for the 490 (7 * 70) triples in each condition. $\dagger$: *Counterfactual.*

For coherence, the data type was a significant factor ($p = .0363$), leading us to reject the null hypothesis that the three conditions were equally coherent. A post-hoc estimated marginal means analysis confirmed that **counterfactual** graphs were rated as less coherent than **factual** graphs when treating the identity of the annotator as a random factor ($p < .0001$), but the comparisons between counterfactual and fictional ($p = .394$) and fictional and factual ($p = .197$) were not significant.

4.3.2 Results for triple coverage

For each of the seven triples in the prompt, annotators also had to check one of three exclusive options; *the text states this fact* (henceforth *present*), *the text does not say anything about this* (*absent*) or *the text states something else that actively goes against this fact* (*hallucinated*). *Absent* corresponds to *omission* in Yin and Wan (2022), with *hallucinated* corresponding to *inaccuracy intrinsic*, *inaccuracy extrinsic* and *positive-negative aspect* (Yin and Wan, 2022).

While the grammaticity and coherence evaluations are subjective and were used in Section 4.3.1, annotators showed poor agreement for the triple coverage task, achieving a Fleiss' Kappa (Fleiss and Cohen, 1973) of only $\kappa \approx 0.016$, at the low end of *slight agreement* on the scale by Landis and Koch (1977). To address this, since we believe that the judgement is objective for most cases, we manually annotated each triple as being present, absent or hallucinated, and discarded the crowdworkers' evaluations for the triple coverage task. The resulting classifications are listed in Table 3.

A χ^2 test confirmed that the distribution of present, absent and hallucinated triple by each condition seen in Table 3 was significantly different from the expected distribution if the condition had had no effect ($\chi^2(4, N = 1470) = 10.5, p = .0328$), leading us to reject that null hypothesis. To analyse the results, we performed repeated Bonferroni-corrected χ^2 tests on each pair of conditions and triple label, applying Yates's correction if any class had an expected occurrence of less than five.

Two post-hoc comparisons were statistically significant ($\alpha = 0.05/9 \approx 0.0056$); the comparison between **present and absent** triples between the **factual and fictional** condition ($\chi^2(1, N = 954) = 8.01, p = .00465$) as well as the comparison between **absent and hallucinated** triples, also between the factual and fictional condition ($\chi^2(1, N = 41) = 10.4, p = .00128$). Residual analysis showed that factual graphs had more present but fewer absent triples than fictional graphs, and that factual graphs had more hallucinated but fewer absent triples than fictional graphs.

4.3.3 Results for hallucinated inserted information

Each of the 210 expressed sets of 7 triples was also annotated for whether it contained any additional information beyond what was stated in the triples, corresponding to what Yin and Wan (2022) call *addition* or what Ji et al. (2023) call *extrinsic hallucinations*. While we had originally set out to also do this via Mechanical Turk, we chose to perform the annotation ourselves after seeing low agreement on pilot tests. We did not choose to annotate cases where the LLM picked an unexpected tense (present tense for something that happened in the past, or vice versa), as we had not specified in the prompt what today's date was. Additionally, cases where the LLM picked a specific gendered pronoun for a fictional character with an ambiguous name were not annotated as hallucinations.

Out of the 70 graphs for each condition, 12 were found to have hallucinated extra information for the **factual** condition, 10 for the **counterfactual** condition and 9 for the **fictional** condition. A χ^2 goodness-of-fit test did not allow us to reject the null hypothesis that the rate of *inserted* hallucinations across all three conditions was the same ($\chi^2(2, N = 31) = 0.452, p = .798$). A list of every hallucination of this type is attached in Appendix E. Recurring issues for all three conditions are unfounded statements that the subject was "survived by" a spouse, child or parent.

5 Discussion

Although LLMs appear to be able to do a relatively good job at generating text expressing arbitrary KG data, the relatively high rate of inserted hallucinated information (around 10-15% in Section 4.3.3) means system designers must be careful before deploying any system using a LLM KG-to-text as a synthesis engine or microplanner. The rate of *addition* previously seen in (Yin and Wan, 2022) has one outlier of an approximate rate of 13%, but most of the high-performance models also seen in the WebNLG 2020 challenge (Castro Ferreira et al., 2020) have a much lower rate of inserting information (Yin and Wan, 2022). This suggests ChatGPT is unusually likely to make these types of mistakes.

Factualness did have an effect on how many triples were present, absent or hallucinated. When expressing factual data, the most common error category was *hallucinated*; expressing triples in a way that was incompatible with the source prompt. When generating text for fictional data, the most common error was instead information missing from the generated text. Yin and Wan (2022) showed that the large pretrained T5 and BART models performed practically no addition or duplication errors on any of the KG datasets they were evaluated on, but that the rates of hallucinations (intrinsic and extrinsic inaccuracy) rose with the amount of pretraining – our results on ChatGPT do not follow this trend, as we see both types of errors on our factual dataset.

We found in Section 3.2 that ChatGPT performed significantly worse on Russian data than on English data. While it is possible that a two-tiered approach that first attempts to use an LLM to translate the triples into the target language, and then generate text for the translated triples, would perform better, we considered such prompt engineering to be outside the scope of this paper. Recent work by (Lai et al., 2023) showed that low-resource languages made ChatGPT perform worse on a zero-shot summary task (with the prompt written in the target language), and while Russian is not necessarily a low-resource language, Lai et al. found that Russian ranked relatively low among high-resource languages.

The main difference between our approach and that of Yuan and Färber (2023) is how we create our prompts. Although the approach by Yuan and Färber is more logically consistent and arguably more minimal, basing their triple representation on previous work by Ribeiro et al. (2019), the authors run into issues with preventing the LLMs from synthesising text beyond what they asked for. It is otherwise difficult to compare the results obtained by Yuan and Färber to ours as their datasets are different from the WebNLG 2020 dataset we utilised in Section 3.2. We do not see the type of hallucinatory text continuation that Yuan and Färber see in their dataset in ours, perhaps because we explicitly tell the LLM to only state what we ask it to state in our prompts (for which see Appendix B).

6 Conclusion

In this paper, we have shown that LLMs can perform the task of arbitrary domain zero-shot knowledge graph-to-text. The model's knowledge of the information for which it is generating text affects how likely it is to misstate or leave out information. This, in combination with the high likelihood that the expressed text contains some information that was not part of the triples that the model was asked to express, calls for caution when deploying LLM-powered systems for in-the-wild KG-to-text synthesis of unseen knowledge graph data on arbitrary domains. For closed comains, on seen knowledge graph data, where the consequences of accidentally omitting or misstating a fact are smaller, the LLM approach may be easier to implement than the models from Castro Ferreira et al. (2020), especially if the topic of the generated text is outside of the scope of typical KG-to-text datasets.

As LLMs with higher number of parameters are trained in the future, some of the issues mentioned in this paper – especially the low performance on Russian data – may be addressed, but the ability of the model to draw parallels between information it has encoded in its parameters and the information it has been asked to express means that issues of triple coverage and hallucination may not cleanly go away in the same fashion. For this reason, we believe that pretrained models that specialise on the KG-to-text task will retain their value.

7 Limitations

The low agreement of our Mechanical Turk annotators on both the coverage of triples and annotating extra hallucinated information in the generated text limited the scale of our evaluation, as we had to manually annotate the data ourselves. With more data, it is possible that more interesting patterns would appear regarding what type of information is dropped and what extra information is hallucinated when generating text for knowledge graphs with LLMs. Additionally, when attempting to express much larger graphs than the size of 7 we used in Section 4.3.2, it became clear that the ability of crowdworkers to annotate large amounts of data as present, absent or hallucinated deteriorated further as the number of triples grew beyond 5-10; this can be addressed by employing professional annotators.

This paper is not intended to be read as a direct review of the performance of ChatGPT or other OpenAI models on the KG-to-text task, but as a generalised analysis using ChatGPT to stand in for LLMs in general. Although some of the deficiencies of ChatGPT on both the WebNLG 2020 task and our WikiData expression task could be addressed by fine-tuning the prompt or using more advanced LLMs such as GPT-4, we believe that the issues of differing performance depending on factualness extend beyond the capacities of the model to understand the data it is reading, and is not necessarily something that improves as the model is able to relate the prompts it is reading to a larger understanding of the context through an increased number of parameters.

The prompts we present in Appendix B may not be the optimal prompts for making ChatGPT express knowledge graph data, and it is possible that different prompt design could significantly affect the ability of an LLM to perform the WebNLG task (Tables 1, 4) or the triple coverage task we presented in Section 4.3.2. We are not aware of a consistent approach to finding an optimal prompt for any task with LLMs.

A large number of recent papers in both the field of evaluating LLMs and in the field of KG-to-text are only available as non-peer-reviewed preprints. This can make it difficult to know the true scale of the field and to know which papers are the most representative for their area – we have made an attempt to do so in this paper.

8 Ethics Statement

Using public LLMs for KG-to-text poses a challenge in extracting explanations for the choices made by the system. Even if LLMs at some point in the near future outperform task-specific models on any NLG task, it may be worth using smaller models specifically to retain control over the model or to achieve explainability.

The use of crowdworkers for the types of annotation and evaluation we presented in Section 4.3.1 did not require ethics approval at our institution.

We made an attempt to filter our WikiData dataset such that it would not contain offensive statements. The Wikidata data synthesis process described in Section 4.2 was rerun when an earlier version of our dataset was found to contain statements about individuals connected to historical events – specifically the Holocaust – that could be interpreted as Holocaust denial. It is nonetheless possible that counterfactual or factual statements in our current dataset, or LLM hallucinations relating to them, could have been perceived as offensive to our Mechanical Turk annotators, on account of the random nature of the process.

9 Data Availability Statement

Data files containing model output as well as annotator judgements have been made available on GitHub at `https://github.com/Agnesion/zero-shot-NLG-from-KGs-data`.

10 Acknowledgements

The authors would like to thank the anonymous INLG reviewers for their insightful comments. This work was supported by the project *Social robots accelerating the transition to sustainable transport* (50276-1), financed by Furhat Robotics & Swedish Energy Agency.

References

Alan Agresti. 2012. *Categorical data analysis*, third edition. Wiley Series in Probability and Statistics. John Wiley & Sons.

Hussam Alkaissi and Samy I McFarlane. 2023. Artificial hallucinations in ChatGPT: Implications in scientific writing. *Cureus*, 15(2):e35179.

Agnes Axelsson and Gabriel Skantze. 2023. Do you follow? A fully automated system for adaptive robot presenters. In *Proceedings of the 2023 ACM/IEEE International Conference on Human-Robot Interaction*, pages 102–111.

Nils Axelsson and Gabriel Skantze. 2020. Using knowledge graphs and behaviour trees for feedback-aware presentation agents. In *Proceedings of the 20th ACM International Conference on Intelligent Virtual Agents*, IVA '20, New York, NY, USA. Association for Computing Machinery.

Satanjeev Banerjee and Alon Lavie. 2005. METEOR: An automatic metric for MT evaluation with improved correlation with human judgments. In *Proceedings of the ACL Workshop on Intrinsic and Extrinsic Evaluation Measures for Machine Translation and/or Summarization*, pages 65–72, Ann Arbor, Michigan. Association for Computational Linguistics.

Thiago Castro Ferreira, Claire Gardent, Nikolai Ilinykh, Chris van der Lee, Simon Mille, Diego Moussallem, and Anastasia Shimorina. 2020. The 2020 bilingual, bi-directional WebNLG+ shared task: Overview and evaluation results (WebNLG+ 2020). In *Proceedings of the 3rd International Workshop on Natural Language Generation from the Semantic Web (WebNLG+)*, pages 55–76, Dublin, Ireland (Virtual). Association for Computational Linguistics.

Boxing Chen and Colin Cherry. 2014. A systematic comparison of smoothing techniques for sentence-level BLEU. In *Proceedings of the Ninth Workshop on Statistical Machine Translation*, pages 362–367, Baltimore, Maryland, USA. Association for Computational Linguistics.

R. H. B. Christensen. 2019. ordinal—regression models for ordinal data. R package version 2019.12-10. https://CRAN.R-project.org/package=ordinal.

Anthony Colas, Ali Sadeghian, Yue Wang, and Daisy Zhe Wang. 2022. Eventnarrative: A large-scale event-centric dataset for knowledge graph-to-text generation. *arXiv preprint arXiv:2111.00276*.

Jacob Devlin, Ming-Wei Chang, Kenton Lee, and Kristina Toutanova. 2019. BERT: pre-training of deep bidirectional transformers for language understanding. In *Proceedings of the 2019 Conference of the North American Chapter of the Association for Computational Linguistics: Human Language Technologies, NAACL-HLT 2019, Minneapolis, MN, USA, June 2-7, 2019, Volume 1 (Long and Short Papers)*, pages 4171–4186. Association for Computational Linguistics.

Li Ding, Rong Pan, Tim Finin, Anupam Joshi, Yun Peng, and Pranam Kolari. 2005. Finding and ranking knowledge on the semantic web. In *The Semantic Web – ISWC 2005*, pages 156–170, Berlin, Heidelberg. Springer Berlin Heidelberg.

Daniel Duma and Ewan Klein. 2013. Generating natural language from linked data: Unsupervised template extraction. In *Proceedings of the 10th International Conference on Computational Semantics (IWCS 2013) – Long Papers*, pages 83–94, Potsdam, Germany. Association for Computational Linguistics.

Lisa Ehrlinger and Wolfram Wöß. 2016. Towards a definition of knowledge graphs. *SEMANTiCS (Posters, Demos, SuCCESS)*, 48(1-4):2.

Joseph L Fleiss and Jacob Cohen. 1973. The equivalence of weighted kappa and the intraclass correlation coefficient as measures of reliability. *Educational and psychological measurement*, 33(3):613–619.

Claire Gardent, Anastasia Shimorina, Shashi Narayan, and Laura Perez-Beltrachini. 2017a. Creating training corpora for nlg micro-planners. In *Proceedings of the 55th Annual Meeting of the Association for Computational Linguistics (Volume 1: Long Papers)*, pages 179–188. Association for Computational Linguistics.

Claire Gardent, Anastasia Shimorina, Shashi Narayan, and Laura Perez-Beltrachini. 2017b. The WebNLG challenge: Generating text from RDF data. In *Proceedings of the 10th International Conference on Natural Language Generation*, pages 124–133, Santiago de Compostela, Spain. Association for Computational Linguistics.

E. Goldberg, N. Driedger, and R.I. Kittredge. 1994. Using natural-language processing to produce weather forecasts. *IEEE Expert*, 9(2):45–53.

Qipeng Guo, Zhijing Jin, Ning Dai, Xipeng Qiu, Xiangyang Xue, David Wipf, and Zheng Zhang. 2020. P^2: A plan-and-pretrain approach for knowledge graph-to-text generation. In *Proceedings of the 3rd International Workshop on Natural Language Generation from the Semantic Web (WebNLG+)*, pages 100–106, Dublin, Ireland (Virtual). Association for Computational Linguistics.

Aidan Hogan, Eva Blomqvist, Michael Cochez, Claudia D'amato, Gerard De Melo, Claudio Gutierrez, Sabrina Kirrane, José Emilio Labra Gayo, Roberto Navigli, Sebastian Neumaier, Axel-Cyrille Ngonga Ngomo, Axel Polleres, Sabbir M. Rashid, Anisa Rula, Lukas Schmelzeisen, Juan Sequeda, Steffen Staab, and Antoine Zimmermann. 2021. Knowledge graphs. *ACM Comput. Surv.*, 54(4).

David M. Howcroft and Verena Rieser. 2021. What happens if you treat ordinal ratings as interval data? human evaluations in NLP are even more underpowered than you think. In *Proceedings of the 2021 Conference on Empirical Methods in Natural Language Processing*, pages 8932–8939, Online and Punta Cana, Dominican Republic. Association for Computational Linguistics.

Ziwei Ji, Nayeon Lee, Rita Frieske, Tiezheng Yu, Dan Su, Yan Xu, Etsuko Ishii, Ye Jin Bang, Andrea Madotto, and Pascale Fung. 2023. Survey of hallucination in natural language generation. *ACM Comput. Surv.*, 55(12).

Mihir Kale and Abhinav Rastogi. 2021. Text-to-text pre-training for data-to-text tasks. *arXiv preprint arXiv:2005.10433*.

Pei Ke, Haozhe Ji, Yu Ran, Xin Cui, Liwei Wang, Linfeng Song, Xiaoyan Zhu, and Minlie Huang. 2021. JointGT: Graph-text joint representation learning for text generation from knowledge graphs. In *Findings of the Association for Computational Linguistics: ACL-IJCNLP 2021*, pages 2526–2538, Online. Association for Computational Linguistics.

Rik Koncel-Kedziorski, Dhanush Bekal, Yi Luan, Mirella Lapata, and Hannaneh Hajishirzi. 2019. Text Generation from Knowledge Graphs with Graph Transformers. In *Proceedings of the 2019 Conference of the North American Chapter of the Association for Computational Linguistics: Human Language Technologies, Volume 1 (Long and Short Papers)*, pages 2284–2293, Minneapolis, Minnesota. Association for Computational Linguistics.

Rik Koncel-Kedziorski, Dhanush Bekal, Yi Luan, Mirella Lapata, and Hannaneh Hajishirzi. 2022. Text generation from knowledge graphs with graph transformers. *arXiv preprint arXiv:1904.02342*.

Ioannis Konstas and Mirella Lapata. 2013. Inducing document plans for concept-to-text generation. In *Proceedings of the 2013 Conference on Empirical Methods in Natural Language Processing*, pages 1503–1514.

Karen Kukich. 1983. Design of a knowledge-based report generator. In *21st Annual Meeting of the Association for Computational Linguistics*, pages 145–150, Cambridge, Massachusetts, USA. Association for Computational Linguistics.

Viet Dac Lai, Nghia Trung Ngo, Amir Pouran Ben Veyseh, Hieu Man, Franck Dernoncourt, Trung Bui, and Thien Huu Nguyen. 2023. Chatgpt beyond english: Towards a comprehensive evaluation of large language models in multilingual learning. *arXiv preprint arXiv:2304.05613*.

J. Richard Landis and Gary G. Koch. 1977. The measurement of observer agreement for categorical data. *Biometrics*, 33(1):159–174.

Ora Lassila and Ralph R. Swick. 1999. Resource description framework (rdf) model and syntax specification. `http://www.w3.org/TR/REC-rdf-syntax/`.

Willem JM Levelt. 1989. *Speaking: From intention to articulation*. MIT Press.

Mike Lewis, Yinhan Liu, Naman Goyal, Marjan Ghazvininejad, Abdelrahman Mohamed, Omer Levy, Veselin Stoyanov, and Luke Zettlemoyer. 2020. BART: Denoising sequence-to-sequence pre-training for natural language generation, translation, and comprehension. In *Proceedings of the 58th Annual Meeting of the Association for Computational Linguistics*, pages 7871–7880, Online. Association for Computational Linguistics.

Junyi Li, Tianyi Tang, Wayne Xin Zhao, Zhicheng Wei, Nicholas Jing Yuan, and Ji-Rong Wen. 2021a. Few-shot knowledge graph-to-text generation with pretrained language models. In *Findings of the Association for Computational Linguistics: ACL-IJCNLP 2021*, pages 1558–1568, Online. Association for Computational Linguistics.

Junyi Li, Tianyi Tang, Wayne Xin Zhao, Zhicheng Wei, Nicholas Jing Yuan, and Ji-Rong Wen. 2021b. Few-shot knowledge graph-to-text generation with pretrained language models. *arXiv preprint arXiv:2106.01623*.

Xintong Li, Aleksandre Maskharashvili, Symon Jory Stevens-Guille, and Michael White. 2020. Leveraging large pretrained models for WebNLG 2020. In *Proceedings of the 3rd International Workshop on Natural Language Generation from the Semantic Web (WebNLG+)*, pages 117–124, Dublin, Ireland (Virtual). Association for Computational Linguistics.

Linyong Nan, Dragomir Radev, Rui Zhang, Amrit Rau, Abhinand Sivaprasad, Chiachun Hsieh, Xiangru Tang, Aadit Vyas, Neha Verma, Pranav Krishna, Yangxiaokang Liu, Nadia Irwanto, Jessica Pan, Faiaz Rahman, Ahmad Zaidi, Mutethia Mutuma, Yasin Tarabar, Ankit Gupta, Tao Yu, Yi Chern Tan, Xi Victoria Lin, Caiming Xiong, Richard Socher, and Nazneen Fatema Rajani. 2021. DART: Open-domain structured data record to text generation. In *Proceedings of the 2021 Conference of the North American Chapter of the Association for Computational Linguistics: Human Language Technologies*, pages 432–447, Online. Association for Computational Linguistics.

Joseph Olive. 2005. Global autonomous language exploitation (gale). DARPA/IPTO Proposer Information Pamphlet.

Kishore Papineni, Salim Roukos, Todd Ward, and Wei-Jing Zhu. 2002. Bleu: a method for automatic evaluation of machine translation. In *Proceedings of the 40th Annual Meeting of the Association for Computational Linguistics*, pages 311–318, Philadelphia, Pennsylvania, USA. Association for Computational Linguistics.

Rivindu Perera and Parma Nand. 2015. A multi-strategy approach for lexicalizing linked open data. In *Computational Linguistics and Intelligent Text Processing*, pages 348–363, Cham. Springer International Publishing.

Maja Popović. 2015. chrF: character n-gram F-score for automatic MT evaluation. In *Proceedings of the Tenth Workshop on Statistical Machine Translation*, pages 392–395, Lisbon, Portugal. Association for Computational Linguistics.

Maja Popović. 2017. chrF++: words helping character n-grams. In *Proceedings of the Second Conference on Machine Translation*, pages 612–618, Copenhagen, Denmark. Association for Computational Linguistics.

Colin Raffel, Noam Shazeer, Adam Roberts, Katherine Lee, Sharan Narang, Michael Matena, Yanqi Zhou, Wei Li, and Peter J. Liu. 2020. Exploring the limits of transfer learning with a unified text-to-text transformer. *J. Mach. Learn. Res.*, 21(1).

Leonardo F. R. Ribeiro, Claire Gardent, and Iryna Gurevych. 2019. Enhancing AMR-to-text generation with dual graph representations. In *Proceedings of the 2019 Conference on Empirical Methods in Natural Language Processing and the 9th International Joint Conference on Natural Language Processing (EMNLP-IJCNLP)*, pages 3183–3194, Hong Kong, China. Association for Computational Linguistics.

Martin Schmitt, Leonardo F. R. Ribeiro, Philipp Dufter, Iryna Gurevych, and Hinrich Schütze. 2021. Modeling graph structure via relative position for text generation from knowledge graphs. In *Proceedings of the Fifteenth Workshop on Graph-Based Methods for Natural Language Processing (TextGraphs-15)*, pages 10–21, Mexico City, Mexico. Association for Computational Linguistics.

Martin Schmitt, Sahand Sharifzadeh, Volker Tresp, and Hinrich Schütze. 2020. An unsupervised joint system for text generation from knowledge graphs and semantic parsing. In *Proceedings of the 2020 Conference on Empirical Methods in Natural Language Processing (EMNLP)*, pages 7117–7130, Online. Association for Computational Linguistics.

Edward W Schneider. 1973. Course modularization applied: The interface system and its implications for sequence control and data analysis. *HumRRO-PP-10-73*. Presented at the meeting of the Association for the Development of Instructional Systems (ADIS), April 1972.

Thibault Sellam, Dipanjan Das, and Ankur Parikh. 2020. BLEURT: Learning robust metrics for text generation. In *Proceedings of the 58th Annual Meeting of the Association for Computational Linguistics*, pages 7881–7892, Online. Association for Computational Linguistics.

Bilin Shao, Xiaojun Li, and Genqing Bian. 2021. A survey of research hotspots and frontier trends of recommendation systems from the perspective of knowledge graph. *Expert Systems with Applications*, 165:113764.

Matthew Snover, Bonnie Dorr, Rich Schwartz, Linnea Micciulla, and John Makhoul. 2006. A study of translation edit rate with targeted human annotation. In *Proceedings of the 7th Conference of the Association for Machine Translation in the Americas: Technical Papers*, pages 223–231, Cambridge, Massachusetts, USA. Association for Machine Translation in the Americas.

Linfeng Song, Ante Wang, Jinsong Su, Yue Zhang, Kun Xu, Yubin Ge, and Dong Yu. 2021. Structural information preserving for graph-to-text generation. *arXiv preprint arXiv:2102.06749*.

Denny Vrandečić and Markus Krötzsch. 2014. Wikidata: a free collaborative knowledgebase. *Communications of the ACM*, 57(10):78–85.

Yashen Wang, Huanhuan Zhang, Yifeng Liu, and Haiyong Xie. 2019. Kg-to-text generation with slot-attention and link-attention. In *Natural Language Processing and Chinese Computing*, pages 223–234, Cham. Springer International Publishing.

Zixiaofan Yang, Arash Einolghozati, Hakan Inan, Keith Diedrick, Angela Fan, Pinar Donmez, and Sonal Gupta. 2020. Improving text-to-text pre-trained models for the graph-to-text task. In *Proceedings of the 3rd International Workshop on Natural Language Generation from the Semantic Web (WebNLG+)*, pages 107–116, Dublin, Ireland (Virtual). Association for Computational Linguistics.

Xunjian Yin and Xiaojun Wan. 2022. How do Seq2Seq models perform on end-to-end data-to-text generation? In *Proceedings of the 60th Annual Meeting of the Association for Computational Linguistics (Volume 1: Long Papers)*, pages 7701–7710, Dublin, Ireland. Association for Computational Linguistics.

Shuzhou Yuan and Michael Färber. 2023. Evaluating generative models for graph-to-text generation. *arXiv preprint arXiv:2307.14712*.

Tianyi Zhang, Varsha Kishore, Felix Wu, Kilian Q. Weinberger, and Yoav Artzi. 2020. Bertscore: Evaluating text generation with BERT. *arXiv preprint arXiv:1904.09675*.

Li Zhou, Jianfeng Gao, Di Li, and Heung-Yeung Shum. 2020. The design and implementation of xiaoice, an empathetic social chatbot. *Comput. Linguist.*, 46(1):53–93.

A WebNLG results, Russian

Team	BLEU	BLEU NLTK	METEOR	CHRF++	TER	BERT Prec.	BERT Recall	BERT F1
bt5	0.516	0.521	**0.676**	**0.683**	0.420	0.909	**0.907**	0.907
cuni-ufal	**0.529**	**0.532**	0.672	0.677	**0.398**	**0.914**	0.905	**0.909**
Huawei Noah's Ark Lab	0.468	0.468	0.632	0.637	0.456	0.899	0.890	0.893
FBConvAI	0.453	0.451	0.617	0.641	0.452	0.903	0.894	0.898
OSU Neural NLG	0.473	0.477	0.616	0.622	0.453	0.897	0.882	0.888
med	0.431	0.430	0.576	0.595	0.487	0.898	0.873	0.884
Baseline-FORGE2020	0.255	0.256	0.467	0.514	0.665	0.841	0.835	0.837
ChatGPT	0.166	0.168	0.403	0.459	0.777	0.815	0.828	0.821

Table 4: ChatGPT's performance on the WebNLG Russian-ALL task.

B Prompts for KG-to-text on WebNLG 2020 data

B.1 English

The *system* prompt was "You are a linguistic robot that translates messages in the form of triples into text."

The *user* prompt was "Please convert these triples into a single piece of clear text. Do not give any comments or explanations, just write the text as your response. Do not include any information or assumptions beyond what is stated in the triples. The order of the triples does not matter.", followed by a newline-separated list of the triples that were part of the prompt. Triples were preprocessed to remove underscores within the names of entities, but otherwise presented in the same format as in the WebNLG 2020 dataset.

B.2 Russian

The *system* prompt was "You are a linguistic robot that translates messages in the form of triples into Russian text."

The *user* prompt was "Please convert these triples into a single piece of clear text in Russian. Your entire response must be in Russian. Your goal is to convert the triples into a piece of Russian text that expresses the meaning of all the triples at the same time, not to translate the triples into Russian. Do not give any comments or explanations, just write this piece of Russian text that expresses the triples as your response. Do not include any information or assumptions beyond what is stated in the triples. The order of the triples does not matter.", followed by a newline-separated list of the triples that were part of the prompt. Triples were preprocessed to remove underscores within the names of entities, but otherwise presented in the same format as in the WebNLG 2020 dataset.

C Prompt for KG-to-text on WikiData corpus

The *system* prompt was "You are a linguistic robot that translates messages in the form of triples into text. You may only return a single sentence and you can't use semicolons as part of your answer."

There were two *user* prompts. The first was "Please convert this triple into a single sentence. Do not insert any other information or commentary.", followed by the first triple in the list of triples.

The second *user* prompt was "Now insert all of the following triples into that sentence. Keep the length as short as possible. Do not insert any other information or commentary than these triples and the previous triple I gave you:", followed by a newline-separated list of the triples beyond the first.

C.1 Instantiated with data from Figure 1

System

You are a linguistic robot that translates messages in the form of triples into text. You may only return a single sentence and you can't use semicolons as part of your answer.

User

Please convert this triple into a single sentence. Do not insert any other information or commentary.
Georgina Cassar / Sport / rhythmic gymnastics

Assistant

Georgina Cassar practices rhythmic gymnastics as her sport.

User

Now insert all of the following triples into that sentence. Keep the length as short as possible. Do not insert any other information or commentary than these triples and the previous triple I gave you:
Georgina Cassar / Participant in / 2010 Commonwealth Games
Georgina Cassar / Date of birth / September 9th, 1993

Assistant

Georgina Cassar, born on September 9th, 1993, practices rhythmic gymnastics as her sport and participated in the 2010 Commonwealth Games.

D Prompt to generate fictional examples of WikiData class

This prompt used GPT-3 and thus is not split into *system, user* and *assistant* like the previous prompts. If we had one example of the class we wanted to generate fictional examples of, the prompt started with:

> "*(the example)*" is an example of "*(the WikiData label of the class)*".

If there was more than one example, it instead started with:

> *(the first N - 1 examples, each in quotes, separated by commas)* and "*(the last example)*" are examples of "*(the WikiData label of the class)*"

The resulting string was then appended with the following template to create the final prompt:

> Please give me *(the number needed to fill in every fictional graph)* fictional examples of "*(the WikiData label of the class)*" for a short story I'm writing. Only give the name or title of the fictional *(the WikiData label of the class)* and no description. I want the names to be completely new and made up so no one recognises them.
>
> 1:

The prompt ended with a tailing *1:* to prompt the LLM into providing the results as a numbered list.

E List of inserted hallucinations

Factual

- Text states the subject was survived by his sibling.
- Text states subject is a former air force colonel and officer, despite no end of employment or position being stated in the triples.
- Text states subject was French, but triples state subject wrote in French and died in Paris.
- Text states that the subject's parents were Buddhist, but the triples state that the subject was Buddhist.
- The text states that the subject died while still employed by TU Dresden, but the triples state the two events independently of each other.
- Text specifies that the subject worked at a company before becoming president, but triples do not specify the order of events.
- Triples don't state when the subject had a child named Fusu, but text states he had the son before becoming king.
- Triples don't state who Raghad Hussein's mother was, but the text makes the connection.
- The triples don't state that Emperor Shun was the subject's predecessor, but the text does.
- Text assumes an order of occupations.
- Triples do not state that the subject was survived by his wife, but text does.
- Text additionally states the subject worked at Fort Sarah Bernhardt, not supported by the triples.

Counterfactual

- Text says Francoise Robin died in 1946; triples do not mention this year at all.
- Text states that the subject participated in the 2008 Summer Olympics as a footballer, but triples are ambiguous about the sport.
- Triples are ambiguous about whether the subject makes or plays music, but text states "composer".
- Text makes unjustified assumption that subject was survived by his son.
- Text states that subject wrote in Russian "despite" being depicted by the Primavera.
- Text states subject's paintings are held in a gallery "despite" being a pharaoh.
- Text states that the Fortin de Kerdonis is located in the 6th arrondissement of Paris, which is not in the triples.
- Text states subject was Belarusian-Canadian, despite the triples not claiming he was Canadian.
- Text states a specific painting is in the collection of Kunstmuseum, despite the triples saying the artist has paintings there, and that the artist also made the specific painting. Artists can have paintings in many places at the same time.
- Text states a specific painting is in the collection of the National Gallery, despite the triples saying the artist has paintings there, and that the artist also made the specific painting. Artists can have paintings in many places at the same time.

Fictional

- Text assumes a marriage happened in the city of Valerusse, triples do not state this.
- Text assumes that the subject replaced her mother as Sultan of the Deep, but triples simply say subject was Sultan of the Deep, and replaced her mother.
- Text states subject was survived by his father and spouse despite neither being claimed by the triples.
- Text states subject is in Ugolaver with her child; triples simply state subject works in Ugolaver and has a child, but child could be old enough to live somewhere else, etc.
- Text states subject was influenced by Defender Kael in a specific field, but triples simply state she was active in that field, and was influenced by Defender Kael.
- Text implies the influence of Unai Moravec led to the subject's death, but triples simply state subject died and was influenced by Unai Moravec.
- Text states subject is archived together with his wife, which is not stated by the triples, which simply state that the subject has archives at a specific location.

Table 5: A summary of every hallucination of the type where the LLM added in information that was not in its prompt that we were able to find in our 210-graph WikiData dataset.

The 2023 WebNLG Shared Task on Low Resource Languages Overview and Evaluation Results (WebNLG 2023)

Liam Cripwell[3,4], Anya Belz[1,6], Claire Gardent[3], Albert Gatt[5], Claudia Borg[2], Marthese Borg[2], John Judge[1], Michela Lorandi[1], Anna Nikiforovskaya[3,4], William Soto-Martinez[3,4], Craig Thomson[6]

[1]ADAPT/DCU, Ireland; [2]University of Malta, Malta; [3]CNRS/LORIA, France; [4]Université de Lorraine, France; [5]Utrecht University, the Netherlands; [6]University of Aberdeen, UK

Abstract

The WebNLG task consists of mapping a knowledge graph to a text verbalising the content of that graph. The 2017 WebNLG edition required participating systems to generate English text from a set of DBpedia triples, while the 2020 WebNLG+ challenge additionally included generation into Russian and semantic parsing of English and Russian texts. In contrast, WebNLG 2023 focuses on four under-resourced languages which are severely under-represented in research on text generation, namely Breton, Irish, Maltese and Welsh. In addition, WebNLG 2023 once again includes Russian. In this paper, we present the organisation of the shared task (data, timeline, evaluation), briefly describe the participating systems and summarise results for participating systems.

1 Introduction

The WebNLG challenges seeks to add to the research on Knowledge Graph verbalisation i.e., how to convert a knowledge graph into a text verbalising its content. This is illustrated in Figure 1 where the text shown conveys the content of the input graph.

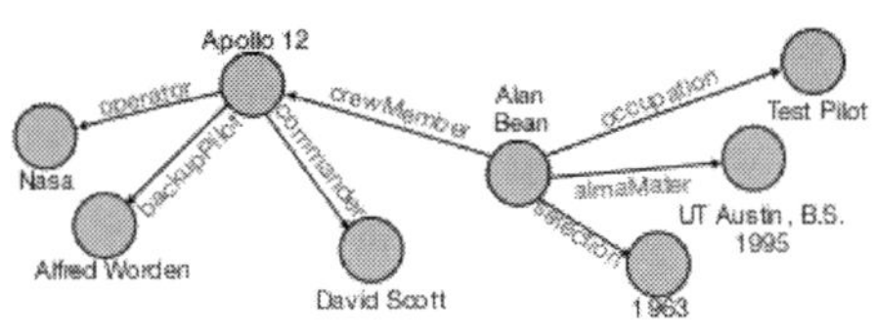

Alan Bean graduated from UT Austin in 1955 with a Bachelor of Science degree. He was hired by NASA in 1963 and served as a test pilot. Apollo 12's backup pilot was Alfred Worden and was commanded by David Scott.

Figure 1: WebNLG Input/Output Example: the generated text should convey the content of the input graph.

The first edition of the challenge, the 2017 WebNLG shared task, required participating systems to generate English text from a set of DBpedia triples (Gardent et al., 2017). The 2020 WebNLG+ challenge encompassed four tasks: RDF-to-English, RDF-to-Russian, English-to-RDF and Russian-to-RDF.

With the development of large-scale pretrained models, research in automatic text generation has acquired new impetus. Yet, the current state-of-the-art is dominated by a handful of languages, for which training data is relatively easy to acquire. At the same time, the field has recently witnessed some encouraging developments which focus on generation for under-resourced and under-represented languages (Abhishek et al., 2022; Team et al., 2022). This trend is paralleled by a growing interest in multilingual models and applications in NLP more broadly.

The WebNLG 2023 Challenge was organised in response to these trends and specifically addresses generation for four under-resourced languages: Breton, Irish, Maltese and Welsh. In addition, WebNLG 2023 once again includes Russian.

Timeline. Noisy training data, gold development data and evaluation scripts were released on February 24, 2023. The test data was made available on June 8th and the deadline for submitting system results was June 15th. Automatic evaluation results were announced on June 13th and the human evaluation results on August 18th. Results were first released anonymously so that participants had the opportunity to withdraw their systems.

In what follows, we summarise the main features of WebNLG 2023. Section 2 describes the datasets used for the challenge. Section 3 briefly presents the participating systems (more detailed descriptions are provided by the participants in separate papers). Section 4 introduces the evaluation methodology, Section 5 discusses the automatic evaluation results for participating systems and Section 6 the human evaluation results. Finally, Sec-

Proceedings of the Workshop on Multimodal, Multilingual Natural Language Generation and Multilingual WebNLG Challenge (MM-NLG 2023), pages 55–66
September 12, 2023 ©2023 Association for Computational Linguistics

Language	Nb. Train Items	Nb. Dev Items	Nb. Test Items
Breton (br)	13,211	1,399	1,778
Welsh (cy)	13,211	1,665	1,778
Irish (ga)	13,211	1,665	1,778
Maltese (mt)	13,211	1,665	1,778
Russian (ru)	5,573	790	1,101

Table 1: Data statistics for each of the supported languages. Training data is 'noisy', i.e. automatically translated; Dev and Test data are translations by professionals of the WebNLG 2020 dev and test English texts .

tion 7 reports correlations between automatic and human-assessed evaluation measures. Section 8 concludes with broad findings and pointers to future developments.

2 Data

To obtain the development and test data for each of the low-resource languages (Breton, Irish, Maltese, and Welsh), we had professional translators manually translate the English text from the WebNLG 2020 development and test sets, given both the English text and the input RDF graph.[1] We only consider the first reference of each test example in the original English dataset when translating, except in the case of Breton which contains 2 translated references for some of the test items. For Russian, we continue to use the WebNLG$^+$ 2020 data.

In addition to the professionally translated dev and test data, we provide optional 'noisy' training data for the low-resource target languages, which was obtained via machine translation of the texts in the English WebNLG 2020 training set. For this, we used the 24-layer Zero machine translation system (Zhang et al., 2020a).[2]

Table 1 provides a summary of the data provided for each language.

3 Participating Systems

This section provides a brief overview of the participating systems and of the runs submitted by the participants to the shared task. Further results obtained after the submission deadline and more details about each systems are available in the system descriptions provided by the participants (Hari et al., 2023; Kazakov et al., 2023; Kumar et al., 2023; Lorandi and Belz, 2023; Mille et al., 2023).

[1]Due to translation constraints, the Breton development set only contains 1,399 entries from the WebNLG 2020 English dev set. These entries were randomly sampled while making sure to cover texts from all triple set size groups.

[2]https://github.com/bzhangGo/zero/tree/master/docs/multilingual_laln_lalt

Seven teams submitted a system run and two teams withdrew after the automatic evaluation results for test set were shared with participants, yielding a final total of five participating teams (Table 2). Of the 5 runs submitted, only one (CUNI-Wue) included output for all languages. Two teams concentrated on a single language (DCU/TCD-FORGe on Irish and Interno on Russian). None of the remaining two participants submitted output for Breton, with one participant (IREL) submitting output for all languages except Breton and the other (DCU-NLG-PBN) for only three languages (Irish, Welsh, Maltese).

In terms of architecture, monolingual submissions were either rule-based (Mille et al., 2023) or a monolingual LLM fine-tuned on the WebNLG data (Hari et al., 2023). Submissions targeting multiple languages predominantly adopted an NLG+MT pipeline approach.

3.1 Monolingual Models

Interno (Kazakov et al., 2023) focuses on Russian and uses the pretrained large language model FRED-T5 (Full-scale Russian Enhanced Denoisers T5[3], 1,700 M Parameters) fine-tuned on the WebNLG 2020 training dataset to convert RDF graphs into Russian texts. Various prompts are experimented with which either consist of the input graphs or of graphs enriched with translation information for entities and relations. Results indicate that the translation data fail to significantly improve results. The system code is available at https://github.com/Ivan30003/webnlg_interno.

DCU/TCD-FORGe (Mille et al., 2023) converts RDF graphs into Irish using a rule-based pipeline consisting of four components: triple lexicalisation, generation of non-inflected Irish text, inflection generation, and post-processing. The pipeline is available at https://github.com/mille-s/DCU_TCD-FORGe_WebNLG23.

[3]https://huggingface.co/ai-forever/FRED-T5-1.7B

Team	Affiliation	Country	Breton	Welsh	Irish	Maltese	Russian
CUNI-Wue	Charles University	Czechia	✓	✓	✓	✓	✓
DCU/TCD-FORGe	ADAPT/DCU/Trinity College	Ireland	-	-	✓	-	-
Interno	Pulkovo Observatory	Russia	-	-	-	-	✓
IREL	IIT Hyderabad	India		✓	✓	✓	✓
DCU-NLG-PBN	ADAPT/DCU	Ireland	-	✓	✓	✓	-

Table 2: WebNLG 2023 Participants.

3.2 NLG+MT Models

IREL (Hari et al., 2023) adopts an NLG+MT approach. RDF graphs are first translated into English using T5-small, fine-tuned on the training split of the WebNLG 2020 dataset for English. The generated English text is then translated to Irish, Maltese, Russian and Welsh using the distilled variant of NLLB (Team et al., 2022). As NLLB does not handle Breton, the approach is not applied to the Breton data. The training code and model checkpoints are available at `https://shorturl.at/hsNO4`.

CUNI-Wue (Kumar et al., 2023) also uses an NLG+MT approach using improved training data, custom decoding and multi-tasking.

As for the Shared Task baseline, the input to MT is the English text generated by the best WebNLG 2020 model (?); the MT system is Zero MT..

Training data for machine translation from English into the Shared Task languages is created as follows. For Maltese, Irish and Welsh, the NLLB MT system is applied to the English texts of WebNLG 2020 (instead of Edinburgh's Zero MT model) while for Breton (which is not handled by NLLB), the translations produced by the Zero MT model for this same data are filtered using a length-based heuristic designed to identify incomplete translations. For Russian, the training data is the data from WebNLG 2020.

The English texts generated by the best WebNLG 2020 model are then converted into Maltese, Irish, Welsh, Russian and Breton using mT5 fine-tuned on the parallel data created from the WebNLG 2020 English texts.

Two further refinements are experimented with: custom decoding (split-and-generate) and multi-task learning. For custom decoding, the input RDF graphs are partitioned and the texts generated from each partition subset are concatenated to produce the final output. Multi-tasking includes, in addition to the RDF-to-Text generation main task, translation from English and RDF-to-English text as auxiliary tasks. The model learns to distinguish tasks by different prompts.

For Maltese, Irish and Welsh the submitted variants are multi-task learning + split-and-generate; for Breton data filtering + split-and-generate; and for Russian a multilingual setup without split-and-generate. The code and submission outputs are available at `https://github.com/knalin55/CUNI_Wue-WebNLG23_Submission`.

3.3 Very Large Language Models, no training

DCU-NLG-PBN (Lorandi and Belz, 2023) experimented with very large language models (GPT-3.5 and 4) without training or finetuning of any kind, testing a range of prompt types and formats on a small sample of example input/output pairs and evaluating the two most promising prompts in two scenarios: (i) direct generation into the under-resourced language, and (ii) generation into English followed by translation into the under-resourced language. The variant submitted to the WebNLG 2023 shared task is the few-shot + translation system variant. All code and results are available at `https://github.com/DCU-NLG/DCU-NLG-PBN`.

4 Evaluation Methodology

4.1 Automatic Metrics

The participating systems were automatically evaluated with some of the most popular text generation metrics. Specifically, we considered BLEU (Papineni et al., 2002), TER (Snover et al., 2006), chrF++ (Popović, 2017) (with word bigrams, character 6-grams and $\beta = 2$), and BERTScore (Zhang et al., 2020b)[4]. We use the SacreBLEU implementation of BLEU[5] (Post, 2018), the pyter implementation of TER[6], and the official implementations of chrF++[7] and BERTScore[8].

[4] We compute BERTScore for all languages except Maltese, as it is not supported.

[5] `https://github.com/mjpost/sacrebleu`

[6] `https://pypi.org/project/pyter/`

[7] `https://github.com/m-popovic/chrF/blob/master/chrF%2B%2B.py`

[8] `https://github.com/google-research/bert/tree/master`

All languages except Breton and Russian contain only a single reference for each test instance, and so only these two languages were evaluated in a multi-reference scenario. Each Breton hypothesis was compared with up to 2 references, and each Russian one with up to 7 references. On average, Breton data has 1.28 references per test instance, and Russian data has 2.52 references per instance. We tokenised the texts using `razdel`[9] for Russian and the NLTK framework (Bird et al., 2009) for the other languages (BERTScore uses its own tokenizer, however).

As a baseline system for the new languages, we use the highest performing RDF-to-English system from the 2020 challenge (Amazon (Guo et al., 2020)) and automatically translate its outputs into the target language using Edinburgh's Zero multilingual MT model (Zhang et al., 2020a). For Russian, we use the baseline (FORGE2020) and highest performing system (CUNI-Ufal (Kasner and Dušek, 2020)) from the 2020 challenge.

4.2 Human Evaluation

The WebNLG 2023 human evaluations assessed system outputs in terms of the quality criteria of Fluency, Absence of Omissions, Absence of Additions, and Absence of Unnecessary Repetition. These were defined and explained to evaluators as can be seen in the instructions document; instructions and other details and resources of the evaluations were published as a preregistration bundle on 25 July 2023.[10]

The same evaluations were carried out for each language except Breton for which only one system was submitted. Once the design was complete, we conducted a pilot evaluation on a set of 10 English WebNLG input/output pairs with six of the authors who were not directly involved in developing the evaluation design. Fleiss's kappa values in the pilot were as follows:

Fleiss's κ for human evaluation methods			
Fluency	−Omissions	−Additions	−Repetitions
0.216	0.908	0.81	0.811

Kappa for Absence of Omissions, Absence of Additions, and Absence of Unnecessary Repetition

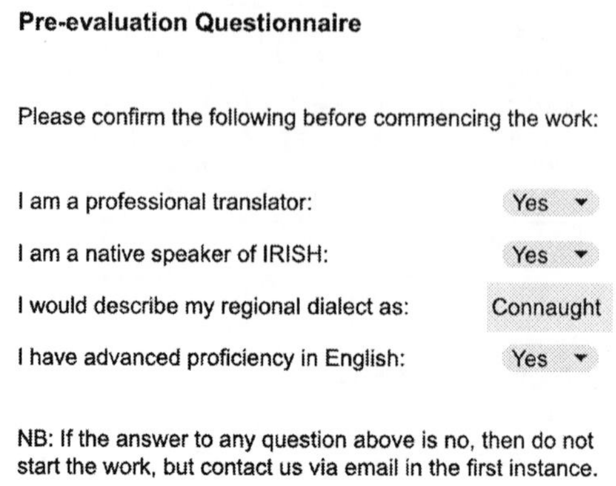

Pre-evaluation Questionnaire

Please confirm the following before commencing the work:

I am a professional translator: Yes

I am a native speaker of IRISH: Yes

I would describe my regional dialect as: Connaught

I have advanced proficiency in English: Yes

NB: If the answer to any question above is no, then do not start the work, but contact us via email in the first instance.

Figure 2: Exclusion questions and dialect check asked of evaluators (here completed by an Irish evaluator).

is high. The lower Fluency kappa is not entirely surprising, as evaluators often disagree on what makes a text (not) fluent. However, as we will see below, kappa was not higher among the authors than among the evaluators which *is* surprising.

The main steps in conducting the evaluation for each language were the following:

1. Recruitment of professional translators via translation agencies.
2. Online training session for evaluators using a Google spreadsheet (Figure 3) and documents and the same 10 English outputs, followed by feedback if the overall kappa for any of the criteria dropped to below 0.7 after the addition of an evaluator's scores to the pilot results.
3. Full evaluation of 100 outputs in the human evaluation test set (see below).
4. Aggregation and analysis of results as described below.

Before commencing the evaluation, translators were asked the questions in Figure 2.

Human evaluation test data: We randomly selected 100 inputs and corresponding system outputs plus human reference text (from the test data itself). Selection was performed with stratification for WebNLG category and number of triples in the input, with the same inputs being used for all low-resource languages (Russian used a different sample of items because of its differing test set).

Allocation of items to evaluators: We used a Repeated Latin Squares design which ensures that each evaluator sees the same number of outputs from each system and for each test set item. For Irish, where we had 5 systems, there were twenty

[9] `https://github.com/natasha/razdel`

[10] Summary on AsPredicted #139263: `https://aspredicted.org/~Mgcdw2J2h6`; full details and resources: `https://github.com/nlgcat/webnlg2023_human_eval_preregistration`

Fluency assessment: please rate the Text shown in terms of Fluency on a scale of 1 to 5 where 5 is the highest (best) score. Highly fluent text 'flows well' and is well connected and free from disfluencies.		*Assessment of similarities and differences between Data and Text: please assess the degree to which a Text expresses the same information as the corresponding Data expression, via the three separate questions below.*				
Text	**FLUENCY**	**Data**	**Text**	**1. Looking at each element of the Data expression in turn, does the Text express all the information in all elements in full (allow synonyms and aggregation)?**	**2. Looking at the Text, is all of its content expressed in the Data expression? (Allow duplication of content.)**	**3. Is the Text free from unnecessary repetition of content?**
Bedford Aerodrome is located in Thurleigh and its ICAO location identifier is EGBF. It has postal code is MK44.	4	location(Bedford_Aerodrome,Thurleigh), icaoLocationIdentifier(Bedford_Aerodrome,EGBF), postalCode(Thurleigh,MK44)	Bedford Aerodrome is located in Thurleigh and its ICAO location identifier is EGBF. It has postal code is MK44.	Yes	Yes	No
The University of Burgundy is located in Dijon, France. The country's leader is Claude Bartolone and its long name is French Republic.	5	country(University_of_Burgundy,France), longName(France,"French Republic"), city(University_of_Burgundy,Dijon), leader(France,Claude_Bartolone)	The University of Burgundy is located in Dijon, France. The country's leader is Claude Bartolone and its long name is French Republic.	Yes	Yes	Yes
Lionsgate is located in the United States.	5	location(Lionsgate,United_States)	Lionsgate is located in the United States.	Yes	Yes	Yes

Figure 3: Human evaluation: Screen shot with items from pilot evaluation with English outputs.

5 × 5 squares, and 2,000 individual judgements (5 evaluators × 4 criteria × 100 outputs), and 400 per system. For the other languages (4 systems) there were twenty-five 4 × 4 squares, and 1,600 individual judgements (4 evaluators × 4 criteria × 100 outputs), again 400 per system.

Aggregation: We used the Fluency assessments unchanged, computing the mean over scores. For the other three criteria, we computed the proportions of Yes scores (equal to the mean of scores mapped Yes=1, No=0).

Analysis: For each language, we carried out four univariate ANOVAs with System as the fixed factor, and Fluency (1–5 ratings), Omission (Yes/No assessments), Addition (Yes/No assessments), and Repetition (Yes/No assessments) as the dependent variables each in one of the ANOVAs. In the results section below, we report F-ratios and their statistical significance, and the homogeneous subsets of systems as determined by a post-hoc Tukey HSD analysis, reflecting significant pairwise differences between systems. The results from the latter are shown, alongside the mean assessment values, in tables where systems whose scores are not significantly different (at the .05 level) share a letter.

We also report Pearson and Spearman correlations with probabilities of statistical significance, between individual Fluency, Omissions, Additions and Repetitions assessments.

5 Results of Automatic Evaluation

In this section, we present results of the evaluation using automatic metrics. These are summarised in Table 3 for each of the four languages under consideration, ordered by chrF++ score. All systems outperform the baselines (or one of the baselines, in the case of Russian), on at least some of the metrics.

As regards the monolingual systems, Interno is ranked (joint) first for Russian on all metric, while DCU/TCD-FORGe is ranked second for BLEU and chrF++, fourth for TER, and third or fourth for BERT P/R/F1. While this suggests that monolingual approaches (whether LLM-based or rule-based) can provide competitive solutions for specific languages, the broader pattern across the four languages shows that combining LLMs with machine translation is more effective in the absence of large amounts of training data.

DCU-NLG-PBN which combines GPT-3.5 with Google Translate and is not trained/finetuned on any WebNLG data, outperforms all systems on all metrics in the three languages it was tested on. It is also instructive to consider the relative performance of IREL and CUNI-Wue, the latter leveraging MT for improved training data, while the former uses it to translate outputs. IREL narrowly outperforms CUNI-Wue on Maltese, Welsh and Irish on all metrics except BLEU on Irish. In summary, these results show a continued role for MT to handle under-resourced languages, even with very large models, as in the case of DCU-NLG-PBN, who report worse performance with direct generation (Lorandi and Belz, 2023).

The inclusion of Russian in WebNLG 2023 provides a point of comparison with the results for the same language in the 2020 edition (Castro Ferreira et al., 2020). In 2020, the CUNI-Ufal system Kasner and Dušek (2020) ranked second on Russian. This year, it is narrowly outperformed by Interno and CUNI-Wue, at least on BLEU and chrF++. On BERTScore, the systems are very close. Indeed, results on Russian for the present edition provide very small improvements over the best results for 2020.

	BLEU	chrF++	TER ↓
DCU-NLG-PBN	21.27	0.52	0.65
IREL	16.49	0.47	0.7
CUNI-Wue	14.02	0.45	0.78
Amazon+Zero	15.60	0.42	0.67

(a) Maltese

	BLEU	chrF++	TER ↓	BERT_P	BERT_R	BERT_F1
Amazon+Zero	9.92	0.33	0.76	0.77	0.73	0.75
CUNI-Wue	10.09	0.33	0.80	0.76	0.73	0.74

(b) Breton

	BLEU	chrF++	TER ↓	BERT_P	BERT_R	BERT_F1
DCU-NLG-PBN	25.11	0.55	0.64	0.83	0.83	0.83
IREL	20.97	0.49	0.67	0.82	0.8	0.81
CUNI-Wue	17.00	0.45	0.79	0.79	0.78	0.79
Amazon+Zero	10.70	0.36	0.77	0.78	0.75	0.76

(c) Welsh

	BLEU	chrF++	TER ↓	BERT_P	BERT_R	BERT_F1
DCU-NLG-PBN	20.40	0.51	0.69	0.81	0.8	0.81
DCU/TCD-FORGe	16.66	0.44	0.75	0.79	0.76	0.77
IREL	15.66	0.44	0.73	0.8	0.77	0.78
CUNI-Wue	15.87	0.43	0.78	0.78	0.77	0.77
Amazon+Zero	11.63	0.36	0.74	0.78	0.74	0.76

(d) Irish

	BLEU	chrF++	TER ↓	BERT_P	BERT_R	BERT_F1
Interno	54.68	0.69	0.37	0.92	0.91	0.92
CUNI-Wue	54.52	0.69	0.38	0.92	0.91	0.91
CUNI-Ufal (2020)	52.9	0.68	0.40	0.91	0.91	0.91
IREL	36.01	0.57	0.53	0.88	0.87	0.87
FORGE (2020)	25.5	0.51	0.67	0.84	0.84	0.84

(e) Russian

Table 3: Results of the automatic evaluation, per language. For each language, results are in descending order of chrF++ score. Baseline results are shaded in light grey: for Russian, we include results from the 2020 version of FORGe (Mille et al., 2019) and for CUNI-Ufal (Kasner and Dušek, 2020), both reported in WebNLG 2020 (Castro Ferreira et al., 2020). Note that BERTScore is not available for Maltese.

6 Results of Human Evaluation

In this section, we present and discuss results from the human evaluations for Irish, Maltese and Welsh. For Russian, we were unable to recruit and train translators able to perform the task reliably, as discussed in the next section below, and in Appendix A.

6.1 Quality assurance checks

For Irish, Maltese and Breton, most evaluators passed the test in the training session easily. One evaluator for Maltese and one for Welsh did not initially pass the threshold. The Welsh evaluator passed the threshold after additional explanation. The Maltese evaluator failed the quality threshold on two of the criteria, and despite prolonged exchange did not manage to pass it, and had to be replaced. The replacement also required repeated additional explanation. All but one evaluator in these languages increased Fleiss's kappa for Fluency when added to the pilot pool of evaluators. On average, compared to the table of pilot kappas (Section 4.2), evaluators increased Fluency to 0.2525, decreased Omissions to 0.855, and slightly decreased Additions and Repetitions to 0.7975 and 0.79, respectively.

The picture was different for Russian, where

three evaluators dropped out after completing the training session, and 3/4 of evaluators who didn't drop out, then failed the quality threshold, two on two criteria, and one on three. Feedback did not succeed in improving kappa; given our recruitment difficulties, we did not have time to replace as many as three evaluators. Concerns from the training session results were corroborated by three further sets of findings for Russian: (a) the effect sizes as per the ANOVAs reported in the appendix for System on scores are very small, and none are significant; (b) there was no correlation between the automatic metrics and the human evaluation measures at all for any measures (Table 9); and (c) there was just a single pairwise significant difference between systems for Russian (Fluency for Interno was better than for IREL), and the reference texts were not significantly better than any system on any scores, and were ranked top only for Absence of Repetitions. The human evaluation results for Russian were therefore not deemed sufficiently reliable, and are presented, for reference, in Appendix A.

6.2 Other checks

Given the overlap between submitting teams and organisers, we took several measures to address conflict of interest, and ensure independence of evaluation. One, we are making all system outputs, original human evaluation scores and scripts, and automatic evaluation scripts available, so that all results can be verified easily. Two, systems and teams were completely obscured in the evaluator spreadsheets. Three, an independent organiser double-checked that the system outputs in the spreadsheets were unchanged compared to original team submission. And four, the same independent organiser also double-checked the edit histories of the evaluator spreadsheets to ensure that any edits were either (a) done outside of the evaluation cells for the purpose of formatting and getting spreadsheets ready, or (b) done inside the evaluation cells by the evaluators only.

6.3 ANOVA and Tukey HSD results

The results of the full evaluations for Irish, Maltese and Welsh can be seen in Table 4. For each language, systems are shown in order of Fluency means, where the human-written reference texts are always ranked top. The means for the other output quality criteria mostly follow the same order, except that DCU-NLG-PBN takes top spot for Additions, Omissions and Repetitions for Maltese and Irish, and Repetitions ranks vary a lot.

The columns containing single capital letters in Table 4 show the homogeneous subsets of systems as determined by a post-hoc Tukey HSD analysis. Systems whose scores are not significantly different (at the .05 level) share a letter.

For **Fluency**, the DCU-NLG-PBN system is in second place after the reference, followed by IREL and then CUNI-Wue, for all three languages. For Irish we also have DCU/TCD-FORGe which comes in at rank 3. For **Absence of Additions**, the references and DCU-NLG-PBN are significantly better than the other two systems for Welsh and Maltese, for the latter IREL is also significantly better than CUNI-Wue; for Irish, the references, DCU-NLG-PBN and DCU/TCD-FORGe are all significantly better than CUNI-Wue; interestingly the references are significantly better only than the lowest-ranked system CUNI-Wue.

For **Absence of Omissions**, the references and DCU-NLG-PBN are significantly better than the other two systems for Welsh and Maltese. The references, DCU-NLG-PBN and DCU/TCD-FORGe are all significantly better than the other two systems for Irish.

For **Absence of Repetitions**, no significant differences were found, and results are generally very close together, for Welsh and Irish. For Maltese, the references and DCU-NLG-PBN were significantly better than CUNI-Wue. From the individual scores it looks as if repetition was simply too sporadic to yield meaningful results.

Table 5 shows the effect sizes and associated p-values for the three languages. The general picture is that for Irish, Maltese and Welsh, there is a strong and highly significant effect of *System* on output quality for all measures, except Repetition, presumably for the reasons discussed above. There are negligible and mostly non-significant effects of *Category* and *Triples* on performance. Finally, there is in all cases except Fluency a small to medium, and mostly significant, effect of *Evaluator* on performance. For Fluency, the effect of Evaluator is very substantial, for the reasons discussed previously.

The correlations between the four human-assessed quality criteria, and between these and the automatic metrics are shown in Tables 6 to 8, and are discussed in a separate section below.

Language	System	Fluency				Addition				Omission			Repetition		
Welsh	Human reference	**3.28**	A			**0.9**	A			**0.84**	A		**0.95**	A	
	DCU-NLG-PBN	3.25	A			0.86	A			0.77	A		0.94	A	
	IREL	2.67		B		0.6		B		0.47		B	0.94	A	
	CUNI-Wue	2.35		B		0.45		B		0.33		B	0.88	A	
Maltese	Human reference	**4.27**	A			0.89	A			0.85	A		0.91	A	
	DCU-NLG-PBN	4.06	A	B		**0.91**	A			**0.86**	A		**0.94**	A	
	IREL	3.74		B		0.69		B		0.56		B	0.87	A	B
	CUNI-Wue	3.34			C	0.52			C	0.46		B	0.76		B
Irish	Human reference	**4.07**	A			0.81	A			0.82	A		0.96	A	
	DCU-NLG-PBN	3.83	A	B		0.83	A			**0.85**	A		**0.97**	A	
	IREL	3.39		B	C	0.65	A	B		0.58		B	0.94	A	
	DCU/TCD-FORGe	3.35			C	**0.84**	A			0.81	A		0.89	A	
	CUNI-Wue	2.98			C	0.55		B		0.51		B	0.92	A	

Table 4: Post-hoc Tukey HSD (alpha = .05) analysis results for Welsh, Maltese and Irish. The columns containing single capital letters show the homogeneous subsets of systems. Human reference results are shaded in light grey.

7 Correlation between Automatic and Human Evaluation Metrics

Tables 6 to 8 are Pearson correlation matrices for all automatic and human-assessed output quality measures. The colour coding goes from vivid green for strong positive correlations to vivid red for strong negative correlations, with both colours growing paler toward 0 (no correlation).

As can be seen very clearly, there are strong correlations between all automatic metrics (note that TER is the only metric where a lower score is better). Otherwise, the strongest correlations are between Omissions and Additions for all languages. In other words, a system that omits information that is in the data from the output is also likely to add information to the output that is not in the data.

In terms of how automatic metrics on the one hand correlate with human-assessed measures on the other, the overall picture is that there are weak to medium correlations between all automatic metrics and Fluency, Additions and Omissions, but not Repetition.

The weakness of the correlations between human and automatic metrics points to an interesting side-effect of building systems for under-resourced languages, in particular when using LLMs. In the past, automatic metrics which tend to assess quality as similarity to a set of test set reference outputs were good predictors of human assessments of outputs of systems which tended to be trained on another part of the same data set. For under-resourced languages, training on reference outputs takes a back seat, hence evaluation on the basis of similarity to reference outputs is a far less effective predictor of human-assessed quality. This effect is exacerbated when using an LLM out-of-the-box as in the case of the DCU-NLG-PBN system.

8 Conclusion

Reflecting on the WebNLG 2023 results overall, it seems remarkable, especially when compared to the two previous WebNLG iterations, that DCU-NLG-PBN, a system that uses GPT-3.5 plus Google Translate in zero-shot mode, with no task-specific adaptation at all, should emerge as the overall winner: its performance is not significantly different from the human-authored reference texts on any of the human-assessed performance measures, and the (automatic metric) margins by which it outperforms systems that have been trained specifically for this task are in many cases substantial.

What is even more surprising is that in the five language/measure combinations where DCU-NLG-PBN is actually ranked higher than the human-written reference texts, the measure in question is never Fluency (which LLMs are supposed to be particularly good at), but Additions, Omissions and Repetitions (which LLMs are supposed to be particularly bad at).

Overall the shared task illustrates the limitations of current neural models when dealing with low resource languages. While fine-tuning existing encoder-decoders or decoders under-perform the NLG+MT pipeline, for languages such as Breton, where machine translation is not available or low quality, the NLG+MT approach similarly shows poor results. In both cases, the scarcity of training data restricts the quality of the generated texts. Approaches which have not been adopted by any of

Language	Fluency				Addition			
	System	Category	# Triples	Evaluator	System	Category	Triples	Evaluator
Welsh	13.64 (p<.001)	1.96 (p=.013)	2.69 (p=.014)	38.48 (p<.001)	26.12 (p<.001)	1.43 (p=.117)	1.37 (p=.226)	7.35 (p<.001)
Maltese	13.87 (p<.001)	2.64 (p<.001)	3.57 (p=.002)	21.72 (p<.001)	20.86 (p<.001)	1.69 (p=.042)	0.93 (p=.476)	2.84 (p=.038)
Irish	12.39 (p<.001)	1.23 (p=.238)	3.14 (p=.005)	50.68 (p<.001)	9.18 (p<.001)	1.1 (p=.351)	1.29 (p=.259)	9.98 (p<.001)

(a) Effect sizes for **Fluency** and **Absence of Additions**.

Language	Omission				Repetition			
	System	Category	# Triples	Evaluator	System	Category	Triples	Evaluator
Welsh	29.77 (p<.001)	1.53 (p=.081)	1.69 (p=.123)	6.0 (p<.001)	1.53 (p=.207)	2.45 (p=.001)	6.87 (p<.001)	5.88 (p<.001)
Maltese	22.05 (p<.001)	2.17 (p=.005)	2.61 (p=.017)	1.71 (p=.165)	5.66 (p<.001)	2.18 (p=.005)	2.11 (p=.052)	3.11 (p=.026)
Irish	13.22 (p<.001)	1.49 (p=.092)	1.95 (p=.071)	11.17 (p<.001)	1.73 (p=.143)	1.13 (p=.324)	2.45 (p=.024)	5.58 (p<.001)

(b) Effect sizes for **Absence of Omissions** and **Absence of Repetitions**.

Table 5: Effect sizes and their statistical significance measures ($\alpha = 0.05$) from one-way ANOVAs for Welsh, Maltese and Irish, with System, Category, Number of triples and Evaluator as factors.

Metric	BLEU	chrF++	TER ↓	Addition	Fluency	Omission	Repetition
BLEU	1.0	0.96	−0.93	0.31	0.23	0.33	0.09
chrF++	0.96	1.0	−0.89	0.36	0.27	0.37	0.09
ter ↓	−0.93	−0.89	1.0	−0.36	−0.29	−0.34	−0.15
Addition	0.31	0.36	−0.36	1.0	0.39	0.61	0.18
Fluency	0.23	0.27	−0.29	0.39	1.0	0.46	0.25
Omission	0.33	0.37	−0.34	0.61	0.46	1.0	0.13
Repetition	0.09	0.09	−0.15	0.18	0.25	0.13	1.0

Table 6: Pearson correlation matrix for all automatic and human-assessed output quality measures for Welsh.

Metric	BLEU	chrF++	TER ↓	Addition	Fluency	Omission	Repetition
BLEU	1.0	0.94	−0.93	0.14	0.25	0.17	0.06
chrF++	0.94	1.0	−0.9	0.17	0.3	0.21	0.09
TER ↓	−0.93	−0.9	1.0	−0.17	−0.28	−0.19	−0.1
Addition	0.14	0.17	−0.17	1.0	0.25	0.74	0.12
Fluency	0.25	0.3	−0.28	0.25	1.0	0.26	0.13
Omission	0.17	0.21	−0.19	0.74	0.26	1.0	0.03
Repetition	0.06	0.09	−0.1	0.12	0.13	0.03	1.0

Table 7: Pearson correlation matrix for all automatic and human-assessed output quality measures for Irish.

Metric	BLEU	chrF++	TER ↓	Addition	Fluency	Omission	Repetition
BLEU	1.0	0.95	−0.78	0.17	0.24	0.23	0.09
chrF++	0.95	1.0	−0.81	0.21	0.29	0.27	0.12
TER ↓	−0.78	−0.81	1.0	−0.25	−0.32	−0.28	−0.24
Addition	0.17	0.21	−0.25	1.0	0.41	0.62	0.29
Fluency	0.24	0.29	−0.32	0.41	1.0	0.43	0.42
Omission	0.23	0.27	−0.28	0.62	0.43	1.0	0.23
Repetition	0.09	0.12	−0.24	0.29	0.42	0.23	1.0

Table 8: Pearson correlation matrix for all automatic and human-assessed output quality measures for Maltese.

the participants but which would be interesting to explore include data augmentation, parameter efficient fine tuning and the development of languages models that are better attuned to specific language families.

The shared task also highlights the practical difficulties involved in training and testing models for low resource languages. As our human evaluation illustrates, recruiting reliable experts to evaluate system outputs is challenging. Similarly, creating development and test data is both costly and complex. We hope that the WebNLG 2023 data will encourage and foster further research on generation into low resource languages.

Acknowledgments

WebNLG 2023 is being organised under the auspices of LT-Bridge, supported by the Horizon 2020 Work Programme Spreading Excellence and Widening Participation (WIDESPREAD) 2018-2020 and the ANR funded xNLG Chair on multilingual, multi-source NLG (Gardent; award ANR-20-CHIA-0003, XNLG "Multi-lingual, Multi-Source Text Generation").

References

Tushar Abhishek, Shivprasad Sagare, Bhavyajeet Singh, Anubhav Sharma, Manish Gupta, and Vasudeva Varma. 2022. Xalign: Cross-lingual fact-to-text alignment and generation for low-resource languages. *CoRR*, abs/2202.00291.

Steven Bird, Ewan Klein, and Edward Loper. 2009. *Natural language processing with Python: analyzing text with the natural language toolkit.* " O'Reilly Media, Inc.".

Thiago Castro Ferreira, Claire Gardent, Nikolai Ilinykh, Chris van der Lee, Simon Mille, Diego Moussallem, and Anastasia Shimorina. 2020. The 2020 bilingual, bi-directional WebNLG+ shared task: Overview and evaluation results (WebNLG+ 2020). In *Proceedings of the 3rd International Workshop on Natural Language Generation from the Semantic Web (WebNLG+)*, pages 55–76, Dublin, Ireland (Virtual). Association for Computational Linguistics.

Claire Gardent, Anastasia Shimorina, Shashi Narayan, and Laura Perez-Beltrachini. 2017. The WebNLG challenge: Generating text from RDF data. In *Proceedings of the 10th International Conference on Natural Language Generation*, pages 124–133, Santiago de Compostela, Spain. Association for Computational Linguistics.

Qipeng Guo, Zhijing Jin, Xipeng Qiu, Weinan Zhang, David Wipf, and Zheng Zhang. 2020. CycleGT: Unsupervised graph-to-text and text-to-graph generation via cycle training. In *Proceedings of the 3rd International Workshop on Natural Language Generation from the Semantic Web (WebNLG+)*, pages 77–88, Dublin, Ireland (Virtual). Association for Computational Linguistics.

Kancharla Aditya Hari, Bhavyajeet Singh, Anubhav Sharma, and Vasudeva Varma. 2023. Webnlg challenge 2023: Domain adaptive machine translation for low-resource multilingual rdf-to-text generation. Technical report, IIT Hyberhadad. WebNLG 2023 System Description.

Zdeněk Kasner and Ondřej Dušek. 2020. Train hard, finetune easy: Multilingual denoising for RDF-to-text generation. In *Proceedings of the 3rd International Workshop on Natural Language Generation from the Semantic Web (WebNLG+)*, pages 171–176, Dublin, Ireland (Virtual). Association for Computational Linguistics.

Maxim Kazakov, Julia Preobrazhenskaya, Ivan Bulychev, and Aleksandr Shain. 2023. Webnlg-interno: Utilizing fred-t5 to address the rdf-to-text problem. Technical report, Pulkovo Observatory. WebNLG 2023 System Description.

Nalin Kumar, Saad Obaid ul Islam, and Ondrej Dusek. 2023. Better translation + split and generate for multilingual rdf-to-text. Technical report, Charles University. WebNLG 2023 System Description.

Michela Lorandi and Anya Belz. 2023. Data-to-text generation for severlay under-resourced languages with gpt-3.5: A bit of help needed from google translate. Technical report, ADAPT, Dublin City University. WebNLG 2023 System Description.

Simon Mille, Stamatia Dasiopoulou, Beatriz Fisas, and Leo Wanner. 2019. Teaching FORGe to verbalize DBpedia properties in Spanish. In *Proceedings of the 12th International Conference on Natural Language Generation*, pages 473–483, Tokyo, Japan. Association for Computational Linguistics.

Simon Mille, Elaine Ui Dhonnchadha, Stamatis Dasiopoulou, Lauren Cassidy, Brian Davis, and Anya Belz. 2023. Dcu/tcd-forge at webnlg'23: Irish rules! Technical report, ADAPT, Dublin City University. WebNLG 2023 System Description.

Kishore Papineni, Salim Roukos, Todd Ward, and Wei-Jing Zhu. 2002. Bleu: a method for automatic evaluation of machine translation. In *Proceedings of the 40th Annual Meeting of the Association for Computational Linguistics*, pages 311–318, Philadelphia, Pennsylvania, USA. Association for Computational Linguistics.

Maja Popović. 2017. chrF++: words helping character n-grams. In *Proceedings of the Second Conference on Machine Translation*, pages 612–618, Copenhagen, Denmark. Association for Computational Linguistics.

Matt Post. 2018. A call for clarity in reporting BLEU scores. In *Proceedings of the Third Conference on Machine Translation: Research Papers*, pages 186–191, Brussels, Belgium. Association for Computational Linguistics.

Matthew Snover, Bonnie Dorr, Richard Schwartz, Linnea Micciulla, and John Makhoul. 2006. A study of translation edit rate with targeted human annotation. In *In Proceedings of Association for Machine Translation in the Americas*, pages 223–231.

NLLB Team, Marta R. Costa-jussà, James Cross, Onur Çelebi, Maha Elbayad, Kenneth Heafield, Kevin Heffernan, Elahe Kalbassi, Janice Lam, Daniel Licht, Jean Maillard, Anna Sun, Skyler Wang, Guillaume Wenzek, Al Youngblood, Bapi Akula, Loic Barrault, Gabriel Mejia Gonzalez, Prangthip Hansanti, John Hoffman, Semarley Jarrett, Kaushik Ram Sadagopan, Dirk Rowe, Shannon Spruit, Chau Tran, Pierre Andrews, Necip Fazil Ayan, Shruti Bhosale, Sergey Edunov, Angela Fan, Cynthia Gao, Vedanuj Goswami, Francisco Guzmán, Philipp Koehn, Alexandre Mourachko, Christophe Ropers, Safiyyah Saleem, Holger Schwenk, and Jeff Wang. 2022. No language left behind: Scaling human-centered machine translation.

Biao Zhang, Philip Williams, Ivan Titov, and Rico Sennrich. 2020a. Improving massively multilingual neural machine translation and zero-shot translation. In *Proceedings of the 58th Annual Meeting of the Association for Computational Linguistics*, pages 1628–1639, Online. Association for Computational Linguistics.

Tianyi Zhang, Varsha Kishore, Felix Wu, Kilian Q. Weinberger, and Yoav Artzi. 2020b. Bertscore: Evaluating text generation with bert. In *International Conference on Learning Representations*.

A Russian Human Evaluations

As explained in the main body of the paper, we are presenting the results from the Russian human evaluation separately in this section, because of concerns about their reliability.

Table 9 is the Pearson correlation matrix for all automatic and human-assessed output quality measures for Russian. As discussed in the paper, the human and automatic measures do not correlate at all.

The results from the one-way ANOVAs for Russian can be seen in Table 10. Systems are shown in order of Fluency means. Unlike the other languages, there are three different system rankings among the four output quality measures.

The columns containing single capital letters in Table 10 show the homogeneous subsets of systems as determined by a post-hoc Tukey HSD analysis. Systems whose scores are not significantly different (at the .05 level) share a letter. Unlike the other languages, there is just one significant difference (Interno's Fluency is significantly better than IREL's.

Table 11 shows the effect sizes and associated p-values for Russian. What we should be seeing is a strong and significant effect of System on each output quality measure, but we're only seeing a slight effect on Fluency, for the other measures, there is no effect, i.e. the scores have a lot of randomness in them.

Metric	BLEU	chrF++	TER ↓	Addition	Fluency	Omission	Repetition
BLEU	1.0	0.96	−0.92	0.06	0.1	0.05	0.07
chrF++	0.96	1.0	−0.92	0.07	0.14	0.08	0.07
TER ↓	−0.92	−0.92	1.0	−0.08	−0.13	−0.06	−0.11
Addition	0.06	0.07	−0.08	1.0	0.35	0.47	0.25
Fluency	0.1	0.14	−0.13	0.35	1.0	0.11	0.37
Omission	0.05	0.08	−0.06	0.47	0.11	1.0	0.16
Repetition	0.07	0.07	−0.11	0.25	0.37	0.16	1.0

Table 9: Pearson correlation matrix for all automatic and human-assessed output quality measures for Russian.

Language	**System**	**Fluency**			**Addition**		**Omission**		**Repetition**	
Russian	Interno	4.13	A		0.83	A	0.91	A	0.9	A
	Human reference	4.02	A	B	0.82	A	0.87	A	0.92	A
	CUNI-Wue	3.99	A	B	0.85	A	0.84	A	0.89	A
	IREL	3.65		B	0.79	A	0.84	A	0.88	A

Table 10: Post-hoc Tukey HSD (alpha = .05) analysis results for Russian. The columns containing single capital letters show the homogeneous subsets of systems. Human reference results are shaded in light grey.

Language	**Fluency**				**Addition**			
	System	Category	# Triples	Evaluator	System	Category	Triples	Evaluator
Russian	3.51 (p=.015)	1.53 (p=.145)	4.39 (p<.001)	77.42 (p<.001)	0.43 (p=.735)	1.81 (p=.075)	1.41 (p=.208)	14.86 (p<.001)

(a) ANOVA results for Fluency and Addition.

Language	**Omission**				**Repetition**			
	System	Category	# Triples	Evaluator	System	Category	Triples	Evaluator
Russian	0.94 (p=.422)	3.16 (p=.002)	2.33 (p=.032)	6.74 (p<.001)	0.31 (p=.815)	1.84 (p=.069)	4.2 (p<.001)	29.32 (p<.001)

(b) ANOVA results for Omission and Repetition .

Table 11: ANOVA results for Russian based on System, Category, Number of triples and Evaluator.

WebNLG-Interno: Utilizing FRED-T5 to address the RDF-to-text problem

Maxim Kazakov
Petal Cloud Technology Co.,Ltd
HSE University
kazakov.maxim@huawei.com

Julia Preobrazhenskaya
Lobachevsky State University
enjulia17@gmail.com

Ivan Bulychev
Lobachevsky State University
halkimic@gmail.com

Aleksandr Shain
Petal Cloud Technology Co.,Ltd
Pulkovo Observatory
alexander.shain@huawei.com

Abstract

We present our solution for the Russian RDF-to-text generation task of the WebNLG Challenge 2023 [1]. We use the pretrained large language model named FRED-T5 (Zmitrovich et al., 2023) to finetune on the train dataset. Also, we propose several types of prompt and run experiments to analyze their effectiveness. Our submission achieves 0.373 TER on the test dataset, taking the first place according to the results of the automatic evaluation and outperforming the best result of the previous challenge by 0.025. The code of our solution is available at the following link: https://github.com/Ivan30003/webnlg_interno

1 Introduction

Recently released large language models (a.k.a. LLMs) like GPT-4 (OpenAI, 2023), BLOOM (Scao et al., 2022), LLaMA (Touvron et al., 2023) and PaLM (Chowdhery et al., 2022) proved the ability of deep neural networks to generate realistic texts, maintain a human-like conversation and answer factual questions based on the information contained in the training data. However, real-life applications of LLMs could benefit from extracting relevant information from external databases to provide a user with a proper answer. Data in databases typically have a structured form, and one of the main challenges is to present extracted information in the natural sentences.

The RDF-to-text track of the WebNLG challenge aims to address that particular problem. Given the data presented in a common RDF format, the task is to generate a natural utterance that conveys information from the structured data. The RDF data format operates with three entities - subject, object and predicate, where the latter represents a type of relations between subject and object. Such entities form a triple, and each data sample is represented as a tripleset consisting of one or several triples (Table 1).

It was mentioned by Kasner and Dušek (2020), such tripleset representation in English can be seen as a noisy version of a target utterance, and denoising autoencoders like T5 (Raffel et al., 2020) and BART (Lewis et al., 2020) may provide a stable solution to the problem. In Russian track of the challenge we additionally expect generated utterances to be in Russian while the triples remain in English. That can be handled either by a two stage solution where translation (of input triples or generated utterances) performed as a separate step, or by an end-to-end solution - for the such case, encoder-decoder architectures are suitable as well (Liu et al., 2020).

The above assumptions are supported by the results of the previous challenge (Castro Ferreira et al., 2020), where 3 out of 6 solutions for the RDF-to-text Russian track were based on a pretrained multilingual BART model (Kasner and Dušek, 2020; Yang et al., 2020; Li et al., 2020), and the winning solution was based on a T5 model pretrained on a large bilingual (*en*, *ru*) corpus of structured data (Agarwal et al., 2020).

In contrast to the previous solutions, we focus solely on the Russian track and use the state-of-the-art LLM for russian language named FRED-T5 (Zmitrovich et al., 2023), assuming that pretraning on a large corpus of Russian texts can benefit the model's ability to generate more realistic utterances. We also experiment with prompt con-

[1] https://synalp.gitlabpages.inria.fr/webnlg-challenge/challenge_2023

Proceedings of the Workshop on Multimodal, Multilingual Natural Language Generation and Multilingual WebNLG Challenge (MM-NLG 2023), pages 67–72
September 12, 2023 ©2023 Association for Computational Linguistics

XML	<entry category="Airport" eid="1309" shape="(X (X (X)))" shape_type="chain" size="2"> < originaltripleset > <otriple>Aarhus_Airport | location | Tirstrup</otriple> <otriple>Tirstrup | country | Denmark</otriple> </ originaltripleset > <modifiedtripleset> <mtriple>Aarhus_Airport | location | Tirstrup</mtriple> <mtriple>Tirstrup | country | Denmark</mtriple> </modifiedtripleset> <lex comment="" lang="en" lid="Id1">Aarhus Airport is located in Tirstrup, Denmark.</lex> <lex comment="" lang="en" lid="Id2">The location of Aarhus Airport is Tirstrup, in Denmark.</lex> <dbpedialinks> <dbpedialink direction="en2ru">Denmark | sameAs | Дания</dbpedialink> </dbpedialinks> <links> <link direction="en2ru">Tirstrup | sameAs | Тирструп</link> <link direction="en2ru">Aarhus Airport | includes | Орхус</link> </links> </entry>
Labels	Аэропорт Орхус расположен в Тирструпе, Дания. Место расположения орхусского аэропорта - Тирструп, в Дании.

Table 1: Example of XML data and labels for Russian track of WebNLG Challenge. *<modifiedtripleset>* is used as linearized triples.

struction enriching tripleset with additional data presented in raw XML. Our final submission is based on a FRED-T5 model finetuned on the train dataset with automatically translated predicates and the properties "links", "dbpedialinks", "category" and "size" included into the prompt. Our submission achieves 0.373 TER on the test dataset, taking the first place according to the results of the automatic evaluation and outperforming the best result of the previous challenge by 0.025.

2 Data

The original dataset for RDF-to-text task is presented in the XML-file format. It is split into train, dev and test sets. RDF-triples were extracted from DBpedia and have the subject-predicate-object structure linearized with vertical bars as separators (Table 1). The number of triples in data samples varies from 1 to 7, and each sample belongs to one of 9 categories: Building, Astronaut, Airport, SportsTeam, ComicsCharacter, CelestialBody, Monument, University, Food.

Category names and triples are initially presented in English. However, links between English and Russian entities from subjects and objects of RDF-triples are provided by *<links>* and *<dbpedialinks>* properties. These links are encoded by two kinds of relations: "includes" and "sameAs", the latter of which can be considered as an explicit translation.

The model's input is the prompt, and we discuss the prompt construction in the next section. As an output, we expect to receive a generated text similar to the text from the label. However, each sample may contain multiple labels that represent a natural language text corresponding to triples (Table 1). Hence we transform each label with the corresponding input into a separate sample for training. In total, the training dataset consists of 14630 samples (from 5573 original samples). Validation and test datasets have 790 and 1102 samples, respectively, on which we performed multi-reference model evaluation.

3 Experimental setup

3.1 Triple Processing

In our approach, data preparation process included two stages - data pre-processing and prompt construction. At data pre-pocessing stage, we converted predicate names and categories from so called 'camel' case to multi-word expressions (e.g. "isPartOf" becomes "is part of"), analogous to (Agarwal et al., 2020). Also, we removed underscore from all occurrences of Object and Subject names in linearized triples, *<links>* and *<dbpedialinks>* (e.g. "Aarhus_Airport" becomes "Aarhus Airport").

At prompt construction stage, we considered three ways of constructing prompt (Table 2). In a "Simple" case, the prompt is presented as a set of pre-processed triples, extracted from the original dataset and separated by semicolon. Unlike the works presented at the challenge in previous years, we did not use any special tokens to indicate the subject, predicate and object.

However, it was noticed that the model faces the problem of translating proper nouns from English to Russian: in some cases the translation was either incorrect or sounded unnatural. To solve this issue, pre-processed links with subjects and

Name	Prompt
Simple	{ Aarhus Airport | location | Tirstrup }; { Tirstrup | country | Denmark }
With links	Соотношения: { Aarhus Airport | location | Tirstrup }; { Tirstrup | country | Denmark }.\nДополнительные соотношения: { Tirstrup = Тирструп }; { Aarhus Airport >= Орхус }.\nСсылки: { Denmark = Дания }.
Full	Категория: Airport.\nЧисло соотношений: 2. Соотношения: { Aarhus Airport | location | Tirstrup }; { Tirstrup | country | Denmark }.\nДополнительные соотношения: { Tirstrup = Тирструп }; { Aarhus Airport >= Орхус }.\nСсылки: { Denmark = Дания }.\nКороткое высказывание:
Translated	Категория: Аэропорт.\nЧисло соотношений: 2. Соотношения: { Aarhus Airport | месторасположение | Tirstrup }; { Tirstrup | страна | Denmark }.\nДополнительные соотношения: { Tirstrup = Тирструп }; { Aarhus Airport >= Орхус }.\nСсылки: { Denmark = Дания }.\nКороткое высказывание:

Table 2: Examples of the proposed prompts. Translation of keywords: Соотношения - Relations; Дополнительные соотношения - Additional relations; Ссылки - Links; Категория - Category; Число соотношений - Number of relations; Короткое высказывание - Short statement.

objects translation from the original dataset were included in the basic version. We preserved original *<links>* and *<dbpedialinks>* division by using keywords "Ссылки" and "Дополнительные соотношения", respectively, and encoded "sameAs" and "includes" relations by "=" and ">=". Moreover, we added a keyword "Соотношения" for the triples to orient a model in the given data. We denote such prompt as "With links".

In order to provide a model with the context and simplify its "perception" process of the received data, it was suggested to add some metadata, such as pre-processed category names and tripleset size, to the prompt. We denote that prompt as "Full".

To prepare our final dataset, we automatically translated predicates and category names (without taking into account the context), expecting that to reduce the number of grammar and morphological mistakes while generating sentences in Russian. The minimum number of characters in our prompt is 171, the maximum is 2179, the average is 450. Examples of each prompt construction is presented in Table 2.

3.2 Training setup

For our experiments we use a large language model named FRED-T5 with 1.7 billion parameters (Zmitrovich et al., 2023). The model is based on T5 architecture (Raffel et al., 2020) and trained on a large corpus of Russian texts using a mixture of denoising objectives analogous to UL2 (Tay et al., 2023). We also experiment with a multilingual mT5 model (Xue et al., 2021) in *Large* (1.2B) and *XL* (3.7B) configurations. Comparing the results of FRED-T5 and mT5, we aim to examine how critical it is for the task to use a model trained specifically for Russian language.

	LoRA trainable # params	Total # params
FRED-T5	7 077 888	1 747 435 008
mT5-Large	4 718 592	1 234 299 904
mT5-XL	9 437 184	3 752 056 832

Table 3: Model size

To start with, we used the pretrained checkpoints [2] [3] [4] and finetuned the models solely on the train dataset for 20 epochs with total $batch\_size = 16$ on $4 \times V100$ GPUs. To make training process more efficient, we used LoRA method (Hu et al., 2022) with $rank = 16, \alpha = 32, dropout = 0.05$ as a commonly used configuration. We used standard

[2]FRED-T5: https://huggingface.co/ai-forever/FRED-T5-1.7B

[3]mT5-Large: https://huggingface.co/google/mt5-large

[4]mT5-XL: https://huggingface.co/google/mt5-xl

Team Name	**BLEU**	**METEOR**	**chrF++**	**TER ↓**	**BERT F1**
WebNLG-Interno (ours)	**54.711**	**0.700**	**0.690**	**0.373**	**0.920**
cuni-ufal (Kasner and Dušek, 2020)	52.930	0.672	0.677	0.398	0.909
bt5 (Agarwal et al., 2020)	51.630	0.676	0.683	0.420	0.907
Baseline (Castro Ferreira et al., 2020)	25.500	0.467	0.514	0.665	0.837

Table 4: Automatic evaluation results of our submission and the leaders of the previous challenge.

cross-entropy loss objective with label smoothing factor $alpha = 0.1$ for model finetuning. It was decided to choose the best checkpoint by the METEOR value on the dev dataset since this metric has been used as an objective in the previous challenge (Castro Ferreira et al., 2020). To obtain the final results, we used beam search with $width = 5$.

4 Results

In this section we provide the results of our experiments. We finetuned FRED-T5 model on the training dataset with different prompts. Table 5 shows the results of automatic evaluation on dev and test splits. Comparing the results of finetuning the model on "Simple" and "With links" prompts, we observe that enriching prompt with *<links>* and *<dbpedialinks>* data leads to a significant gain in generation quality on average. However, this gain is not consistent as we noticed drop in performance for a big portion of samples. Also, we cannot confirm that using *<links>* and *<dbpedialinks>* data contributes to a better translation of named entities, although it does help for some samples. It seems that the additional data simply enables a better convergence. The same conclusion was made for the "Full" prompt, although the gain is not so noticeable.

Also, we conducted the same experiments with translated predicates and categories. To our surprise, this did not lead to a significant improvement, and for the "Simple" prompt it even worsened the model's performance. The possible explanation for this is that the target labels are quite different from the translated predicates, and FRED-T5 already has a decent translation ability.

In order to understand what advantages FRED-T5 has over multilingual LLMs, we finetuned mT5-Large and mT5-XL models on the train dataset with "Full Translated" prompt. From Table 6 we can conclude that mT5-XL and FRED-T5 demonstrate comparable performance, while FRED-T5 is more than twice smaller than mT5-XL (Table 3). At the same time, mT5-Large is closer to FRED-T5 in terms of model size, but converges with lower accuracy, especially on the dev dataset. Considering the fact that from architecture perspective all models are based on T5, we may assume that FRED-T5 benefits from its pretraining scheme and the target language corpora.

In our submission we used FRED-T5 model finetuned on the train dataset with "Full Translated" prompt. Table 4 shows automatic evaluation results on the test dataset in comparison to the leaders of the previous challenge (Castro Ferreira et al., 2020). Our model outperforms existing solutions by a significant margin, although does not yield a drastic improvement.

5 Conclusion

We presented a solution for the RDF-to-text problem in Russian. Our solution is based on FRED-T5 large language model, utilizes additional information from raw XML data and is aided by machine translation. The developed solution achieves 0.373 TER on the WebNLG-2023 test dataset and outperforms existing solutions by a large margin. Furthermore, conducted experiments demonstrated that translated data is not crucial for the solution and provides only a small gain, while a proper pretraining plays a major role.

Acknowledgements

We would like to express our gratitude to Wenshuai Yin and Alexey Trushkov for their support in our participation in the challenge, and to Leonid Beynenson for his valuable technical advices.

References

Oshin Agarwal, Mihir Kale, Heming Ge, Siamak Shakeri, and Rami Al-Rfou. 2020. Machine translation aided bilingual data-to-text generation and semantic parsing. In *Proceedings of the 3rd International Workshop on Natural Language Generation from the Semantic Web (WebNLG+)*, pages 125–130, Dublin,

	Dev					
	Simple		**With links**		**Full**	
	Original	**Translated**	**Original**	**Translated**	**Original**	**Translated**
BLEU	49.338	48.286	50.356	**51.020**	50.630	50.708
METEOR	0.65	0.64	**0.66**	**0.66**	**0.66**	**0.66**
chrF++	0.66	0.65	**0.67**	**0.67**	**0.67**	**0.67**
TER ↓	0.442	0.443	0.423	0.419	0.421	**0.416**
BERT-SCORE P	0.90	0.90	**0.91**	**0.91**	**0.91**	**0.91**
BERT-SCORE R	**0.90**	0.89	**0.90**	**0.90**	**0.90**	**0.90**
BERT-SCORE F1	0.90	0.90	0.90	0.90	0.90	**0.91**

	Test					
	Simple		**With links**		**Full**	
	Original	**Translated**	**Original**	**Translated**	**Original**	**Translated**
BLEU	54.173	54.028	54.449	**54.960**	54.956	54.711
METEOR	0.69	0.69	0.69	0.69	**0.70**	**0.70**
chrF++	**0.69**	0.68	**0.69**	**0.69**	**0.69**	**0.69**
TER ↓	0.386	0.389	0.381	0.381	0.379	**0.373**
BERT-SCORE P	**0.92**	**0.92**	**0.92**	**0.92**	**0.92**	**0.92**
BERT-SCORE R	**0.91**	**0.91**	**0.91**	**0.91**	**0.91**	**0.91**
BERT-SCORE F1	0.91	0.91	0.91	**0.92**	**0.92**	**0.92**

Table 5: FRED-T5 results. Best checkpoint is chosen by METEOR value on dev split. The completions obtained using beam search with $width = 5$.

	Dev		
	FRED-T5	**mT5 XL**	**mT5 Large**
BLEU	**50.708**	50.362	48.588
METEOR	**0.66**	0.65	0.64
chrF++	**0.67**	0.66	0.66
TER ↓	0.416	**0.411**	0.434
BERT P	**0.91**	**0.91**	**0.91**
BERT R	**0.90**	**0.90**	**0.90**
BERT F1	**0.91**	0.90	0.90

	Test		
	FRED-T5	**mT5 XL**	**mT5 Large**
BLEU	**54.711**	54.688	54.121
METEOR	**0.70**	0.69	0.69
chrF++	**0.69**	**0.69**	**0.69**
TER ↓	**0.373**	0.380	0.377
BERT P	**0.92**	**0.92**	**0.92**
BERT R	**0.91**	**0.91**	**0.91**
BERT F1	**0.92**	0.91	**0.92**

Table 6: Results of the models finetuned using the "Full Translated" prompt. Best checkpoint is chosen by METEOR value on dev split. The completions obtained using beam search with $width = 5$.

Ireland (Virtual). Association for Computational Linguistics.

Thiago Castro Ferreira, Claire Gardent, Nikolai Ilinykh, Chris van der Lee, Simon Mille, Diego Moussallem, and Anastasia Shimorina. 2020. The 2020 bilingual, bi-directional WebNLG+ shared task: Overview and evaluation results (WebNLG+ 2020). In *Proceedings of the 3rd International Workshop on Natural Language Generation from the Semantic Web (WebNLG+)*, pages 55–76, Dublin, Ireland (Virtual). Association for Computational Linguistics.

Aakanksha Chowdhery, Sharan Narang, Jacob Devlin, Maarten Bosma, Gaurav Mishra, Adam Roberts, Paul Barham, Hyung Won Chung, Charles Sutton, Sebastian Gehrmann, et al. 2022. Palm: Scaling language modeling with pathways. *arXiv preprint arXiv:2204.02311*.

Edward J Hu, Yelong Shen, Phillip Wallis, Zeyuan Allen-Zhu, Yuanzhi Li, Shean Wang, Lu Wang, and Weizhu Chen. 2022. LoRA: Low-rank adaptation of large language models. In *International Conference on Learning Representations*.

Zdeněk Kasner and Ondřej Dušek. 2020. Train hard, finetune easy: Multilingual denoising for RDF-to-text generation. In *Proceedings of the 3rd International Workshop on Natural Language Generation from the Semantic Web (WebNLG+)*, pages 171–176, Dublin, Ireland (Virtual). Association for Computational Linguistics.

Mike Lewis, Yinhan Liu, Naman Goyal, Marjan Ghazvininejad, Abdelrahman Mohamed, Omer Levy, Veselin Stoyanov, and Luke Zettlemoyer. 2020. BART: Denoising sequence-to-sequence pre-training for natural language generation, translation, and comprehension. In *Proceedings of the 58th Annual Meeting of the Association for Computational Linguistics*, pages 7871–7880, Online. Association for Computational Linguistics.

Xintong Li, Aleksandre Maskharashvili, Symon Jory Stevens-Guille, and Michael White. 2020. Leveraging large pretrained models for WebNLG 2020. In *Proceedings of the 3rd International Workshop on Natural Language Generation from the Semantic Web (WebNLG+)*, pages 117–124, Dublin, Ireland (Virtual). Association for Computational Linguistics.

Yinhan Liu, Jiatao Gu, Naman Goyal, Xian Li, Sergey Edunov, Marjan Ghazvininejad, Mike Lewis, and Luke Zettlemoyer. 2020. Multilingual denoising pre-training for neural machine translation. *Transactions of the Association for Computational Linguistics*, 8:726–742.

OpenAI. 2023. GPT-4 technical report. *arXiv preprint arXiv:2303.08774*.

Colin Raffel, Noam Shazeer, Adam Roberts, Katherine Lee, Sharan Narang, Michael Matena, Yanqi Zhou, Wei Li, and Peter J Liu. 2020. Exploring the limits of transfer learning with a unified text-to-text transformer. *The Journal of Machine Learning Research*, 21(1):5485–5551.

Teven Le Scao, Angela Fan, Christopher Akiki, Ellie Pavlick, Suzana Ilić, Daniel Hesslow, Roman Castagné, Alexandra Sasha Luccioni, François Yvon, Matthias Gallé, et al. 2022. Bloom: A 176b-parameter open-access multilingual language model. *arXiv preprint arXiv:2211.05100*.

Yi Tay, Mostafa Dehghani, Vinh Q. Tran, Xavier Garcia, Jason Wei, Xuezhi Wang, Hyung Won Chung, Dara Bahri, Tal Schuster, Steven Zheng, Denny Zhou, Neil Houlsby, and Donald Metzler. 2023. UL2: Unifying language learning paradigms. In *The Eleventh International Conference on Learning Representations*.

Hugo Touvron, Thibaut Lavril, Gautier Izacard, Xavier Martinet, Marie-Anne Lachaux, Timothée Lacroix, Baptiste Rozière, Naman Goyal, Eric Hambro, Faisal Azhar, et al. 2023. Llama: Open and efficient foundation language models. *arXiv preprint arXiv:2302.13971*.

Linting Xue, Noah Constant, Adam Roberts, Mihir Kale, Rami Al-Rfou, Aditya Siddhant, Aditya Barua, and Colin Raffel. 2021. mT5: A massively multilingual pre-trained text-to-text transformer. In *Proceedings of the 2021 Conference of the North American Chapter of the Association for Computational Linguistics: Human Language Technologies*, pages 483–498, Online. Association for Computational Linguistics.

Zixiaofan Yang, Arash Einolghozati, Hakan Inan, Keith Diedrick, Angela Fan, Pinar Donmez, and Sonal Gupta. 2020. Improving text-to-text pre-trained models for the graph-to-text task. In *Proceedings of the 3rd International Workshop on Natural Language Generation from the Semantic Web (WebNLG+)*, pages 107–116, Dublin, Ireland (Virtual). Association for Computational Linguistics.

Dmitry Zmitrovich, Andrei Kalmykov, Vitaly Kadulin, Mikhail Novikov, and Alexey Khoroshilov. 2023. FRED: Full-scale russian enhanced denoisers T5.

Better Translation + Split and Generate for Multilingual RDF-to-Text

Nalin Kumar[♣], **Saad Obaid ul Islam**[♠], **Ondřej Dušek**[♣]
[♣]Charles University, Faculty of Mathematics and Physics, Prague, Czechia
[♠]Center For Artificial Intelligence and Data Science, University of Würzburg, Germany
kumarnal@student.cuni.cz, saad.obaid-ul-islam@uni-wuerzburg.de, odusek@ufal.mff.cuni.cz

Abstract

This paper presents system descriptions of our submitted outputs for WebNLG Challenge 2023. We use mT5 in multi-task and multilingual settings to generate more fluent and reliable verbalizations of the given RDF triples. Furthermore, we introduce a partial decoding technique to produce more elaborate yet simplified outputs. Additionally, we demonstrate the significance of employing better translation systems in creating training data.

1 Introduction

State-of-the-art in natural language generation (NLG) recently has benefited from self-supervised pretrained language models (PLMs) such as BART, T5, and GPT-2 (Lewis et al., 2020; Raffel et al., 2020; Radford et al., 2019), which provided performance improvements on many NLG tasks (Zhang et al., 2020b; Wei et al., 2021; Kale and Rastogi, 2020). One of the most prominent NLG tasks is data-to-text generation (Wiseman et al., 2017), with multiple public datasets, including WebNLG (Colin et al., 2016), ToTTo (Parikh et al., 2020), or DART (Nan et al., 2021). A significant problem of these datasets is their limitation to English only, which effectively rules out their application to other languages; incorporating low-resource languages in NLG is generally an open problem (Ruder, 2019).

Researchers addressed this by multilingual PLMs like mT5 (Xue et al., 2021) and mBART (Liu et al., 2020) pre-trained on massively multilingual corpora like Common Crawl 101.[1] Unfortunately, given the disproportionate representation of low-resource languages in multilingual datasets,[2] the efficacy of PLMs on these languages is compromised. Efforts are being made to improve PLM performance for low-resource languages via cross-lingual transfer (Conneau et al., 2020). To assess the state-of-the-art performance and spur development in data-to-text NLG techniques for low-resource languages, the WebNLG 2023 challenge features five non-English languages – four entirely new low-resource ones: Maltese (*Mt*), Welsh (*Cy*), Irish (*Ga*) and Breton (*Br*), with the addition of Russian (*Ru*) from the 2020 iteration (Castro Ferreira et al., 2020). While development and test sets for the low-resource languages were created by hand, training sets are machine-translated.

In our submission of WebNLG 2023 challenge, we use the power of mT5 (Xue et al., 2021), a multilingual transformer model trained in a multi-task fashion. To boost performance on low-resource languages, we employ several additional steps in finetuning and inference: (1) We improve WebNLG 2023 training data by re-translating with a stronger machine translation (MT) model (Costa-jussà et al., 2022). (2) We finetune either individual models for each language (single-task setting), or a single model for all languages (multi-task setting). (3) We generate text by splitting the input RDF triples and decoding a subset of triples at a time. We publish our code and submitted outputs on GitHub.[3]

2 Related Works

A lot of non-English NLG works addresses either surface realization (Mille et al., 2018; Fan and Gardent, 2020) or text-to-text tasks such as summarization (Straka et al., 2018; Scialom et al., 2020; Hasan et al., 2021) or question generation (Shakeri et al., 2021). In data-to-text generation, Dušek and Jurčíček (2019) trained a RNN-based model for Czech, van der Lee et al. (2020) apply a similar architecture for Dutch. A RNN decoder has also been applied to Japanese in a multimodal setup (Ishigaki et al., 2021). Recent works mostly

[1]https://commoncrawl.org/

[2]https://commoncrawl.github.io/cc-crawl-statistics/plots/languages

[3]https://github.com/knalin55/CUNI_Wue-WebNLG23_Submission

Proceedings of the Workshop on Multimodal, Multilingual Natural Language Generation and Multilingual WebNLG Challenge (MM-NLG 2023), pages 73–79
September 12, 2023 ©2023 Association for Computational Linguistics

use transformer-based architectures. Kale and Roy (2020) applied a custom transformer pretrained for MT to a Czech data-to-text task. Several systems targeted WebNLG 2020's Russian task (Castro Ferreira et al., 2020). Agarwal et al. (2020)'s system features a custom-trained bilingual T5-derived transformer, the works of Kasner and Dušek (2020) and Zhou and Lampouras (2021) build on the standard mBART model. Our approach combines the use of MT for preprocessing with standard multilingual PLMs and adds multi-task learning and sentence-level generation.

3 WebNLG 2023 Task Description

The WebNLG challenge focuses on generating text from a set of RDF triples. Input RDF triples are extracted from DBpedia (Auer et al., 2007) and the corresponding reference texts are gathered through crowdsourcing. Previous iterations (Gardent et al., 2017; Castro Ferreira et al., 2020) focused on English and Russian. The 2023 WebNLG challenge includes 4 low-resource languages (*Mt*, *Cy*, *Ga*, *Br*), along with Russian (*Ru*). The development and test sets are manually translated from English, but the training data is a result of MT by the Edinburgh Zero translation system (Zhang et al., 2020a).

3.1 Automatic Metrics

WebNLG 2023 has been evaluated by automatic metrics so far. These include BLEU (Post, 2018), METEOR (Lavie and Agarwal, 2007), chrF++ (Popović, 2015), and TER (Snover et al., 2006). Comparison against multiple references is used for *Ru*, other languages use a single reference per instance.

3.2 Organizer Baselines

The organizer-provided baselines for *Ru* include Kasner and Dušek (2020)'s finetuned mBART and the 2020 Challenge baseline, the FORGE system (Mille et al., 2019) coupled with Google Translate. The baseline for *Mt*, *Ga*, *Cy*, *Br* is the 2020 Challenge English system of Guo et al. (2020), coupled with Edinburgh Zero MT (Zhang et al., 2020a).

4 Proposed Approaches

Our own approach builds on multilingual transformer PLMs, but improves input data processing in the low-resource languages by better translation or filtering (Section 4.1) and employs two simple yet effective strategies to improve generation: multitask learning (Section 4.2) and splitting complex inputs for decoding (Section 4.3).

4.1 Better Translation & Data Filtering

To improve on the challenge's generate-and-translate baseline (see Section 3.2) and show the effect of the quality of MT-processed training data on the outputs in low-resource languages, we replace or filter the baseline MT system outputs. We then use these improved MT outputs both in an alternative generate-and-translate baseline and as improved training data for our direct NLG methods.

Specifically, for *Mt*, *Ga*, and *Cy*, we replace the Edinburgh Zero System (Zhang et al., 2020a) with the state-of-the-art NLLB system (Costa-jussà et al., 2022). Additionally, we modify the translation process. The original training data was created by translating *whole En verbalizations*. However, based on our inspection, the resulting translations are often incomplete. We counter this problem by translating *individual En sentences* using NLLB.

For *Br* where NLLB is unavailable, we filter out inconsistent examples from the existing MT-processed training data. Since each input set of triples in the training set typically corresponds to multiple verbalizations, we calculate the ratios of lengths of all *En* verbalizations to their corresponding *Br* translations. Subsequently, we filter out the *Br* verbalizations with ratios (to their corresponding *En* original) smaller than half the maximum ratio for the given input triple set.

4.2 Multitask Learning (MTL)

Multitask learning (MTL) trains models on diverse tasks simultaneously, improving generalization to different tasks and domains (Liu et al., 2019; Raffel et al., 2020; Sanh et al., 2022). We apply MTL to improve the model's understanding of input triples: In addition to data-to-text generation in the target language, we use translation from English and data-to-text in English as auxiliary tasks. The model learns to distinguish tasks by different prompts.

4.3 Split and Generate (SaG)

Due to data quality problems being more common in larger input triple sets, PLMs struggle to generate fluent and accurate outputs for complex inputs. In a previous study, Narayan et al. (2017) introduced a split and rephrase approach for sentence simplification. Their method involved creating parallel data by finding the verbalizations of a subset of input

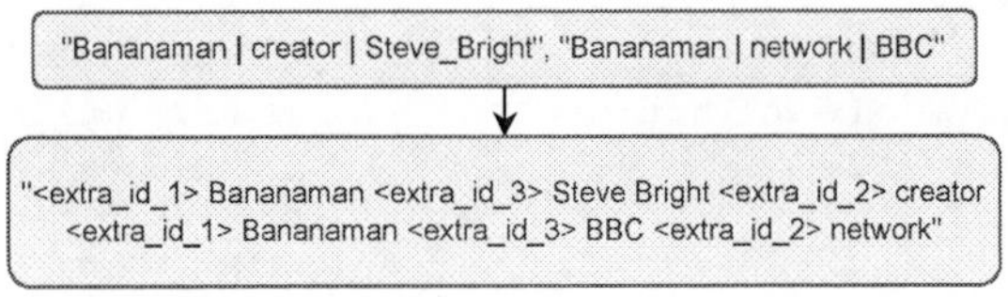

Figure 1: An instance of the preprocessing step

triples in the WebNLG dataset. Building upon this concept and following earlier works on sentence-by-sentence verbalization (Moryossef et al., 2019; Ferreira et al., 2019), we employ a straightforward decoding strategy: We split the input triple sets into subsets based on the same triple subject, generate outputs for the individual subsets, and subsequently concatenate the generated texts. We further experiment with a subset size limit – we partition the subset S into further subsets if its size exceeds a pre-set value n.

5 Experiments

5.1 Data preprocessing

As is common in PLM-based RDF-to-text systems, we linearize the input triples. We use three special tokens (newly added to the model) to mark subjects, objects, and predicates. We remove underscores from entities. The triples are concatenated using a subject-object-verb order (see Figure 1). Following mT5 pretraining methodology, we use prompts to distinguish tasks. For RDF triple verbalization, we adopt the prompt format: "*RDF-to-text in <lang>: <input>*" where *<lang>* is the target language and *<input>* denotes the input triples.

5.2 Model Parameters

We use the base variant of mT5 (Xue et al., 2021).[4] We train all our models for 30 epochs with batch sizes of 8 and select our best model based on validation loss. We use beam search decoding with beam size 4. To prevent repetitive outputs, we also use a repetition penalty $rp = 3.5$ (Keskar et al., 2019).[5]

5.3 Model Variants

We experiment with the following system variants (in both training and inference):

baseline For each language, we simply fine-tune mT5 on the organizer-provided training data.

base-(NLLB/DF) For *Mt*, *Ga* and *Cy*, we retranslate the training dat using NLLB (Costa-jussà et al., 2022) and for *Br*, we apply simple data filtering, as described in Section 4.1. We do not apply this step for *Ru* where the training data is of sufficient quality. Since the performance of retranslated and filtered data is better than the baseline (see Tables 1b to 1d, Table 2), we use it as our primary training data in all further experiments.

MTL We finetune separate mT5 models using MTL for *Mt*, *Ga*, and *Cy* (using NLLB-retranslated data) and *Ru* (on original data), with translation to English and English RDF-to-text as auxiliary tasks (see Section 4.2). For translation from English, we use the prompt "*Translate from En to <lang>: <input>*", and the prompt for English text generation is "*RDF-to-text in English: <input>*".

Multilingual Model (MLM) We finetune a single mT5 model on data created from combining NLLB-retranslated *Mt*, *Ga*, and *Cy* datasets with the existing *Ru* data. Since the *Br* data is lower quality, we do not include it in this setting.

SaG We optionally employ SaG during inference to ensure simpler and more fluent outputs (see Section 4.3). We only use the subset size limit n in *Br*, as we observed no performance improvements in other languages. For *Br*, we find that setting $n = 2$ yields the best performance.

6 Results

Table 1 shows comprehensive evaluation scores of our experiments on *Ru*, *Mt*, *Ga* and *Cy*. Generally, we see a substantial improvement for *base-NLLB* from *baseline* for *Mt*, *Ga*, and *Cy*. This is the most notable boost as using NLLB represents the largest change in the setup.

For *Ru* (Table 1a), we observe an improvement with the *MTL* and *MLM* setups, but *SaG* decoding seems to hurt performance. As *Ru* is a comparatively high-resource language, we suspect the model is already well-suited to process complex outputs in a single step, and splitting the inputs means losing context in the individual steps.

Unlike *Ru*, *Mt* (Table 1b) sees a performance drop of *MTL*/*MLM* over *base-NLLB*. Adding SaG helps slightly, but not enough to match *base-NLLB*. The organizers' baseline and generate-and-translate with NLLB are better than any of our models.

For both *Ga* and *Cy*, we observe an improvement in the performance of *MTL* and *MTM* over *base-*

[4] https://huggingface.co/google/mt5-base

[5] The value was found by development data trials.

Model	BLEU	MET	ChrF	TER
WebNLG 2023 best	54.71	-	0.69	0.37
(Kasner and Dušek, 2020)	52.9	-	0.68	0.40
(Mille et al., 2019) + GT	25.5	-	0.51	0.67
baseline	51.39	0.37	0.67	0.41
MTL	53.48	0.39	0.68	0.4
MLM ◇	**54.52**	**0.39**	**0.69**	**0.38**
MTL + SaG	50.15	0.38	0.67	0.44
MLM + SaG	50.12	0.38	0.68	0.44

(a) Russian (*Ru*) – 2nd of 4 submitted systems

Model	BLEU	MET	ChrF	TER
WebNLG 2023 best	21.27	-	0.52	0.65
(Guo et al., 2020) + Edin	15.60	-	0.42	**0.67**
(Guo et al., 2020) + NLLB	**16.07**	0.26	**0.47**	0.71
baseline	12.37	0.2	0.36	0.72
base-NLLB	14.08	0.25	0.44	0.77
MTL	13.95	0.25	0.44	0.78
MLM	13.91	0.25	0.45	0.77
MTL + SaG ◇	14.02	0.26	0.45	0.78
MLM + SaG	14.02	**0.29**	0.45	0.79

(b) Maltese (*Mt*) – 3rd of 5 submitted systems

Model	BLEU	MET	ChrF	TER
WebNLG 2023 best	20.40	-	0.51	0.69
(Guo et al., 2020) + Edin	11.63	-	0.36	0.74
(Guo et al., 2020) + NLLB	**17.95**	0.23	**0.46**	**0.70**
baseline	6.53	0.13	0.27	0.77
base-NLLB	15.65	0.22	0.43	0.78
MTL	15.65	0.22	0.43	0.77
MLM	15.70	0.22	0.43	0.78
MTL + SaG ◇	15.87	0.22	0.43	0.78
MLM + SaG	15.15	**0.32**	0.42	0.8

(c) Irish (*Ga*) – 3rd/4th of 5 submitted systems

Model	BLEU	MET	ChrF	TER
WebNLG 2023 best	25.11	-	0.55	0.64
(Guo et al., 2020) + Edin	10.70	-	0.36	0.77
(Guo et al., 2020) + NLLB	**18.77**	0.25	**0.48**	**0.7**
baseline	7.80	0.15	0.29	0.78
base-NLLB	16.13	0.24	0.44	0.79
MTL	16.73	0.24	0.45	0.78
MLM	16.65	0.24	0.44	0.80
MTL + SaG ◇	17.01	0.24	0.45	0.79
MLM + SaG	16.28	**0.35**	0.45	0.81

(d) Welsh (*Cy*) – 3rd of 4 submitted systems

Table 1: Automatic Evaluation Scores for *Ru*, *Mt*, *Ga*, *Cy*. "MET" stands for METEOR. We include the scores for the best WebNLG 2023 system and baseline systems above the dividing line in each table. For *Ru*, these come from WebNLG 2020. The English outputs of (Mille et al., 2019)'s system were processed by Google Translate (GT). For *Mt*, *Ga*, *Cy*, the English outputs of (Guo et al., 2020)'s system were processed by Edinburgh Zero (Zhang et al., 2020a) (Edin) and re-processed by ourselves using NLLB (Costa-jussà et al., 2022), see Section 4.1. ◇ denotes our system used for the challenge submission. The rankings of our submission and the number of submitted systems are included in each sub-caption.

Model	BLEU	MET	ChrF	TER
(Guo et al., 2020) + Edin	9.92	-	0.32	**0.77**
baseline	7.02	0.14	0.27	0.79
base-DF	8.84	0.15	0.29	0.91
base-DF + SaG ◇	10.09	0.17	0.33	0.80
base-DF + SaG ($n = 2$)	**11.31**	**0.19**	**0.36**	0.83

Table 2: Automatic evaluation scores for *Br* (see Table 1 for explanations). Our submission was the only one competing in the challenge.

NLLB (Tables 1c and 1d), similar to *Ru*. There is a slight improvement in the performance of *SaG* decoding over *MTL*, but not in the *MTM* case. While our direct translation models outperform the challenge baseline, they fare worse than generate-and-translate with NLLB.

The scores for *Br* are shown in Table 2. Using *SaG* decoding with base-DF slightly enhances the performance over the organizer's baseline, and unlike other languages, *Br* sees a decent performance boost over the method without *SaG* decoding.

7 Conclusion

In this work, we describe our submitted systems for the WebNLG 2023 Challenge. The provided silver training dataset for the under-resourced languages sometimes contains incomplete translations. To address this, we create alternate parallel data using NLLB, which seems to provide the biggest performance boost. Furthermore, we gain additional minor improvements by using a multi-task and multilingual training settings, coupled with a split-and-generate decoding method, which produces simpler and more verbose outputs. Our systems mostly score in the middle of the challenge scoreboard; our *Br* submission was the only competitor in the challenge. For *Ru*, *Ga* and *Cy*, our submitted systems perform substantially better than the organizers' baseline. A non-submitted variant of our system for *Br* also surpasses the baseline. However, in *Mt*, *Ga*, and *Cy*, our approaches underperform a simple generate-and-translate baseline with the improved NLLB MT system.

Acknowledgements

This work was supported by the European Research Council (Grant agreement No. 101039303 NG-NLG). It used resources provided by the LINDAT/CLARIAH-CZ Research Infrastructure (Czech Ministry of Education, Youth and Sports project No. LM2018101).

References

Oshin Agarwal, Mihir Kale, Heming Ge, Siamak Shakeri, and Rami Al-Rfou. 2020. Machine Translation Aided Bilingual Data-to-Text Generation and Semantic Parsing. In *Proceedings of the 3rd International Workshop on Natural Language Generation from the Semantic Web (WebNLG+)*, pages 125–130, Dublin, Ireland (Virtual). Association for Computational Linguistics.

Sören Auer, Christian Bizer, Georgi Kobilarov, Jens Lehmann, Richard Cyganiak, and Zachary Ives. 2007. Dbpedia: A nucleus for a web of open data. In *international semantic web conference*, pages 722–735. Springer.

Thiago Castro Ferreira, Claire Gardent, Nikolai Ilinykh, Chris van der Lee, Simon Mille, Diego Moussallem, and Anastasia Shimorina. 2020. The 2020 bilingual, bi-directional WebNLG+ shared task: Overview and evaluation results (WebNLG+ 2020). In *Proceedings of the 3rd International Workshop on Natural Language Generation from the Semantic Web (WebNLG+)*, pages 55–76, Dublin, Ireland (Virtual). Association for Computational Linguistics.

Emilie Colin, Claire Gardent, Yassine M'rabet, Shashi Narayan, and Laura Perez-Beltrachini. 2016. The WebNLG challenge: Generating text from DBPedia data. In *Proceedings of the 9th International Natural Language Generation conference*, pages 163–167, Edinburgh, UK. Association for Computational Linguistics.

Alexis Conneau, Kartikay Khandelwal, Naman Goyal, Vishrav Chaudhary, Guillaume Wenzek, Francisco Guzmán, Edouard Grave, Myle Ott, Luke Zettlemoyer, and Veselin Stoyanov. 2020. Unsupervised cross-lingual representation learning at scale. In *Proceedings of the 58th Annual Meeting of the Association for Computational Linguistics*, pages 8440–8451, Online. Association for Computational Linguistics.

Marta R Costa-jussà, James Cross, Onur Çelebi, Maha Elbayad, Kenneth Heafield, Kevin Heffernan, Elahe Kalbassi, Janice Lam, Daniel Licht, Jean Maillard, et al. 2022. No language left behind: Scaling human-centered machine translation. *arXiv preprint arXiv:2207.04672*.

Ondřej Dušek and Filip Jurčíček. 2019. Neural Generation for Czech: Data and Baselines. In *Proceedings of the 12th International Conference on Natural Language Generation (INLG 2019)*, pages 563–574, Tokyo, Japan. ArXiv: 1910.05298.

Angela Fan and Claire Gardent. 2020. Multilingual AMR-to-Text Generation. In *Proceedings of the 2020 Conference on Empirical Methods in Natural Language Processing (EMNLP)*, pages 2889–2901, Online. Association for Computational Linguistics.

Thiago Castro Ferreira, Chris van der Lee, Emiel van Miltenburg, and Emiel Krahmer. 2019. Neural data-to-text generation: A comparison between pipeline and end-to-end architectures. In *2019 Conference on Empirical Methods in Natural Language Processing (EMNLP) and 9th International Joint Conference on Natural Language Processing (IJCNLP)*, Hong Kong. ArXiv: 1908.09022.

Claire Gardent, Anastasia Shimorina, Shashi Narayan, and Laura Perez-Beltrachini. 2017. The WebNLG challenge: Generating text from RDF data. In *Proceedings of the 10th International Conference on Natural Language Generation*, pages 124–133, Santiago de Compostela, Spain. Association for Computational Linguistics.

Qipeng Guo, Zhijing Jin, Ning Dai, Xipeng Qiu, Xiangyang Xue, David Wipf, and Zheng Zhang. 2020. P2: A Plan-and-Pretrain Approach for Knowledge Graph-to-Text Generation. In *Proceedings of the 3rd International Workshop on Natural Language Generation from the Semantic Web (WebNLG+)*, pages 100–106, Dublin, Ireland (Virtual). Association for Computational Linguistics.

Tahmid Hasan, Abhik Bhattacharjee, Md. Saiful Islam, Kazi Mubasshir, Yuan-Fang Li, Yong-Bin Kang, M. Sohel Rahman, and Rifat Shahriyar. 2021. XL-Sum: Large-Scale Multilingual Abstractive Summarization for 44 Languages. In *Findings of the Association for Computational Linguistics: ACL-IJCNLP 2021*, pages 4693–4703, Online. Association for Computational Linguistics.

Tatsuya Ishigaki, Goran Topic, Yumi Hamazono, Hiroshi Noji, Ichiro Kobayashi, Yusuke Miyao, and Hiroya Takamura. 2021. Generating Racing Game Commentary from Vision, Language, and Structured Data. In *Proceedings of the 14th International Conference on Natural Language Generation*, pages 103–113, Aberdeen, Scotland, UK. Association for Computational Linguistics.

Mihir Kale and Abhinav Rastogi. 2020. Text-to-text pre-training for data-to-text tasks. In *Proceedings of the 13th International Conference on Natural Language Generation*, pages 97–102, Dublin, Ireland. Association for Computational Linguistics.

Mihir Kale and Scott Roy. 2020. Machine Translation Pre-training for Data-to-Text Generation – A Case Study in Czech. In *Proceedings of the 13th International Conference on Natural Language Generation*, Online. ArXiv: 2004.02077.

Zdeněk Kasner and Ondřej Dušek. 2020. Train Hard, Finetune Easy: Multilingual Denoising for RDF-to-Text Generation. In *Proceedings of the 3rd International Workshop on Natural Language Generation from the Semantic Web (WebNLG+)*, pages 171–176, Online.

Nitish Shirish Keskar, Bryan McCann, Lav R Varshney, Caiming Xiong, and Richard Socher. 2019. Ctrl: A conditional transformer language model for controllable generation. *arXiv preprint arXiv:1909.05858*.

Alon Lavie and Abhaya Agarwal. 2007. METEOR: An automatic metric for MT evaluation with high levels of correlation with human judgments. In *Proceedings of the Second Workshop on Statistical Machine Translation*, pages 228–231, Prague, Czech Republic. Association for Computational Linguistics.

Mike Lewis, Yinhan Liu, Naman Goyal, Marjan Ghazvininejad, Abdelrahman Mohamed, Omer Levy, Veselin Stoyanov, and Luke Zettlemoyer. 2020. BART: Denoising sequence-to-sequence pre-training for natural language generation, translation, and comprehension. In *Proceedings of the 58th Annual Meeting of the Association for Computational Linguistics*, pages 7871–7880, Online. Association for Computational Linguistics.

Xiaodong Liu, Pengcheng He, Weizhu Chen, and Jianfeng Gao. 2019. Multi-task deep neural networks for natural language understanding. In *Proceedings of the 57th Annual Meeting of the Association for Computational Linguistics*, pages 4487–4496.

Yinhan Liu, Jiatao Gu, Naman Goyal, Xian Li, Sergey Edunov, Marjan Ghazvininejad, Mike Lewis, and Luke Zettlemoyer. 2020. Multilingual denoising pretraining for neural machine translation. *Transactions of the Association for Computational Linguistics*, 8:726–742.

Simon Mille, Anja Belz, Bernd Bohnet, Yvette Graham, Emily Pitler, and Leo Wanner. 2018. The First Multilingual Surface Realisation Shared Task (SR'18): Overview and Evaluation Results. In *Proceedings of the First Workshop on Multilingual Surface Realisation*, pages 1–12, Melbourne, Australia.

Simon Mille, Stamatia Dasiopoulou, Beatriz Fisas, and Leo Wanner. 2019. Teaching FORGe to Verbalize DBpedia Properties in Spanish. In *Proceedings of the 12th International Conference on Natural Language Generation*, pages 473–483, Tokyo, Japan. Association for Computational Linguistics.

Amit Moryossef, Yoav Goldberg, and Ido Dagan. 2019. Step-by-Step: Separating Planning from Realization in Neural Data-to-Text Generation. In *NAACL*, Minneapolis, MN, USA. ArXiv: 1904.03396.

Linyong Nan, Dragomir Radev, Rui Zhang, Amrit Rau, Abhinand Sivaprasad, Chiachun Hsieh, Xiangru Tang, Aadit Vyas, Neha Verma, Pranav Krishna, Yangxiaokang Liu, Nadia Irwanto, Jessica Pan, Faiaz Rahman, Ahmad Zaidi, Mutethia Mutuma, Yasin Tarabar, Ankit Gupta, Tao Yu, Yi Chern Tan, Xi Victoria Lin, Caiming Xiong, Richard Socher, and Nazneen Fatema Rajani. 2021. DART: Open-domain structured data record to text generation. In *Proceedings of the 2021 Conference of the North American Chapter of the Association for Computational Linguistics: Human Language Technologies*, pages 432–447, Online. Association for Computational Linguistics.

Shashi Narayan, Claire Gardent, Shay B. Cohen, and Anastasia Shimorina. 2017. Split and rephrase. In *Proceedings of the 2017 Conference on Empirical Methods in Natural Language Processing*, pages 606–616, Copenhagen, Denmark. Association for Computational Linguistics.

Ankur P Parikh, Xuezhi Wang, Sebastian Gehrmann, Manaal Faruqui, Bhuwan Dhingra, Diyi Yang, and Dipanjan Das. 2020. Totto: A controlled table-to-text generation dataset. *arXiv preprint arXiv:2004.14373*.

Maja Popović. 2015. chrF: character n-gram F-score for automatic MT evaluation. In *Proceedings of the Tenth Workshop on Statistical Machine Translation*, pages 392–395, Lisbon, Portugal. Association for Computational Linguistics.

Matt Post. 2018. A call for clarity in reporting BLEU scores. In *Proceedings of the Third Conference on Machine Translation: Research Papers*, pages 186–191, Brussels, Belgium. Association for Computational Linguistics.

Alec Radford, Jeffrey Wu, Rewon Child, David Luan, Dario Amodei, Ilya Sutskever, et al. 2019. Language models are unsupervised multitask learners. *OpenAI blog*, 1(8):9.

Colin Raffel, Noam Shazeer, Adam Roberts, Katherine Lee, Sharan Narang, Michael Matena, Yanqi Zhou, Wei Li, and Peter J Liu. 2020. Exploring the limits of transfer learning with a unified text-to-text transformer. *The Journal of Machine Learning Research*, 21(1):5485–5551.

Sebastian Ruder. 2019. The 4 biggest open problems in nlp. `https://www.ruder.io/4-biggest-open-problems-in-nlp/`.

Victor Sanh, Albert Webson, Colin Raffel, Stephen H Bach, Lintang Sutawika, Zaid Alyafeai, Antoine Chaffin, Arnaud Stiegler, Teven Le Scao, Arun Raja, et al. 2022. Multitask prompted training enables zero-shot task generalization. In *ICLR 2022-Tenth International Conference on Learning Representations*.

Thomas Scialom, Paul-Alexis Dray, Sylvain Lamprier, Benjamin Piwowarski, and Jacopo Staiano. 2020. MLSUM: The Multilingual Summarization Corpus. In *Proceedings of the 2020 Conference on Empirical Methods in Natural Language Processing (EMNLP)*, pages 8051–8067, Online. Association for Computational Linguistics.

Siamak Shakeri, Noah Constant, Mihir Kale, and Linting Xue. 2021. Towards Zero-Shot Multilingual Synthetic Question and Answer Generation for Cross-Lingual Reading Comprehension. In *Proceedings of the 14th International Conference on Natural Language Generation*, pages 35–45, Aberdeen, Scotland, UK. Association for Computational Linguistics.

Matthew Snover, Bonnie Dorr, Rich Schwartz, Linnea Micciulla, and John Makhoul. 2006. A study of translation edit rate with targeted human annotation. In *Proceedings of the 7th Conference of the Association for Machine Translation in the Americas: Technical Papers*, pages 223–231, Cambridge, Massachusetts, USA. Association for Machine Translation in the Americas.

Milan Straka, Nikita Mediankin, Tom Kocmi, Zdeněk Žabokrtský, Vojtěch Hudeček, and Jan Hajič. 2018. SumeCzech: Large Czech News-Based Summarization Dataset. In *Proceedings of the Eleventh International Conference on Language Resources and Evaluation (LREC 2018)*, Miyazaki, Japan. European Language Resources Association (ELRA).

Chris van der Lee, Chris Emmery, Sander Wubben, and Emiel Krahmer. 2020. The CACAPO Dataset: A Multilingual, Multi-Domain Dataset for Neural Pipeline and End-to-End Data-to-Text Generation. In *Proceedings of the 13th International Conference on Natural Language Generation*, pages 68–79, Dublin, Ireland. Association for Computational Linguistics.

Jason Wei, Maarten Bosma, Vincent Y Zhao, Kelvin Guu, Adams Wei Yu, Brian Lester, Nan Du, Andrew M Dai, and Quoc V Le. 2021. Finetuned language models are zero-shot learners. *arXiv preprint arXiv:2109.01652*.

Sam Wiseman, Stuart Shieber, and Alexander Rush. 2017. Challenges in data-to-document generation. In *Proceedings of the 2017 Conference on Empirical Methods in Natural Language Processing*, pages 2253–2263, Copenhagen, Denmark. Association for Computational Linguistics.

Linting Xue, Noah Constant, Adam Roberts, Mihir Kale, Rami Al-Rfou, Aditya Siddhant, Aditya Barua, and Colin Raffel. 2021. mT5: A massively multilingual pre-trained text-to-text transformer. In *Proceedings of the 2021 Conference of the North American Chapter of the Association for Computational Linguistics: Human Language Technologies*, pages 483–498, Online. Association for Computational Linguistics.

Biao Zhang, Philip Williams, Ivan Titov, and Rico Sennrich. 2020a. Improving massively multilingual neural machine translation and zero-shot translation. *arXiv preprint arXiv:2004.11867*.

Jingqing Zhang, Yao Zhao, Mohammad Saleh, and Peter Liu. 2020b. Pegasus: Pre-training with extracted gap-sentences for abstractive summarization. In *International Conference on Machine Learning*, pages 11328–11339. PMLR.

Giulio Zhou and Gerasimos Lampouras. 2021. Generalising Multilingual Concept-to-Text NLG with Language Agnostic Delexicalisation. In *Proceedings of the 59th Annual Meeting of the Association for Computational Linguistics and the 11th International Joint Conference on Natural Language Processing (Volume 1: Long Papers)*, pages 114–127, Online. Association for Computational Linguistics.

Data-to-text Generation for Severely Under-Resourced Languages with GPT-3.5: A Bit of Help Needed from Google Translate

Michela Lorandi and **Anya Belz**
ADAPT Research Centre
Dublin City University, Ireland
{michela.lorandi,anya.belz}@adaptcentre.ie

Abstract

LLMs like GPT are great at tasks involving English which dominates in their training data. In this paper, we look at how they cope with tasks involving languages that are severely under-represented in their training data, in the context of data-to-text generation for Irish, Maltese, Welsh and Breton. During the prompt-engineering phase we tested a range of prompt types and formats on GPT-3.5 and 4 with a small sample of example input/output pairs. We then fully evaluated the two most promising prompts in two scenarios: (i) direct generation into the under-resourced language, and (ii) generation into English followed by translation into the under-resourced language. We find that few-shot prompting works better for direct generation into under-resourced languages, but that the difference disappears when pivoting via English. The few-shot + translation system variants were submitted to the WebNLG 2023 shared task where they outperformed competitor systems by substantial margins in all languages on all metrics. We conclude that good performance on under-resourced languages can be achieved out-of-the box with state-of-the-art LLMs. However, our best results (for Welsh) remain well below the lowest ranked English system at WebNLG'20.

1 Introduction

Pretrained large language models (LLMs) are everywhere, achieving state-of-the-art-results across many application areas. LLMs display strong out-of-the-box abilities at a wide range of different tasks far beyond language-based tasks. However, these abilities have been explored mostly for English which dominates text online, hence the data on which LLMs are trained. In the work reported here, we explore to what extent state-of-the-art LLMs can help with tasks involving severely under-resourced languages which by definition would have been very scarce in their training data.

More specifically, we address the challenging task of data-to-text generation for four severely under-resourced languages: Irish, Maltese, Welsh and Breton. Developing any new system is difficult in a severely under-resourced scenario, more so where the task has language-specific input/output combinations as in data-to-text and text-to-text.

The paper is structured as follows. Section 2 describes data and task, Section 3 presents the general approach, prompt engineering, and the specific systems we fully evaluated. Experimental set-up and results are outlined in Section 4, and Section 5 provides discussion and conclusions.

All code and results are available on Github: https://github.com/DCU-NLG/DCU-NLG-PBN.

2 Data and Task

The WebNLG'23 (?) data consists of 1,778 dev items for each language, 1,399 test items for Breton, and 1,665 for Welsh, Irish and Maltese, that were manually translated by professional translators from the English originals. Additionally 13,211 training items are provided where texts were automatically translated from English.

As in all WebNLG shared tasks, WebNLG 2023 systems must map from the data (RDF triples) to a suitable output text, as in the example from the WebNLG'23 website[1] in Figure 2. This is a data-to-text generation task which is well established in the natural language generation (NLG) field.

3 General Approach and Specific Systems

The general approach we take is to use a state-of-the-art LLM in its out-of-the-box state, to either (i) generate texts directly from the data in the target language, or (ii) generate texts in English and then translate them into the target language. More specifically, the LLM we used was the Instruct-GPT model identified as text-davinci-003, and the

[1] https://synalp.gitlabpages.inria.fr/webnlg-challenge/docs

Proceedings of the Workshop on Multimodal, Multilingual Natural Language Generation and Multilingual WebNLG Challenge (MM-NLG 2023), pages 80–86
September 12, 2023 ©2023 Association for Computational Linguistics

(a) Set of RDF triples

```
<entry category="Company" eid="Id21" shape="(X (X) (X) (X) (X))" shape_type="sibling" size="4">
    <modifiedtripleset>
        <mtriple>Trane | foundingDate | 1913-01-01</mtriple>
        <mtriple>Trane | location | Ireland</mtriple>
        <mtriple>Trane | foundationPlace | La_Crosse,_Wisconsin</mtriple>
        <mtriple>Trane | numberOfEmployees | 29000</mtriple>
    </modifiedtripleset>
</entry>
```

(b) English text

Trane, which was founded on January 1st 1913 in La Crosse, Wisconsin, is based in Ireland. It has 29,000 employees.

Figure 1: WebNLG example of input triples and output text in English.

MT system was Google Translate which covers all WebNLG'23 languages except Breton.

In all cases, we fed a prompt representing the generation task to text-davinci-003, and collected the system completion as the output which we then cleaned up by simple post-processing procedures.

3.1 Prompt testing and selection

We conducted three prompt testing phases, in each phase using a different random sample of 20 data/text pairs, stratified for triple size, with outputs in all target languages, from the dev set. These small subsets of the dev set represent all the data we used during system development.

Phase 1: In the first prompt testing phase, we tested seven prompt variants on text-davinci-003 on all four target languages and a subset of four prompts on GPT-4 on Irish and Breton. The prompts were of three types: **zero-shot minimal instruction**, **few-shot in-context learning**, and **chain-of-thought** (?).

On GPT-3.5, we tested each prompt in two scenarios: (i) generating the texts directly into the target languages, (ii) generating all texts into English and then translating them into each target language. In all prompts, the input triples were surrounded by triple quotes as per best-practice recommendations; we tested removing these quotes for the zero-shot prompt. On GPT-4, we tested zero-shot and few-shot with and without translation, and chain-of-thought (CoT) without translation.

The clearest results immediately were that (i) generation into English plus translation worked better than direct generation into the target languages, and (ii) the CoT prompts performed far worse than the others, a difference that was exacerbated when using GPT-4. Zero-shot looked better for Irish, but few-shot had the edge for the other three languages.

BLEU, METEOR and ChrF++ for zero-shot looked overall slightly better on GPT-4, but TER was substantially worse and moreover the emerging patterns were less clear. Leaving out the triple quotes did not appear to work better (although this was tested on only one language).

Phase 2: As we were testing on a very small sample, the risk was poor representativeness of the data as a whole. Therefore, in the second prompt testing phase, we used a fresh sample of 20 pairs to further test the most promising zero-shot and few-shot prompts in both +/- translation scenarios. We dropped the chain-of-thought prompts and GPT-4, as the Phase 1 results had been less promising.

Results confirmed better performance for few-shot, this time in all scenarios with all evaluation metrics (although for a small number of results, scores were virtually the same). Again having quotes worked better than leaving them out.

At this point we tested a postprocessing method on most of the previous experiments. This revealed clear improvements in almost all cases. The method replaces HTML with ASCII characters (e.g. &quot is replaced with "). Furthermore, we remove underscores, and quotes that wrap the entire text.

Phase 3: In the third prompt testing phase, we tested just the zero-shot and few-shot prompts into English with translation, on Irish and Welsh. At this stage the aim was to further investigate the difference between the two so far most promising types of prompts, on another fresh data sample, on these two languages because results were most similar for different prompt variants for them. However, Phase 3 results for zero-shot and few-shot + MT for Irish and Welsh were again overall tied.

3.2 Prompt types used in final systems

Prompt testing had revealed zero-shot and few-shot prompts with triple quotes generating into English plus MT as clearly the most promising. Figure 2 shows examples of these two prompt variants in terms of the prompt template, few-shot examples (where applicable), and system completion. For more example prompts, see appendix, Section A.

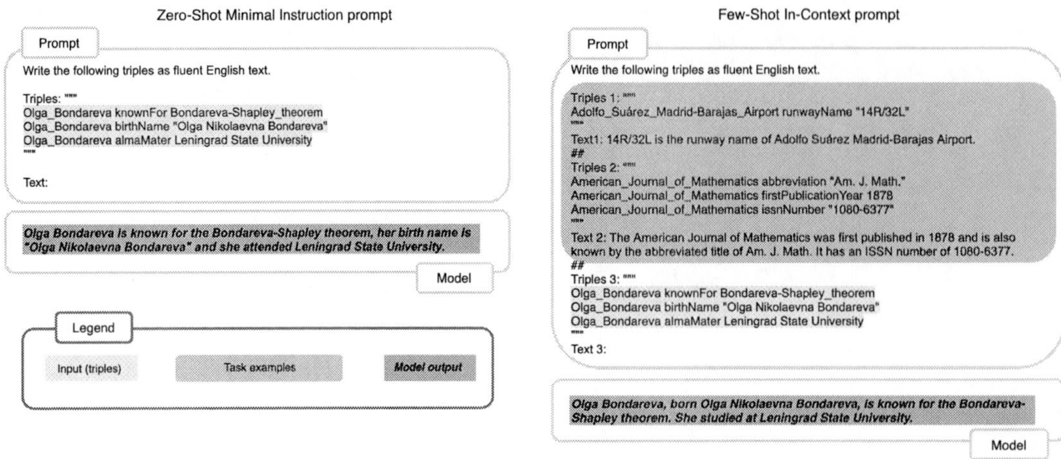

Figure 2: The two prompt types used in the final systems. Given Input (triples) highlighted in yellow, model output in blue. The few-shot in-context prompt also incorporates examples (highlighted green).[2]

Zero-shot minimal instruction prompts are simple requests to perform a task without details or examples, in our case consisting of a brief sentence describing the task and the input to the task. **Few-shot in-context learning** prompts are composed of a brief description of the task and a list of examples providing both inputs and target outputs, ending in just an input, for which the system response is taken to be the output.

The final prompt formats follow best practice for prompt engineering provided by OpenAI;[3] input triples are recast as *subject predicate object*.

3.3 System variants evaluated

In the full evaluations on the WebNLG'23 test set reported below, we tested our selected zero-shot and few-shot prompts in both +/- MT scenarios, giving us four system variants as follows:

1. Zero-shot generation into each language;
2. Few-shot generation into each language;
3. Zero-shot generation into English + translation into each language;
4. Few-shot generation into English + translation into each language.

4 Experimental Set-up and Results

We executed our experiments using the paid-for OpenAI API to access text-davinci-003,[4] and the free Google Translate API,[5] in early June 2023.

In all experiments, we set text-davinci-003 parameters to *temperature*=0, *top p*=1 (default) to consider all possible tokens, *frequency penalty*=0 and *presence penalty*=0 (default value) to slightly reduce repetitive tokens, *best of*=1 (default) to get only 1 completion for each prompt, and *maximum length* to 500. All generated texts are post-processed as described above.

Table 1 presents BLEU (**?**), ChrF++ (**?**) and TER (**?**) for our four systems, and the baseline reported by the WebNLG organisers (**?**): the winning system for English from WebNLG'20 combined with the Zero MT system.

Comparing zero-shot results with corresponding few-shot results, it is clear that the addition of examples to the prompt helps the model perform the task better in all languages: BLEU and TER are always higher for the few-shot variant than the zero-shot variant, while ChrF++ is always higher for few-shot where translation is *not* used, and virtually identical where translation *is* used.

When generating the texts in English plus translation, we don't see the same strong benefit achieved by the addition of few-shot examples noted above. Even where there is a benefit, it is small. In fact, we observe similar performance between zero-shot + MT and few-shot + MT throughout, while both clearly outperform versions without translation; this is the case in all three languages where we have translation (Irish, Maltese, and Welsh).

It might be speculated that providing few-shot

[3] https://help.openai.com/en/articles/6654000-best-practices-for-prompt-engineering-with-openai-api

[4] https://platform.openai.com/docs/models/gpt-3-5

[5] https://cloud.google.com/translate

Language	Method	BLEU ↑	ChrF++ ↑	TER ↓
Irish	Zero-Shot Irish	12.9931	0.4124	0.9298
	Few-Shot Irish	15.3477	0.4303	0.8451
	Zero-Shot English + Google Translate	**20.5176**	**0.5146**	0.7122
	Few-Shot English + Google Translate	20.4001	0.51	**0.6894**
	WebNLG 2023 Baseline	11.63	0.36	0.74
Maltese	Zero-Shot Maltese	13.0311	0.445	0.8496
	Few-Shot Maltese	15.4315	0.4536	0.7605
	Zero-Shot English + Google Translate	20.3528	**0.5263**	0.67
	Few-Shot English + Google Translate	**21.2656**	0.5249	**0.6465**
	WebNLG 2023 Baseline	15.60	0.42	0.67
Welsh	Zero-Shot Welsh	15.8695	0.4619	0.822
	Few-Shot Welsh	18.9512	0.4742	0.7192
	Zero-Shot English + Google Translate	24.7126	**0.5496**	0.6659
	Few-Shot English + Google Translate	**25.115**	0.5484	**0.6435**
	WebNLG 2023 Baseline	10.70	0.36	0.77
Breton	Zero-Shot Breton	15.2498	0.4217	0.82
	Few-Shot Breton	**17.207**	**0.4394**	**0.739**
	WebNLG 2023 Baseline	9.92	0.33	0.76

Table 1: Results for our system variants (Section 3), and the WebNLG'23 baseline results provided by the organisers. Highest score in each column for each language in boldface.

examples partially compensates for the comparatively smaller amount of knowledge that the LLM has about the under-resourced languages. This would explain why the benefit disappears when pivoting via English, where examples can add little to the knowledge the LLM already has.

5 Discussion and Conclusion

We submitted the three few-shot + MT systems to the WebNLG Challenge 2023,[6] in the Welsh, Irish and Maltese tracks. Based on the metric evaluation results (test set) shared by WebNLG organisers, these systems outperform all other submitted systems by sizeable margins; moreover, few-shot Breton without translation (*) also outperforms the one submitted system substantially:

	Few-Shot + GTransl			Nearest system		
	BLEU	chrF++	TER	BLEU	chrF++	TER
Irish	20.4	0.51	0.69	16.66	0.44	0.75
Maltese	21.27	0.52	0.65	16.49	0.47	0.7
Welsh	25.12	0.55	0.64	20.97	0.49	0.67
Breton*	17.21	0.44	0.74	13.11	0.33	0.76

At the time of writing, we do not know what kinds of systems produced the runner-up results, except that the Irish runner-up is the handcrafted rule-based FORGe system extended for Irish (?). There are interesting differences between FORGe and our system. FORGe took a considerable amount of person time, but uses no paid-for resources. To create and test our system took next to no time, and US$91.82 in API costs. For FORGe, the system and how it was created is known. For our system, we don't have access to the model itself, and only incomplete knowledge about its exact technical details at the particular time we access it; on another day, results may differ. This makes experiments non-repeatable, and generalising to future use of the same approach difficult. Moreover, it's not a system that can be deployed in this form, because of the changing nature of what's at the other end of the LLM and MT APIs.

This raises important general questions about (i) how scientific research is to be conducted with LLMs served as-a-service that deliver best performance, but whose technical details aren't known and moreover change over time; and (ii) how such research results can be utilised in developing systems for real-world deployment.

In this paper we have explored different prompt types and formats for data-to-text generation for under-resourced languages, with out-of-the-box LLMs with and without machine translation. We found that few-shot + MT achieves new state-of-the-art metric performance at the WebNLG'23 RDF-to-text generation task for the severely under-resourced languages Irish, Maltese, Welsh and Breton. However, given the caveats above, results presented here must be treated as a rough indication of what is achievable with an LLM+MT approach.

[6] https://synalp.gitlabpages.inria.fr/webnlg-challenge/challenge_2023/docs

Acknowledgements

The cost of accessing the GPT API was covered by financial support from the DCU-NLG Research Group at DCU. Michela Lorandi's work was conducted with the financial support of the Science Foundation Ireland Centre for Research Training in Digitally-Enhanced Reality (d-real) under Grant No. 18/CRT/6224. Both authors benefit from being members of the ADAPT SFI Research Centre at Dublin City University, funded by the Science Foundation Ireland under Grant Agreement No. 13/RC/2106_P2. For the purpose of Open Access, the author has applied a CC BY public copyright licence to any Author Accepted Manuscript version arising from this submission.

A Prompts

We provide all the prompts used in our experiments, specifying the template and one example for each prompt. In Table 2 we provide the zero-shot minimal instruction prompt, while in Table 3 we provide the few-shot in-context prompt with the same set of examples we used in our experiments.

<table>
<tr><th colspan="2">Zero-Shot minimal instruction</th></tr>
<tr><td>Template:</td><td>Write the following triples as fluent English | Irish | Welsh | Maltese | Breton text.

Triples: """
{set of triples in the format subject predicate object and each triple in a new line}
"""

Text: [MODEL]</td></tr>
<tr><td>Example Prompt:</td><td>Write the following triples as fluent English text.

Triples: """
AC_Hotel_Bella_Sky_Copenhagen owner Bella_Center
AC_Hotel_Bella_Sky_Copenhagen tenant Marriott_International
AC_Hotel_Bella_Sky_Copenhagen architect 3XN
AC_Hotel_Bella_Sky_Copenhagen floorCount 23
"""

Text:</td></tr>
<tr><td>Model output:</td><td>The AC Hotel Bella Sky Copenhagen is owned by Bella Center, and is rented by Marriott International. It was designed by 3XN and has 23 floors.</td></tr>
</table>

Table 2: Zero-Shot minimal instruction prompt. Template of the prompt and complete example in English.

<table>
<tr><th colspan="2">Few-Shot in-context</th></tr>
<tr><td>Template:</td><td>Write the following triples as fluent English | Irish | Welsh | Maltese | Breton text.

Triple 1: """
{set of triples in the format *subject predicate object* and each triple in a new line}
"""
Text 1: {verbalisation of Triple 1}
##
Triple 2: """
{set of triples in the format *subject predicate object* and each triple in a new line}
"""
Text 2: {verbalisation of Triple 2}
##
Triple 3: """
{set of triples in the format *subject predicate object* and each triple in a new line}
"""
Text 3: [MODEL]</td></tr>
<tr><td>Example Prompt:

Model output:</td><td>Write the following triples as fluent English text.

Triple 1: """
Adolfo_Suárez_Madrid–Barajas_Airport runwayName "14R/32L"
"""
Text 1: 14R/32L is the runway name of Adolfo Suárez Madrid-Barajas Airport.
##
Triple 2: """
American_Journal_of_Mathematics abbreviation "Am. J. Math."
American_Journal_of_Mathematics firstPublicationYear 1878
American_Journal_of_Mathematics issnNumber "1080-6377"
"""
Text 2: The American Journal of Mathematics was first published in 1878 and is also known by the abbreviated title of Am. J. Math. It has an ISSN number of 1080-6377.
##
Triple 3: """
AC_Hotel_Bella_Sky_Copenhagen owner Bella_Center
AC_Hotel_Bella_Sky_Copenhagen tenant Marriott_International
AC_Hotel_Bella_Sky_Copenhagen architect 3XN
AC_Hotel_Bella_Sky_Copenhagen floorCount 23
"""
Text 3:
The AC Hotel Bella Sky Copenhagen is owned by Bella Center and is tenanted by Marriott International. It was designed by 3XN and has 23 floors.</td></tr>
<tr><td>Irish texts:</td><td>Text 1: 14R/32L is ainm do rúidbhealach Aerfort Adolfo Suárez Madrid-Barajas
Text 2: Foilsíodh an American Journal of Mathematics don chéad uair in 1878 agus aithnítear leis an ainm giorraithe Am. J. Math. chomh maith é. Tá an uimhir ISSN 1080-6377 aige.</td></tr>
<tr><td>Breton texts:</td><td>Text 1: Anv leurenn bradañ aerborzh Adolfo Suárez Madrid-Barajas zo 14L/32R.
Text 2: Finland zo bro ar Finniz hag hini ar skorndorrer Aleksey Chirikov bet savet e chanter-bigi Arctech en Helsinki.</td></tr>
<tr><td>Maltese and Welsh Triples:</td><td>Triple 1: Albennie_Jones birthPlace Errata,_Mississippi

Triple 2: GMA_New_Media industry Entertainment
GMA_New_Media type Media_company
GMA_New_Media product World_Wide_Web</td></tr>
<tr><td>Maltese texts:</td><td>Text 1: Albennie Jones twieldet f'Errata Mississippi.
Text 2: GMA New Media hija kumpanija tal-midja tal-industrija tad-divertiment li toffri servizzi li jikkonċernaw il-World Wide Web.</td></tr>
<tr><td>Welsh texts:</td><td>Text 1: Ganed Albennie Jones yn Errata, Mississippi.
Text 2: Mae GMA New Media yn gwmni cyfryngau yn y diwydiant adloniant sy'n cynnig gwasanaethau sy'n ymwneud â'r We Fyd Eang.</td></tr>
</table>

Table 3: Few-Shot In-context prompt. **Top** Template and complete example in English. **Center** Examples' texts in Irish and Breton. **Bottom** Examples' triple set and texts in Maltese and Welsh.

DCU/TCD-FORGe at WebNLG'23: Irish rules!

Simon Mille
ADAPT, Dublin City University
simon.mille@adaptcentre.ie

Elaine Uí Dhonnchadha
Trinity College, Dublin
uidhonne@tcd.ie

Stamatia Dasiopoulou
Independent Researcher
stamatia.dasiopoulou@gmail.com

Lauren Cassidy
ADAPT, Dublin City University
lauren.cassidy@adaptcentre.ie

Brian Davis
ADAPT, Dublin City University
brian.davis@adaptcentre.ie

Anya Belz
ADAPT, Dublin City University
anya.belz@adaptcentre.ie

Abstract

In this paper, we describe the submission of Dublin City University (DCU) and Trinity College Dublin (TCD) for the WebNLG 2023 shared task. We present a fully rule-based pipeline for generating Irish texts from DBpedia triple sets which comprises 4 components: triple lexicalisation, generation of non-inflected Irish text, inflection generation, and post-processing. Our whole pipeline is available at https://github.com/mille-s/DCU_TCD-FORGe_WebNLG23

1 Introduction

The WebNLG dataset is a benchmark for data-to-text Natural Language Generation (NLG) consisting of {input, output} pairs, where the input is a set of n triples ($1 \leq n \leq 7$) and the output a set of m texts that verbalise each triple set. The triples are extracted from DBpedia and represent relationships between DBpedia resources, namely subjects (*DB-Subj*) and objects (*DB-Obj*), via respective properties e.g. for the property *country*: `Texas | country | United_States`. The WebNLG'23 shared task focuses on four languages for which the existing resources are limited: Irish, Welsh, Breton and Maltese; we submitted Irish outputs only.

Large Language Models are becoming more and more used for NLG, but it is well known that they are heavily dependent on the quantity and quality of data they are trained on. On the other hand, rule-based systems although limited in terms of coverage and/or fluency are usually easier to adapt to low-resource languages. For our DCU/TCD-FORGe submission, our pipeline consists of 4 fully rule-based modules, which are described in the remainder of the paper: **Lexicalisation of input triples**: instantiation of predicate-argument templates with DB-Subj and DB-Obj values (Section 2); **Generation of non-inflected Irish sentences**: a sequence of graph transducers that progressively specify the linguistic structures into their surface-oriented form (FORGe, Section 3); **Generation of morphological inflections**: finite-state transducers to produce inflections via two-level morphology (Section 4); and **Post-processing**: cleaning and formatting of the text (Section 5). DCU/TCD-FORGe uses disk space of ~8MB and runs with less than 1GB of RAM; it generates the WebNLG test set (1,779 texts) in ~15 min (~0.5 sec/text) and achieved 0.167 BLEU.

2 Lexicalisation of Input Triples

In this section, we detail the steps involved in the lexicalisation of the WebNLG inputs: we start with the predicate-argument (PredArg) templates and their instantiation (2.1), and continue with the adaptations carried out for Irish generation (2.2).

2.1 PredArg templates and their instantiation

For lexicalisation, we follow the approach of the FORGe submission at WebNLG'19 (Mille et al., 2019), i.e. we use PredArg templates in the PropBank style (Kingsbury and Palmer, 2002) that correspond to each individual property and instantiate them by replacing the DB-Subj and DB-Obj placeholders with their respective lexicalisations (see Section 2.2). The instantiated templates are then grouped based on their DB-Subj and ordered in descending frequency of appearance of the DB-Subj

Proceedings of the Workshop on Multimodal, Multilingual Natural Language Generation and Multilingual WebNLG Challenge (MM-NLG 2023), pages 87–92
September 12, 2023 ©2023 Association for Computational Linguistics

in the input triple set (e.g. the triples with a DB-Subj that has 3 mentions come before those with 2 mentions). Figure 1 shows a PredArg template, instantiated in Figure 3 in Appendix A.

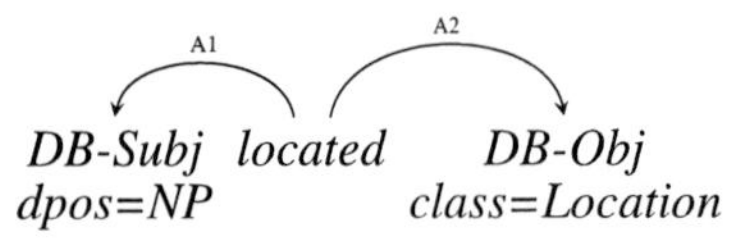

Figure 1: Sample PredArg template corresponding to the *country* property.

2.2 Adaptations for Irish

Lexicalisation of properties. We handcrafted templates for all properties already covered by FORGe, i.e. the training, development and test properties of WebNLG'20 (Castro Ferreira et al., 2020); there were no new properties in the 2023 dataset, so our generator is able to generate all the 2023 inputs. There are 411 different properties, and since several properties can be verbalised the same way,[1] the total number of unique templates is lower (381).
Lexicalisation of DB-Subj and DB-Obj values. For each triple, the property and its pertinent domain and range classes determine whether the DB-Subj and DB-Obj values will be lexicalised using their English or Irish label (human readable name). To obtain the latter, we take advantage of the *owl:sameAs* relation that links the DB-Subj (DB-Obj) entity of the English DBpedia to its equivalent entity in the Irish DBpedia version; if no equivalent entity is contained in the localised DBpedia version, we fall back to Google translate,[2] giving as input the English label without any further context.

3 Generation of non-inflected sentences

In this section, we describe FORGe (3.1) and provide an overview of its extensions for Irish (3.2).

3.1 FORGe

FORGe (Mille et al., 2019) is a rule-based generator that takes as input minimal PredArg structures. It realises the last four consecutive steps of the traditional NLG pipeline (Reiter and Dale, 1997) (sentence aggregation, lexicalisation,[3] referring expression generation and linguistic realisation), except that for WebNLG'23, the output of FORGe is a sequence of lemmas with morphological information instead of inflected words (see Section 4). Each of the four steps is implemented as one or more graph transducer(s) that successively map the input PredArg onto different dependency-based intermediate linguistic representations, loosely following the different levels of Meaning-Text Theory (Mel'čuk, 1973); see Mille et al. (2023) for details of levels of representation, and Table 1 for the list of modules that produce these intermediate levels.

A mix of language-independent and language-specific rules build the intermediate representations using additional knowledge contained in language-specific dictionaries. Language-specific rules are needed either because a language phenomenon is highly idiosyncratic in its own nature (e.g. *a* before a vowel in English becomes *an*), or because the conditions of application of a more general phenomenon are idiosyncratic (e.g. the introduction of determiners). From the perspective of multilingualism, there are 3 types (T1-T3) of rules in FORGe: fully language-independent rules (T1, ~82% of all rules); rules that apply to a subset of languages (T2, ~6.5 languages on average, ~3% of rules); and language-specific rules, which apply to one single language (T3, ~15% of rules).

FORGe uses three types of dictionaries to store:

- Mappings between concepts and lexical units, e.g. *located {GA={lex=lonnaithe_JJ_01}}*.
- Lexical unit descriptions, e.g. *lonnaithe_JJ_01 {lemma = lonnaithe; pos = JJ; preposition_arg2 = i }*, where *i* 'in' is required on the second argument of *lonnaithe*: *lonnaithe i X* 'located in X'.
- Generic language-specific knowledge, such as the type of word order or morphological agreement triggered by surface-oriented dependencies (e.g. a direct object is by default after its governing verb in the sentence, and a determiner receives case, number and gender from its governing noun).

3.2 Extensions for Irish

With respect to dictionaries, we added 457 mappings between concepts and lexical units and as many lexical unit descriptions, and we manually crafted the generic language-specific dictionary. For rules, we implemented 76 rules that apply exclusively to Irish (T3), which represents 2.78% of

[1] Properties such as *municipality*, *district*, or *state* are mapped to the same template as *country*, shown in Figure 1.

[2] We used the publicly available *Translator* module of the *googletrans* (version 3.1.0a0) library.

[3] We refer to a more surface-oriented lexicalisation here, with, e.g., function words, as opposed to the "deep" lexicalisation of the main concepts described in Section 2.

ID	FORGe module	# rl	# T3 GA rl	% T3 GA rl
1	Text planning	553	0	0
2	Lexicalisation	183	0	0
3	Communicative structuring	258	0	0
4	Deep sentence structuring	345	3	0.87
5	Surface sentence structuring	477	17	3.56
6	Syntactic aggregation	215	0	0
7	Referring Expression Generation	237	0	0
8	Word order and agreement resolution	265	17	6.42
9	Morphology processing	201	39	19.4
	All modules	2,734	76	2.78

Table 1: Number of rules, and number and % of Irish-specific (T3) rules (rl) per per FORGe module.

rules; Table 1 shows the breakdown of language-agnostic and language-specific rules per module. We also activated 65 existing T2 rules for Irish.

As Table 1 shows, 4 modules require Irish-specific rules: deep sentence structuring, surface sentence structuring, word order and agreement resolution and morphology processing; next we list the phenomena that required T3 and most T2 rules.

Deep sentence structuring

Relative particles (T3): the particle *a* is introduced to link the modified noun and the main verb in relative clauses; in case of prepositional relatives, the particle has a different form depending on the tense of the verb (present *a*, past *ar*).

Passive (T3): in Irish there are two alternative constructions where a passive form would be used in English. If the data refers to an action/event, an autonomous main verb form is used, e.g. for the triple `Acharya_Institute_of_Technology | established | 2000`, *bunaíodh*, the autonomous form of the verb *bunaigh* 'to establish' is used, as in *Bunaíodh Institiúid Teicneolaíochta Acharya sa bhliain 2000*, 'Acharya Institute of Technology was established in the year 2000'. Alternatively, where a state/location is referred to, e.g. for the triple `MotorSport_Vision|city|Longfield`, we have *tá*, the present tense of the auxiliary verb *bí* 'to be', and the past participle *lonnaithe* 'located', as in *Tá MotorSport Vision lonnaithe i gcathair Longfield*, 'MotorSport Vision is located in Longfield'.

Non-verbal copula (T3): Irish has two copular constructions. The verbal copula is used for changeable properties whereas the non-verbal copula *is* is used for more permanent properties; e.g. for `The_Fellowship_of_the_Ring | author | J._R._R._Tolkien` we have *Is é J.R.R. Tolkien a scríobh The Fellowship of the Ring* where *is* connects the author and the book, and the pronoun *é* agrees with the gender and number of the author.

Surface sentence structuring

Determiners (T3): a definite determiner is only introduced on a noun *N* if *N*'s dependent is not a definite noun or a proper noun.

Dependencies (T2, 22 rules in common with Catalan, Greek, Spanish, French, Italian and Portuguese): surface-oriented dependencies are introduced as, e.g., *subject, direct object, modifier*, etc.

Word order and agreement resolution

Genitive chains (T3): in a chain of genitive elements, only the last element maintains the genitive case, e.g. in the case of 'the length of the runway of the aerodrome', only the last element 'aerodrome' has genitive case as in *Is é fad rúidbhealach an aeradróim 1,095m.*

Word order class (T3): when an element is established as a member of a class, the class name goes right after the copula, as in *Is milseog é Bionico* 'Bionico is a dessert'.

Possessive pronoun agreement (T3): the semantic number and gender of a possessor triggers agreement on the possessed. In the case of the triple `India | leader | T._S._Thakur`, the copular construction generates the text *Tá T.S. Shakur ina cheannaire ar an India*, 'T. S. Thakur is a leader of India', where we have the present tense of the verbal copula *bí*, followed by the subject *'T. S. Thakur'* and the subject complement *'ina cheannaire ar an India'*. The complement has a possessive pronoun *ina* that agrees in gender and number with the subject, i.e. *ina* is masculine singular reflecting the subject 'T. S. Thakur' and it triggers masculine singular agreement on the noun *cheannaire* 'leader'.

Ellipsis (T3): some rules look for pronouns to elide, in particular in relative and non-verbal copular constructions. In addition, Irish is a VSO language so a specific rule checks for repeated subjects on the right of the verb and replaces them with pronouns.[4]

Order between siblings (T2, 29 rules in common with Catalan, Greek, Spanish, French, Portuguese and sometimes Italian): for instance, in many languages, the determiner usually goes before all other dependents of the noun.

Morphology processing

Concatenations (T3): *don* is a contraction of *do an* 'for the' as in *Scríobh Nicholas Brodszky an ceol don scannán* meaning 'Nicholas Brodszky wrote the music **for the** film'.

Prefixes (T3): vowel-initial masculine nouns following the determiner *an* receive a *t-* prefix as in *Rugadh an* ***t-aisteoir*** *Bill Oddie in Rochdale* meaning 'The actor Bill Oddie was born in Rochdale'. The preposition *le* triggers a prefix *h-* on following nouns starting with a vowel, and some past verbs get the prefix *d'*.

Mutations (T3): word-initial mutations are common in Irish and fulfil many grammatical functions, for example the noun *cathair* 'city' has various mutations depending on the number and gender of the possessive pronoun, e.g. there is lenition in *mo* ***ch****athair* 'my city', eclipsis in *ár* ***gc****athair* 'our city' and no mutation in *a cathair* 'her city'.

Verbal Adj/N, Prep. declension, V flags (T3): other rules cover the conversion of some adjectives and nouns into their verbal counterparts, the inflection of some prepositions and the insertion of a tag that flags vowel-initial verbs, as required by the morphology generator.

4 Generation of morphological inflections

We describe here the morphology generation (4.1) and its interface with FORGe (4.2).

4.1 Irish NLP Tools

The Irish NLP tools suite[5] includes finite-state transducers for Irish morphology generation (Dhonnchadha et al., 2003). These tools handle tokenisation and morphological analysis/generation of the inflected forms of Irish headwords coded in the finite-state lexicons. The tools were initially developed using xfst (Xerox finite state tools) (Beesley and Karttunen, 2003) and later converted to use foma tools (Hulden, 2009).[6] Finite-state transducers model a two-level morphology where a lexical description is mapped to a surface form, e.g. déan+Verb+VT+FutInd maps to the future tense form *déanfaidh* of the transitive verb *déan* 'make'. The transducers can be used to generate inflected forms of words for NLG and CALL applications, and the same transducers work in the opposite direction for morphological analysis as part of NLP applications including PoS tagging and parsing.

4.2 Interfacing FORGe with Irish NLP tools

In order to match the inputs expected by Irish NLP tools, we process FORGe outputs with regular expressions so as to replace reserved characters, introduce a '+' separator between morphological tags, and insert single line breaks between consecutive words of the same text and double line breaks between consecutive texts.

5 Post-processing

The post-processing consists of regular expressions to revert reserved characters to their original form, true-case and clean the texts, and take care of prefixing, hyphenation, contraction, lenition and eclipsis phenomena triggered by the inflected forms of words; see Appendix A for an example.

6 Discussion and Conclusion

We have presented DCU/TCD-FORGe, a fully rule-based pipeline of four modules for Irish text generation at WebNLG'23; sample inputs and outputs for all modules are provided in Appendix A. The BLEU score provided by the organisers[7] (0.167) is significantly lower than FORGe's scores on English at WebNLG'20 (0.406 (Castro Ferreira et al., 2020)); this is likely because we created our lexicalisations without reference to train and dev Irish texts, i.e. surface similarity is likely to be low. However, the gap in BLEU scores between our system (0.167) and the highest-scoring GPT-based system (0.204) (Lorandi and Belz, 2023) is less than 0.04 points; this compares to a corresponding gap of 0.13 points between FORGe and the best English system at WebNLG'20. We will be able to draw more reliable conclusions when the results of the human evaluation are released.

[4]Strictly speaking, this rule belongs to the REG module but since it has the same conditions of application as ellipsis in other languages, it was left in this module for the time being.

[5]https://www.scss.tcd.ie/~uidhonne/irish.utf8.htm

[6]https://fomafst.github.io/

[7]https://github.com/WebNLG/2023-Challenge/tree/main/evaluation/automatic/scripts

Acknowledgements

Mille's contribution was funded by the European Union under the Marie Skłodowska-Curie grant agreement No 101062572 (M-FleNS).

References

Kenneth R Beesley and Lauri Karttunen. 2003. Finite-state morphology: Xerox tools and techniques. *CSLI, Stanford.*

Thiago Castro Ferreira, Claire Gardent, Nikolai Ilinykh, Chris van der Lee, Simon Mille, Diego Moussallem, and Anastasia Shimorina. 2020. The 2020 bilingual, bi-directional WebNLG+ shared task: Overview and evaluation results (WebNLG+ 2020). In *Proceedings of the 3rd International Workshop on Natural Language Generation from the Semantic Web (WebNLG+)*, pages 55–76, Dublin, Ireland (Virtual). Association for Computational Linguistics.

Uí Dhonnchadha, Caoilfhionn Nic Pháidín, and Josef Van Genabith. 2003. Design, implementation and evaluation of an inflectional morphology finite state transducer for Irish. *Machine Translation*, 18:173–193.

Mans Hulden. 2009. Foma: a finite-state compiler and library. In *Proceedings of the Demonstrations Session at EACL 2009*, pages 29–32, Athens, Greece. Association for Computational Linguistics.

Paul Kingsbury and Martha Palmer. 2002. From TreeBank to PropBank. In *Proceedings of the Third International Conference on Language Resources and Evaluation (LREC'02)*, Las Palmas, Canary Islands - Spain. European Language Resources Association (ELRA).

Michela Lorandi and Anya Belz. 2023. Data-to-text generation for severely under-resourced languages with GPT-3.5: A bit of help needed from Google Translate. In *Proceedings of the Workshop on Multimodal, Multilingual Natural Language Generation and Multilingual WebNLG Challenge*, page tbd, Prague, Czech Republic.

Igor A. Mel'čuk. 1973. Towards a linguistic 'Meaning ↔ Text' model. *Trends in Soviet theoretical linguistics*, pages 33–57.

Simon Mille, Stamatia Dasiopoulou, and Leo Wanner. 2019. A portable grammar-based nlg system for verbalization of structured data. In *Proceedings of the 34th ACM/SIGAPP Symposium on Applied Computing*, pages 1054–1056.

Simon Mille, François Lareau, Anya Belz, and Stamatia Dasiopoulou. 2023. Mod-D2T: A Multi-layer Dataset for Modular Data-to-Text Generation. In *Proceedings of the 16th International Conference on Natural Language Generation*, page tbd, Prague, Czech Republic.

Ehud Reiter and Robert Dale. 1997. Building applied natural language generation systems. *Natural Language Engineering*, 3(1):57–87.

A Sample input and output structures

The figures in the next page illustrate the generation process starting from an input triple set that corresponds to the following English text:

Agra Airport, operated by Indian Air Force, is located in India. Its ICAO location identifier is VIAG.

Figure 2 shows a WebNLG'23 input, and Figure 3 shows the output of the lexicalisation module. The FORGe, morphology and post-processing outputs are shown in a one-word-per-line format in Table 2. The output Irish text is the following:

Tá Agra Airport, reáchtáilte ag Indian Air Force, lonnaithe ins An India. Tá VIAG in a aitheantóir suímh ICAO.

```
<entry category="Airport" eid="719" shape="(X (X) (X) (X))" shape_type="sibling" size="3">
  <modifiedtripleset>
    <mtriple>Agra_Airport | location | India</mtriple>
    <mtriple>Agra_Airport | operatingOrganisation | Indian_Air_Force</mtriple>
    <mtriple>Agra_Airport | icaoLocationIdentifier | &quot;VIAG&quot;</mtriple>
  </modifiedtripleset>
</entry>
```

Figure 2: A sample WebNLG input with 3 triples

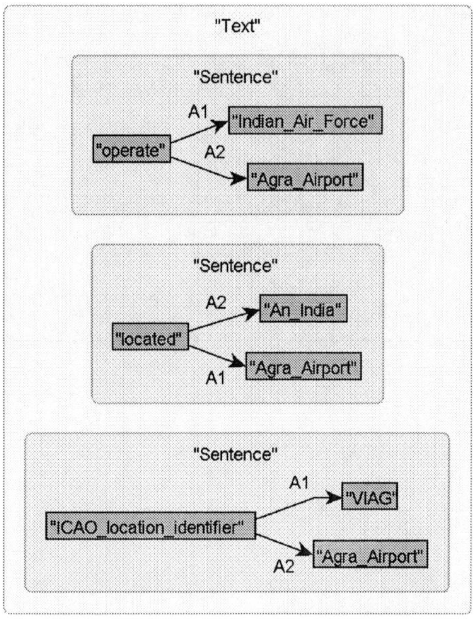

Figure 3: Lexicalisation output: instantiated PredArg templates

FORGe	Morphology	Post-processing
bí+Verb+PresInd	tá	Tá
Agra_Airport+Noun+Masc+Com+Sg	Agra_Airport	Agra Airport
,	,	,
reáchtáilte	reáchtáilte	reáchtáilte
ag	ag	ag
Indian_Air_Force+Noun+Masc+Com+Sg	Indian_Air_Force	Indian Air Force
,	,	,
lonnaithe+Adj+Masc+Com+Sg	lonnaithe	lonnaithe
i	i	ins
An_India+Noun+Masc+Com+Sg	An_India	An India
.	.	.
bí+Verb+PresInd	tá	Tá
VIAG+Noun+Masc+Com+Sg	VIAG	VIAG
i	i	in
a	a	a
aitheantóir+Noun+Masc+Com+Sg	aitheantóir	aitheantóir
suímh	suímh	suímh
ICAO+Noun+Masc+Com+Sg	ICAO	ICAO
.		

Table 2: FORGe, morphology and post-processing outputs (one word per line for convenience)

WebNLG Challenge 2023: Domain Adaptive Machine Translation for Low-Resource Multilingual RDF-to-Text Generation

Kancharla Aditya Hari
IIIT Hyderabad

Bhavyajeet Singh
IIIT Hyderabad

Anubhav Sharma
IIIT Hyderabad

Vasudeva Varma
IIIT Hyderabad

Abstract

This paper presents our submission to the WebNLG Challenge 2023 for generating text in several low-resource languages from RDF-triples. Our submission focuses on using machine translation for generating texts in Irish, Maltese, Welsh and Russian. While a simple and straightfoward approach, recent works have shown that using monolingual models for inference for multilingual tasks with the help of machine translation (*translate-test*) can outperform multilingual models and training multilingual models on machine-translated data (*translate-train*) through careful tuning of the MT component. Our results show that this approach demonstrates competitive performance for this task even with limited data.

1 Introduction

The multilingual RDF-to-Text generation task involves generating verbalizations of RDF triples in different languages. It represents an important problem, as it can allow for the rapid generation and enrichment of informative texts in different languages by leveraging existing knowledge graphs and databases. This is of particular relevance for low-resource languages which are typically less represented.

Recent methods for RDF-to-Text generation rely on neural methods, which require availability of high quality data for training. However, this is challenging for low-resource languages due to the lack of such data. Manual curation of such datasets requires expert human supervision, and is expensive and time-consuming. Thus, utilizing machine translated data available in different languages is naturally motivated. The *translate-train* method relies of translating the training data to the target language, while the *translate-test* method translate the test data to English and using a monolingual model for inference.

Recent works have shown that through careful adaption of the MT component, the *translate-test* method can perform significantly better than previously shown results, even outperforming *translate-train* and multilingual models across different classification tasks (Artetxe et al., 2023). Our submission investigates the performance of *translate-test* method for generation. In particular, we use domain adaption to improve the MT component and generate high quality texts in the target language with very little training data. We first generate text in English using a monolingual, English generation model, and then translate the generated text to the target text using the MT component.

2 Experimental Setup

2.1 Pre-trained model

We use the T5 model (Raffel et al., 2020) for RDF-to-Text generation in English. The task is thus modeled as a text-to-text generation task, with the input RDF triples serialized to strings. The small, 60M parameter variant of T5 is used. The model is finetuned on the training split of WebNLG 2020 challenge's English dataset.

2.2 MT component

For the MT component, we use the distilled variant of NLLB (Team et al., 2022) with 600M parameters. Beam search with a beam size of 5 is used as the decoding strategy.

In (Artetxe et al., 2023), the authors investigate augmenting the training data using rount-trip translation. This is motivated by the idea that the model at inference takes translated data as input. However, due to the crosslingual nature of this problem, the input is always in English, rendering this process irrevelant. Hence we only investigate domain adaption. For domain adaption, we finetune this model on translating the text pairs made available in the development set of WebNLG challenge 2023 for Irish, Maltese, Russian, and Welsh. We do not use

Proceedings of the Workshop on Multimodal, Multilingual Natural Language Generation and Multilingual WebNLG Challenge (MM-NLG 2023), pages 93–94
September 12, 2023 ©2023 Association for Computational Linguistics

Language	BLEU	chrF++	TER
Irish	15.66	0.44	0.73
Maltese	16.49	0.47	0.7
Russian	36.01	0.57	0.53
Welsh	20.97	0.49	0.67

Table 1: Results of translate-test with domain adaption

Breton as this language is not present in NLLB's pretraining corpus. We translate at a document level, without segmenting the texts into individual sentences. At test time, the generations of the T5 model are translated to the target text by the fine-tuned NLLB model, again at a document level.
We also make available the training code and model checkpoints[1]

2.3 Dataset

The T5 model for generating text in English prior to MT is trained on the training split of the English language data made available in WebNLG Challenge 2020.
The MT component is finetuned on only the development set of all languages except Breton made available in WebNLG Challenge 2023. We withold 20% of this dataset for evaluating the MT component. In total, 1332 samples are used for training and 333 samples are used for evaluation.

3 Results

Table 1 shows the automatic evaluation results of our approach. Despite relying on just the few samples available for the low-resource languages, this approach demonstrates strong performance.

References

Mikel Artetxe, Vedanuj Goswami, Shruti Bhosale, Angela Fan, and Luke Zettlemoyer. 2023. Revisiting machine translation for cross-lingual classification.

Colin Raffel, Noam Shazeer, Adam Roberts, Katherine Lee, Sharan Narang, Michael Matena, Yanqi Zhou, Wei Li, and Peter J. Liu. 2020. Exploring the limits of transfer learning with a unified text-to-text transformer. *Journal of Machine Learning Research*, 21(140):1–67.

NLLB Team, Marta R. Costa-jussà, James Cross, Onur Çelebi, Maha Elbayad, Kenneth Heafield, Kevin Heffernan, Elahe Kalbassi, Janice Lam, Daniel Licht, Jean Maillard, Anna Sun, Skyler Wang, Guillaume Wenzek, Al Youngblood, Bapi Akula, Loic Barrault, Gabriel Mejia Gonzalez, Prangthip Hansanti, John Hoffman, Semarley Jarrett, Kaushik Ram Sadagopan, Dirk Rowe, Shannon Spruit, Chau Tran, Pierre Andrews, Necip Fazil Ayan, Shruti Bhosale, Sergey Edunov, Angela Fan, Cynthia Gao, Vedanuj Goswami, Francisco Guzmán, Philipp Koehn, Alexandre Mourachko, Christophe Ropers, Safiyyah Saleem, Holger Schwenk, and Jeff Wang. 2022. No language left behind: Scaling human-centered machine translation.

[1]https://shorturl.at/hsN04

AUTHOR INDEX

Association for Computational Linguistics
209 N. Eighth Street
Stroudsburg, Pennsylvania 18360

CURRAN ASSOCIATES INC.
proceedings.com

ISBN 978-1-7138-9033-1